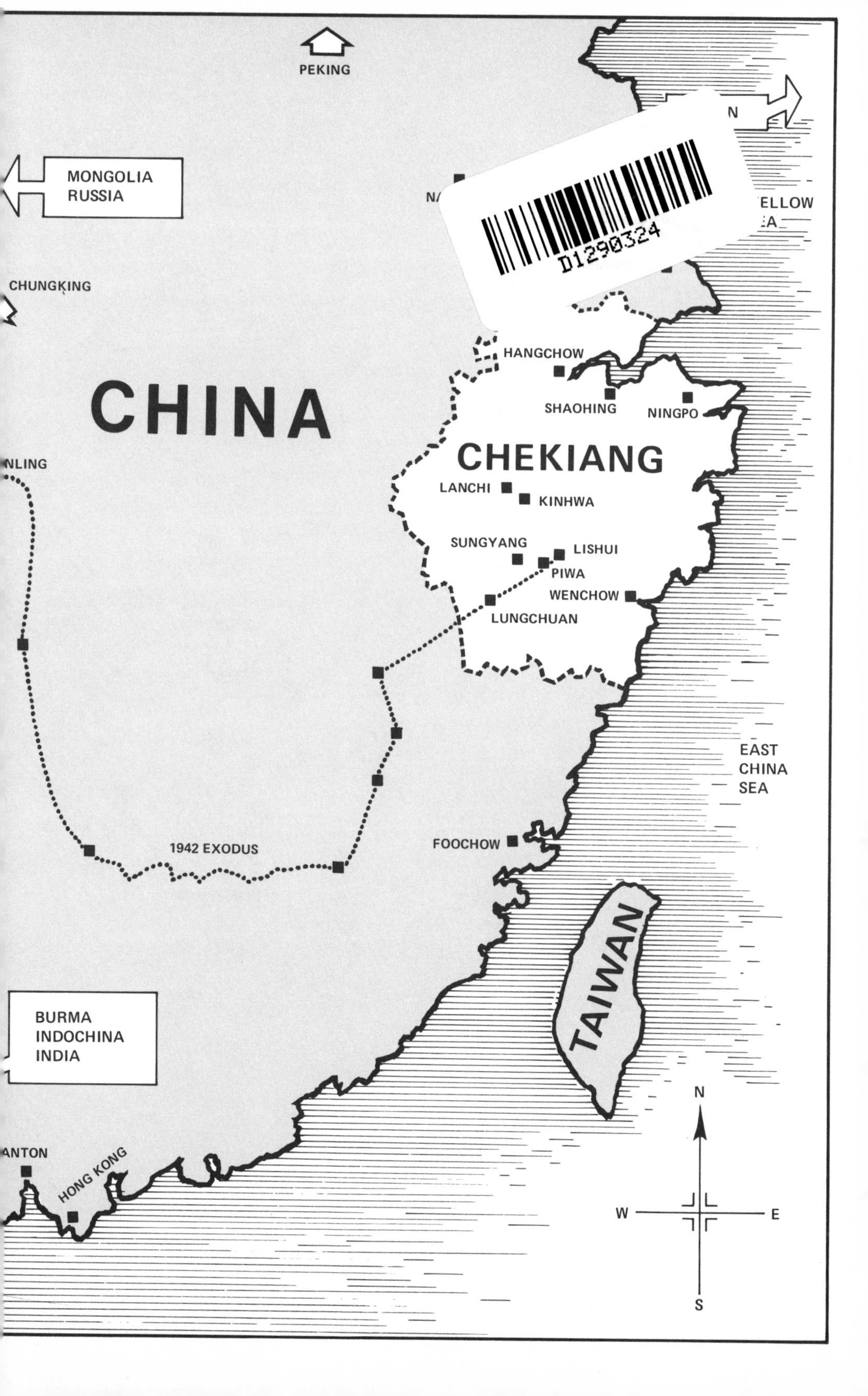
PEKING
MONGOLIA
RUSSIA
CHUNGKING
CHINA
HANGCHOW
SHAOHING
NINGPO
CHEKIANG
LANCHI
KINHWA
SUNGYANG
LISHUI
PIWA
WENCHOW
LUNGCHUAN
EAST
CHINA
SEA
FOOCHOW
1942 EXODUS
TAIWAN
BURMA
INDOCHINA
INDIA
HONG KONG
N
W
E
S

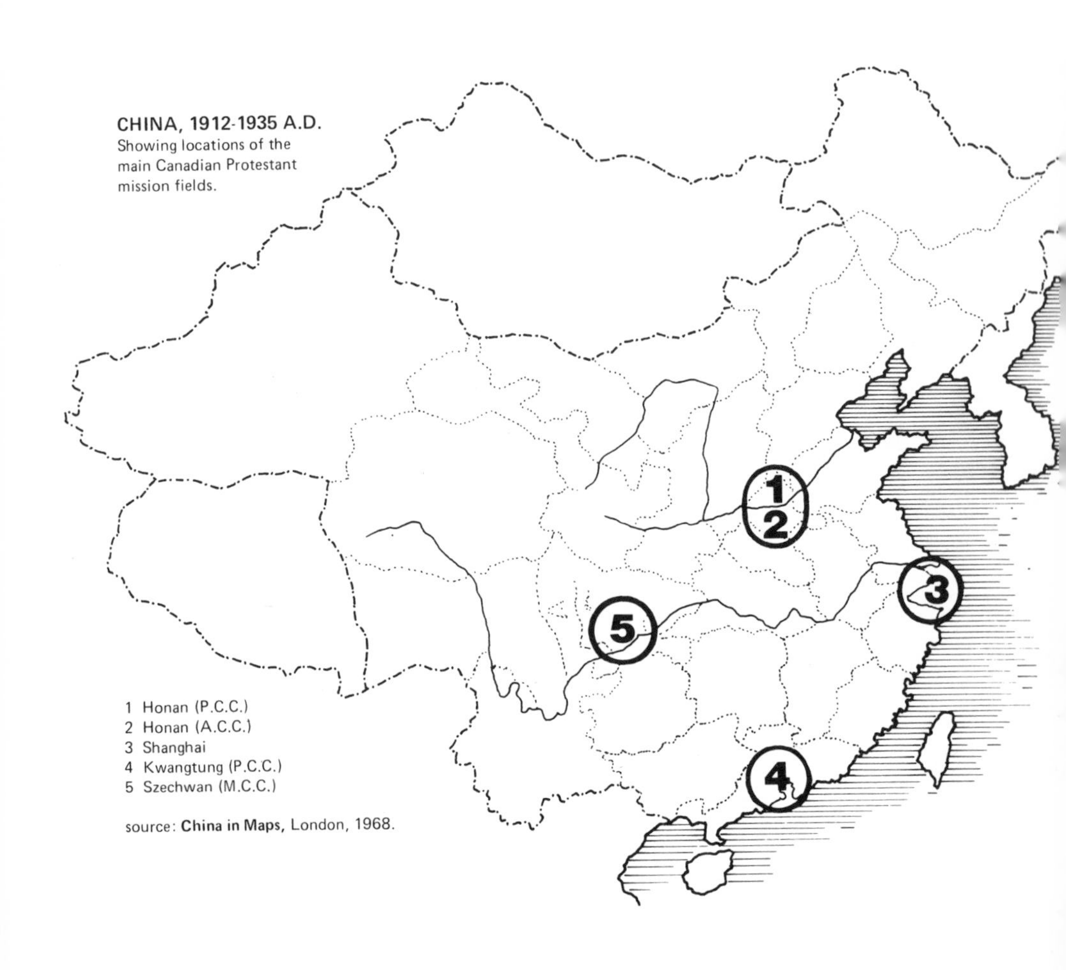
CHINA, 1912-1935 A.D.
Showing locations of the main Canadian Protestant mission fields.
1
2
3
4
5
1 Honan (P.C.C.)
2 Honan (A.C.C.)
3 Shanghai
4 Kwangtung (P.C.C.)
5 Szechwan (M.C.C.)
source: China in Maps, London, 1968.

ASSIGNMENT IN CHEKIANG

71 Canadians
in China
1902 • 1954

by
Grant Maxwell

Endorsement

As a friend of Scarboro Missions, Grant Maxwell has told the story of the Scarboro Fathers-Grey Sisters involvement in China in a balanced way. It is a story of the dedication and dreams of these 71 Canadians whose faith led them to a strange and distant land.

As well as being a history, this book describes the changes that took place in their attitudes regarding their mission among the Chinese. While they never once questioned their goal, they constantly questioned the methods used. Thus, their story affords a glimpse into the development that has been taking place in mission methods and motivation — one touching the very foundations of Christianity's understanding of the Lord's command to 'Go and teach all nations'.

Grant has made a significant contribution to the story of the Canadian mission effort and to the ongoing history of mission.

The General Council,
Scarboro Foreign Mission Society.

May 1982

Published by: Scarboro Foreign Mission Society,
2685 Kingston Road,
Scarborough, Ontario. M1M 1M4
Canada.

Printed by: Thorn Press Limited,
135 Railside Road,
Don Mills, Ontario. M3A 1B7
Canada.

Cover and Layout by: Ron Wilson

ISBN 0-9691173-0-2

Foreword

Perhaps no aspect of the "foreign intrusion" upon China during the last two centuries is more shrouded in myth, misunderstanding and disputatiousness than the role of the missionaries. Controversy attended their unexpected arrival and dogged their unceremonious departure. From the early Jesuits who saw an image of the peaceable kingdom marred only by an absence of faith in Jesus Christ to the "red Protestants" of the late nineteen-forties who felt Chairman Mao Tse-tung and the Communist Party of China were the logical heirs of their endeavors, the contact between the Christian faith and the Chinese reality has been a radicalizing experience.

In deploring the lies that have been manufactured by the Communists to discredit the missionary movement in China, it is not necessary to minimize the legitimate grievances some Chinese have traditionally held against the "church militant." Nor is it necessary, or honest, to ascribe all the misunderstanding to Communist propaganda. Among professing Christians, it comes as no surprise that some of their number who proclaimed the gospel in "a heathen land" — including the more fervent variety — did so with unchristian arrogance.

No one can deny that the church sinned in China from time to time and in place to place. Communist propaganda has been adept at exploiting the reluctance of many missionaries to distance themselves from the extra-territorial perquisites of the "unfair treaties" and it is an effective criticism. The very sin of disunion and denominational rancour must not only have confused the Chinese but seriously distorted the revolutionary message of Christ, which is one of forgiveness and reconciliation. Both the Christian Church and the Communist Party believe that confession is good for the soul. What the party cannot grant absolution for, however, are the positive accomplishments of the missionaries, accomplishments that look better and better as time passes by and the faction-ridden Communist Party of China becomes increasingly burdened with its own list of almost cosmic sins.

During the time that I lived in China and tried to fathom the complex logic of party policy, it became increasingly clear why Communist ideology employed a mailed fist to Christian theology.

Certainly the number of converts the missionaries managed to come up with were, numerically, unimpressive compared to the vast sea of unconverted. The same thing can be said, curiously, about the party itself, for its own proselytes have been conspicuously unsuccessful in convincing the majority of Chinese people that it is capable of conjuring up heaven on earth. At the root of all this is the simple, stark fact that Communism is out stalking the same quarry as the church — the human soul.

Here, then, is where all the parallels and fascinating conjecture on similarities ends, because we must consider both means and ends. The guilt which weighed so heavily on many liberal Christians after the Communist takeover of China in 1949 has been much ameliorated by the record of what came to pass. Once again, one need not make extravagant claims of goodness for some of the church's social work, from universities and hospitals to the fight against feudalism by preaching the dignity of peasants and women. That the responsible missionaries should have identified social ills and tried to help correct them seems natural within the context of the social gospel, even if it is second line work compared to the primary goal of redemption. Early on, the party sought to co-opt Christian reform and hitch it to its own version of redemption. The means used, however, brought a fearful cost in material and spiritual decrepitude. The party has a lot more to confess than it is prepared to do in the current period of "readjustment." And the actual ends, for the most part, were ignoble and craven: the nation Mao bequeathed the long-suffering Chinese masses continues to be a ruthless totalitarian state almost unequalled in hypocrisy and self-righteousness.

So it is both useful and timely that we re-examine the role of the missionary. Grant Maxwell has provided a sober but nevertheless moving account of people who, at their best, had an awesome respect for the tradition and potential of an amazing country and a remarkable people. We need to know more about them because what brought many to the Middle Kingdom in the first place and kept them there was not "class warfare" or "proletarian dictatorship" but something far more volatile, something called love.

June 1982 John Fraser

John Fraser, **Globe & Mail** *correspondent in China in 1977-79, is the author of THE CHINESE — PORTRAIT OF A PEOPLE.*

Contents

"Imagine a sower going out to sow . . ." (Matthew 13:4) Here is a story of an uncertain sowing and an unknown harvest. Still, a prophet long ago heard the Lord say: " . . . the word that goes out of my mouth does not return to me empty, without carrying out my will and succeeding in what it was sent to do." (Isaiah 55:11)

Introduction

"How many people do something they really believe in?"

— Terry Fox, 1981

First impressions by passersby are likely to be negative. Here is a sprawling complex of institutional buildings spread along the 2600 block of Kingston Road in Scarborough, Ontario. The oriental looking sign in front of the complex reads "SCARBORO FOREIGN MISSIONS". Understandably, very few of the thousands who daily pass by stop long enough to inquire within as to who lives there and what they are doing.

But first impressions are misleading in this instance, as in so many others. Those who do venture inside 2685 Kingston Road receive a friendly welcome from Society members and associates who daily co-ordinate an enterprise that, while small in numbers, is active in a dozen countries on three continents. All across Canada hundreds have come to know and prize the Scarboro Society complex for its hospitality — including the modest facilities and good food it provides at low prices to church groups and other voluntary organizations holding retreats and meetings there.

Few of these guests, however, and still fewer other Canadians know about the Society's origins, the pioneer daring of its founder, and of the labors of the 55 missionary priests and 15 nursing and teaching sisters who followed J.M. Fraser to pre-Maoist China.

This little known story deserves to be shared widely for the same reasons that the related sagas of French-Canadian Catholic and Canadian Protestant missionaries in China merit wider telling. Each of these stories has made an unique contribution to Canadian history while having some small impact on the much longer and more complex narrative of the peoples of China. Inevitably, these Western messengers' witness to Christianity in the Orient was a divided one, given their different denominational, language and other cultural inheritances; yet a sincere and dedicated witness for all that.

Like the companion stories, the Scarboro-Grey Sisters' record is an eventful one. And it is instructive — especially to Christians with an interest in the now debatable question of overseas missions, and to all those wanting to learn more about how much social perceptions and religious practices have evolved since the beginning of this century. Furthermore, at a personal level this Canadian endeavor challenges us to reassess our own beliefs regarding the meaning of life and the values we live by.

These are some of the reasons why I accepted an invitation from the Scarboro Society to write a journalist's account of their years in the China that was.

A "mix" of several approaches has been used to recount the story: chronological narrative, interrupted here and there by "flashbacks" and "previews" of earlier and later developments; descriptions of the historical background and changing contexts of church and world; biographies of some principal figures and collective histories of the Scarboro and Grey Sisters' communities; and some analysis of Christian missiology. The result is an interpretive report, not a definitive study.

So far as possible the priests' and sisters' experiences and reactions are described in the participants' own words — as selected from the printed record of articles, letters and a few books, and from recent interviews with many surviving members.

Their correspondence and reports from Chekiang province in east central China usually were characterized by a certainty of tone. The writers knew what they were about, why they were there. They believed they had been called by God and they tried to evaluate all else in the light of what this calling demanded of them. They did not spend time, at least publicly, analyzing their attitudes or taking their emotional temperatures. They got on with the job at hand — however endless and hopeless it must often have appeared.

These 71 men and women — mostly from Ontario and the Atlantic provinces — saw themselves as instruments of eternal miracles in their work as missionaries. As celibates, they gave up what the large majority in every generation prizes so much: marriage and family life, career and material success. Admittedly, for those seeking them, there were some alternative compensations, such as clerical status and group security.

The Scarboro-Grey Sisters' venture, initiated by John Mary Fraser of Toronto, was one full of contradictions: ambitious goals and limited achievements, continual disappointment and persisting hope, internal tension and external conflict, church politics and personal piety. Even so the men and women who composed this story by their dreams and sweat, their prayers and labors, persisted because they passionately believed in what they had set out to do.

A very human story, in short — one inspired and empowered by their faith. Whether or not their efforts "made sense" is something readers will judge for themselves.

Those judgments are certain to range the spectrum. One indication: "feedback" from more than 40 readers who previewed the first drafts of this text brought very diverse suggestions and criticisms.

Most of these criticisms and suggestions made possible important additions and corrections to the manuscript. Other criticisms tended to cancel one another. Often as not these objections focused on quotations from the writings or later recollections of the men and women who had staffed the China mission. Some critics felt the selected quotations favored one school of thought; other respondents argued that the choices favored different points of view, and yet another reader felt that I was "hiding" behind the quotations.

Not hiding but letting participants speak for themselves: this was my primary purpose. Admittedly, the selection of quotations itself involved subjective judgments. I attempted to make a balanced choice from the innumerable perceptions and conclusions on record, while not allowing personal reactions, pro or con, to color this selectivity unduly. Of course, every other writer would have made a different selection from the sources at hand.

So far as these and other limiting circumstances allowed, I have shared the story of the 71 Canadians as fairly and frankly as possible.

Many people made preparation of this interpretive report possible. I am indebted most to the patient guidance of the SFM General Council of Kenneth MacAuley, Fred Wakeham, and especially Gerald Curry as principal editorial adviser; to Scarboro archivists, Robert Cranley and Richard Veltri; to Michael O'Hearn, editor of **Scarboro Missions**; to Sisters Bernadette Kinsella, superior and Lucille Martin, former superior, and to Sisters Catherine Fairbairn and Gladys Brennan of the Grey Sisters in Pembroke; and to Dr. Katharine Hockin, United Church missiologist; to C.J. Eustace of Toronto and Pat Jamieson of Ottawa, for their valuable research studies; and to the veterans of the China Years, both men and women, who shared their memories generously and expressed their opinions candidly.

December 1981 *G.M.*

Chronological Guide

Civil Events		Religious Affairs
	Before the modern era	
China's historical record predates the birth of Christ by more than 20 centuries — reaching back, for example, to Confucius in the 6th Century B.C.; and in the Christian era to Marco Polo's visit there in the 13th Century, which happened 300 years before the first Christian missionaries arrived for a prolonged, if uncertain stay.		
	16th Century	
	1550s	Francis Xavier pioneers as a Jesuit missionary in the Far East.
	1580s	Well received by the Ming dynasty, Matteo Ricci SJ promotes Christian adaptations to China's culture.
	17th Century	
	1640s	Jesuit missionaries from France work in Huronia (Northern Ontario) until martyred or driven out.
Manchu dynasty takes power as China's ruling emperors.	1644	

Civil Events		Religious Affairs
	18th Century	
Emperor decrees an end to Christian missions after the Vatican reverses Ricci's adaptive approach.	1723	
	19th Century	
	1807	Robert Morrison of Britain becomes the first Protestant missionary in China.
Opium War between Britain and China.	1839-42	
Britain, France, U.S. and Russia sign treaties with China extending foreign privileges.	1858-60	
Canada becomes a self-governing Dominion of the British Empire.	1867	
	1877	Future founder of Scarboro Foreign Mission Society, John Andrew (later Mary) Fraser born in Toronto.
	1880s	First Protestant missionaries from Canada arrive in China. By 1925 their cumulative total will reach 350.
Indentured laborers are imported from China to help construct the Canadian Pacific Railway.	1881-85	
China's Boxer Uprising against "foreign devils" crushed by Western forces.	1899-1900	

Civil Events		Religious Affairs
	20th Century	
	1902-10	Father Fraser's first years in China as the first English-speaking Catholic missionary from Canada.
	1903	Death of Pope Leo XIII. Election of Pius X.
Revolution led by Sun Yat-sen overthrows Manchu dynasty and sets up a Republic in China.	1911-12	J. M. Fraser campaigns for funds for a China mission college. Visits the U.S., Italy, Ireland, Scotland, and England.
	1912-18	Back in China, Fraser still solicits funds for China mission college in Canada.
World War I — "the war to end wars" begins.	1914	Death of Pius X. Election of Benedict XV.
Bolshevik Revolution in Russia overthrows Czar and establishes Soviet Republic.	1917	
November 11 Armistice ends World War I.	1918	November 9 sees the China mission college starting in Almonte, Ontario. (Celebrated now as "Foundation Day" of the future SFM Society.)
	1919	First issue of **China** magazine published by new China Mission College in October.
Chinese Communist Party is established.	1921	J. M. Fraser purchases new college site in Scarborough, Ontario — now the Guild Inn.
	1922	Death of Benedict XV. Election of Pius XI.

Civil Events		Religious Affairs
First "United Front" between Nationalist and Communist Parties in China.	1924	Present Scarboro headquarters opened on Kingston Road. Its president: Father John E. McRae.
Death of Sun Yat-sen, founder of China's Republic. Disciples include Chiang Kai-shek and Mao Tse-tung.	1925	Vatican City assigns Chuchow/Lishui region in Chekiang Province to Scarboro missionaries.
	1926	First Scarboro mission band — Fathers Fraser, Morrison and Serra — reaches Chuchow.
Chiang Kai-shek takes control of China's Nationalist (Kuomintang) Party.	1928	
	1929	First Grey Sisters of Pembroke arrive in Chekiang as nursing and teaching partners in the Scarboro missions.
Japan invades Chinese Manchuria	1931	
	1932	J. M. Fraser is named pastor of Kinhwa, next door to the Scarboro missions in the Lishui region.
Mao Tse-tung leads Marxist "Long March" into Honan Province to regroup and challenge Chiang's rule.	1932-34	
Mao emerges as main leader of Chinese Communism.	1935	

Civil Events		Religious Affairs
	1937	Lishui and Kinhwa are bombed repeatedly by Japanese planes. Canadian mission teams assist the wounded.
	1938	Scarboro sends 10 men to China, largest mission band ever.
Outbreak in Europe of World War II.	1939	Death of Pius XI. Election of Pius XII.
World War II spreads to the Far East when Japan attacks Pearl Harbour, sweeps across East Asia and into the Philippines.	1941	1st General Chapter of the Scarboro Foreign Mission Society. Msgr. J. E. McRae elected superior general.
	1942	Some Scarboro men are interned by Japanese in Peking and Hong Kong, while Father Fraser takes refuge with the Archbishop of Manila in the Philippines. Most SFM priests and Grey Sisters evacuate the Lishui area ahead of Japanese invaders. Refugees disperse widely, some travelling 1,500 miles into Hunan Province.
	1944	Lishui region missions are reopened.
World War II ends with the surrender by Nazi Germany in May and by Japan after atomic bombing of Hiroshima and Nagaski in August.	1945	J. M. Fraser returns to Canada — but not for long.

Civil Events		Religious Affairs
China's civil war resumes between Chiang's Nationalists and Mao's Marxists.	1946	14 Scarboro members and six Grey Sisters are back in the Lishui prefecture and Father Fraser returns to nearby Kinhwa.
	1948	Kenneth Turner SFM is named Bishop of the new Diocese of Lishui.
Communists win civil war. People's Republic of China proclaimed by Mao Tse-tung.	1949	2nd General Chapter of the SFM Society.
Korean War sees United Nations units, including Canadians, opposing North Korean and Chinese armies.	1950	J. M. Fraser begins pastoral work in his first Japanese mission in Nagasaki.
	1950-53	Exit visas are granted to some Canadian Catholic missionaries in China, while others are confined to quarters or imprisoned — including Scarboro's Arthur Venadam and Paul Kam.
	1954	Last members of the Scarboro team (excepting Father Kam) and of the French-Canadian Société des Missions — Étrangères leave China for Canada. Meanwhile over 100 SFM members are missioning in six nations of Asia, Latin America and the West Indies.
	1955	Death of Msgr. J. E. McRae.
	1958	Death of Pius XII. Election of Pope John XXIII.

Civil Events		Religious Affairs
Globe & Mail negotiates exchange of resident correspondents with the New China News Agency in Peking.	1959	3rd General Chapter of SFM.
	1962	John XXIII opens Vatican II. Msgr. J. M. Fraser, 85, dies in Osaka, Japan.
Assassination of President J. F. Kennedy.	1963	Death of John XXIII. Election of Paul VI.
China explodes its first atomic bomb.	1964	
	1965	Vatican II ends after issuing 16 decrees promoting Catholic renewal, Christian co-operation and international justice.
"Cultural Revolution" in China is spearheaded by Red Guards. Remaining religious activities are suppressed or driven underground.	1965-68	
	1968	Latin America's Catholic bishops meeting at Medellin, Colombia adopt a twofold approach of "evangelization and liberation". Meanwhile, the 4th General Chapter of SFM adopts new missionary directions in the light of Vatican II and mission experiences on three continents.
The Canadian government establishes full diplomatic relations with Vatican City and the Peoples Republic of China.	1970	

Civil Events		Religious Affairs
U.S. President Nixon visits China to inaugurate Sino-American rapprochment.	1972	
	1974	5th General Chapter of SFM. Supporting funds are voted for the Canada-China Programme of the Canadian Council of Churches.
Deaths of Mao Tse-tung and Chou En-lai are followed by a power struggle. New leaders arrest, try and imprison "Gang of Four", including Mao's widow. Now China encourages more exchanges with Western nations, including religious delegations, in the interests of more rapid industrialization.	1978-81	
	1978	Deaths of Paul VI and John Paul I. Election of John Paul II. 6th General Chapter of SFM.
	1979	At Puebla, Mexico a majority of Latin American bishops affirm a twofold pastoral approach of "evangelization and liberation". Meantime, Dr. K. T. Ting (also known as Bishop Ding), vice-chairman of the Three Self Movement among China's Protestants, visits Canada. His tour is co-ordinated by the Canada-China Programme of the CCC.

Civil Events		Religious Affairs
	1981	While visiting the Philippines, Pope John Paul II looks to future conciliation with China but the Peking government and the Patriotic Catholics Association condemn the Vatican for naming a new archbishop of Canton. In the same year a delegation organized by the Canadian Council of Churches, a few Catholics among them, meets with religious leaders in China. Later a Chinese delegation confers with Canadians at an ecumenical exchange in Montreal.
	1982	7th General Chapter of the Scarboro Foreign Mission Society.

1 WHY THEY WENT: MOTIVES FOR MISSION

This Canadian adventure — some would say misadventure — began very early in the twentieth century. The setting was an ancient civilization in the throes of disorderly change — a China exploited by foreign commerce, terrorized by feuding warlords and marauding bandits, later ravaged by Japanese invasion, and torn by intermittent civil war between Nationalists and Communists. By the early 1950s the missionary enterprise of Scarboro priests and Grey Sisters — like a small foreign island in hostile waters — was terminated.

A similar fate befell the French-Canadian Société des Missions — Etrangères, whose last member had to leave Manchuria in 1954. And most Canadian Protestants missioning in China departed in the years following.

Three decades passed. Still no one knew when, if ever, the interrupted Scarboro story in Chekiang province might resume. One thing was clear by the 1980s: past mission experiences in China provided valuable insights and painfully instructive lessons for all Canadians willing to learn and interested in our country's future relations with the world's most populous and someday possibly most powerful nation.

* * *

Many of the Canadian Catholics who crossed the Pacific intent on "making converts" among China's millions were inspired by the example of French missionaries who three centuries earlier had ventured over the Atlantic to bring the same faith to North American Indians, including the Hurons around Georgian Bay.

In 1925, not long before the first mission band of Scarboro men embarked for the Orient, the Roman Catholic Church celebrated the beatification ("blessed state") of eight Jesuit priests and lay helpers who in the 1640s had died as martyrs in what are now Northern Ontario and New York State. Their official recognition as the continent's first saints came in 1930. Ever since these official proclamations, many thousands of pilgrims and tourists have visited the Martyrs' Shrine at Midland, Ontario and another in Auriesville, New York.

On the saints' feast day in 1938 a "faithful protégé in Christ" named Craig Strang wrote an imaginative letter from the Church of Canadian Martyrs in Pihu, China. The Newfoundlander, who had arrived in Chekiang in the 1934 mission band from Scarboro, addressed his letter of September 26 to "John Brebeuf, Isaac Jogues and Company, Choir of Martyrs, Heaven." He saluted these mentors as "Blessed and Reverend Gentlemen."

His letter, featured in **China,** the Scarboro mission magazine, provides readers now with revealing glimpses of the perceptions and motivations which fueled Canadians like Father Strang and his contemporaries, just as similar aspirations had moved Jesuit missionaries to risk their lives in seventeenth century Canada. A few paragraphs of the Strang letter give the flavor of his ardent commitment:

> *We are in receipt of, and herein gratefully acknowledge, a multitude of favors, ranging from the date some centuries ago when you sealed our heritage with your blood, to this year of grace, 1938, on this your feast day, and in this place overseas, so far from your beloved France and the loved Canadian land of your adoption. . . .*
>
> *It is this sweet experience we court as we try to follow your noble example in the same work of saving pagan souls. You have convinced us that parting from the homeland is but the first and entirely separate sacrifice in the life of a missionary. . . .*
>
> *You will be gratified to know (at least, humanly speaking, it is gratifying to us) that the pagans here have not the barbarous ways that made it so hard for you to get your subjects to embrace Christian peace, and which, eventually, was the cause of your noble and painful death. The pagans here have a culture all their own, which is marvellous in its perfection, sagacity and antiquity, considering its pagan source. Its adherents oppose us with the best of worldly culture and see no need of added Divine revelation.*
>
> *Still, as everything worldly without any superior power to guide it, it has in many instances fallen from the high ideals of its founder, and thus we have to instil Christian virtues into those who would not, or could not practice the humanitarian ones handed down by their forefathers.*

Chinese street scene.

The letter described in some detail the missionary labors of Craig Strang and his colleague John Maurice. A large brick church had been erected by the previous pastor, Bernard Boudreau, also of Scarboro. Several ordinary Chinese houses served as chapels in outlying districts, and there was a mission school in Pihu. Native catechists assisted the priests as they "catered to the spiritual needs" of some 1,000 Chinese Christians in their pastoral charge.

* * *

Two dozen priests and a half dozen religious sisters had preceded Father Strang to the Orient, beginning with the zealous founder of what became the Scarboro Foreign Mission Society.

A few days before Christmas in 1902 this Toronto-born Scottish-Canadian arrived in China. As a recently ordained priest still in his twenties, John Mary Fraser was certain why he was there. He had crossed the ocean to teach and baptize as many "heathen Chinese" as he possibly could in order to "save their souls from eternal loss".

Father Fraser was not alone in this conviction. It was held by contemporary Protestant as well as Catholic missionaries. In fact the

Grey Sisters with four of their pupils.

first Protestant missionaries from Canada had arrived in China in the 1880s with mass conversions in mind. All major churches held that "The Great Commissioning" described in Matthew's Gospel (Cf. Mt. 28:19-20) was to be taken literally. The Good News of salvation brought by Jesus Christ was to be proclaimed to peoples in every pagan country, just as the Jewish Christian apostles 20 centuries before had brought the message to the pagan Gentiles of the Eastern Mediterranean.

Fraser's determination to rescue those he considered spiritually lost propelled him through a long lifetime and attracted more than 200 missionary followers. Many of them were ministering on three continents by the time their founder died in 1962.

Soon after beginning his career in China, J. M. Fraser wrote a letter to his family describing an experience which showed, he said, that "God will send an angel or a missionary to instruct and baptize" all good-living non-believers. Forced by a coming storm to take shelter in a small town he had not planned to visit, the missionary hurried by mistake into a "pagan's house". There he saw a haggard old man lying on a bed. "I could tell by his look that he was near the end". Fraser asked the dying man if he would like to become a Catholic:

> *To my great joy he replied, "Yes." I then sent the catechist to instruct him in the necessary doctrine, and in a half an hour he returned saying that the man wanted to be baptized . . . . I found upon inquiries that he had been a good man, never injuring anyone. After saying a few words of consolation, I poured the saving water over his head.*

More than three decades later Father Fraser was no less certain of the efficacy of administering the sacraments of the Roman Catholic rite, including Extreme Unction (as it was then called) for persons approaching death. This was so even if it meant extra expense, which was something the frugal missionary ordinarily avoided. In his autobiographical memoir, Fraser recalled that in 1937 he had received an urgent sick call to a Chinese Christian living 25 miles distant:

> *There was nothing for it but to go without delay. I hired a rickshaw and took a houseboy with me . . . . Arriving at the bus terminal I wished to hire the only auto in sight, but it was out of order. They were expecting parts from Shanghai.*
>
> *The next thing would be to charter a bus, but the price was prohibitive — 10 United States dollars — but we would have*

to be back before dark or else it would be dearer. Well, the cost should not be counted when it is a matter of a soul to be saved . . . . We bumped over the road in the empty bus and arrived in time to administer the Last Sacraments, and also to baptize a four-months old baby . . . . It was well worth the expense.

* * *

Like many intrepid men and women before and since, J. M. Fraser personified Christianity's history as one of the two major religions having the most vigorous missionary thrust, the other being Islam. "Spreading the Faith" has been a Christian tradition since the first Pentecost. And from the beginning there were different views as to how this message should be proclaimed. Should first preference in missioning be given to fellow Jews or to pagan Gentiles? Should Gentile converts be circumcised? How should the dietary prescriptions of Judaism be interpreted in New Testament times? The Book of Acts describes these and other disputes involving Peter, Paul, James and the other apostles of the Risen Christ.

Those initial disputes and periodic disagreements about evangelization in succeeding centuries were not unlike squabbles in a close-knit family. The Scarboro men in China and their leaders in Canada were no exception. They argued then, as their successors argue today, about mission. At its root this continuing debate is an argument between differing perceptions of "reality" and differing opinions as to what criteria should be used to assess these diverse versions of reality.

Among those inspired by John Mary Fraser there always were some who doubted whether their founder's narrowly focused approach to Christian evangelizing really was, in his words, "well worth the expense".

These loyal dissenters did not think so. Not, that is, in terms of what they perceived as the full scope of Christ's instruction to make and baptize disciples everywhere. Had not the Messiah himself espoused an integrated approach when he cited Isaiah's prophecy, "He has sent me to bring Good News to the poor"; and then declared that this mission was "being fulfilled today even as you listen"? (Cf. Luke 4:16-30; 7:22-23)?

Seen in its historical context, Father Fraser's method of evangelization was no more narrow than that of his Protestant contemporaries. Dr. John Foster, national staff member of the

J. M. Fraser (centre) and pioneer Scarboro missionaries in Chekiang.

United Church of Canada, has written:

> *The sorts of deep questions regarding economic and social reform which were coming to concern churchmen in Canada in the early twentieth century were not yet so clearly apparent in the foreign societies which obsessed the mission-minded. The task there seemed somehow more simple and urgent: to bring Gospel light where there was darkness.*

* * *

Whatever their individual views on how best to evangelize, life for the Scarboro men and Grey Sisters in Chekiang province rarely unfolded as they had hoped. And soon after the Marxist People's Republic was proclaimed in 1949, all their proselytizing activities came to an end. No doubt the Korean War in the early 1950s was a contributing factor. This conflict saw China and North Korea allied against South Korea, which was supported by United Nations forces, including Canadian units.

One of the Canadian missioners directly affected by these political-military developments was Sister Mary Catherine Doyle, a rather outspoken member of the usually reticent Grey Sisters. Mary Catherine was of the same mind about mission when she had to leave Chekiang in 1952 as she had been on first arriving in 1929. This is indicated by her later description of her arrest and expulsion:

> *. . . one morning in April (1950) several Red soldiers appeared at the convent (in Lishui) to inform me that I was under arrest. With rifles pointing at my back they marched me up the street before them . . . . The charge against me was disobedience, as I had admitted and baptized a dying woman, one of our catechumens. They were unable to decide on my punishment as they pretended to believe I had killed the patient . . . . They soon dismissed me but warned that they had not as yet decided on my punishment . . . .*
>
> *After two years of ceaseless interrogations and harassment we were ordered to leave. By truck and rail we reached the coast. As we crossed Freedom Bridge over the narrow gap separating the mainland of China from Hong Kong we realized that this was our greatest sacrifice to be faced — to leave our missionary homeland where we left our hearts.*

* * *

Craig Strang, SFM.

A quarter century passes. By 1978 Clair Yaeck was one of those asking new questions as the Scarboro Society observed its 60th anniversary year. After a summer visit to the People's Republic, this veteran missionary to Japan and past member of the SFM General Council wondered:

> *If God is acting in history, how do we see His activity in the people of China today? Are they living out the Gospel in a way more authentic than some so-called Christian countries, as some Christian scholars assert? If that is so, what does it mean for the Church?*

* * *

In 1981 Pope John Paul II himself discerned new directions for a missioning mandate as old as the Christian story itself. When visiting the Philippines in February, 1981 the Holy Father addressed neighboring China in conciliatory terms. The Pope acknowledged China's greatness, especially in "the wealth of its culture and . . . moral values". He paid significant tribute to the sixteenth century efforts of the pioneer Jesuit missionary, Matteo Ricci, who had attempted to adapt Christian teaching and practice to the Chinese culture. Of the man whose pioneer innovations were condemned by the Vatican early in the eighteenth century, John Paul would say nearly 300 years later that "his example should serve as an inspiration to many". And furthermore:

> *Others, at times, did not show the same understanding. But whatever difficulties there may have been, they belong to the past, and now it is the future that we have to look to.*

* * *

Scarboro members were looking both to the future and interpreting the past as the Pope toured in the Far East. Any "harsh judgments" of the missionary methods used by J. M. Fraser and other pioneers in earlier decades would be "grossly unfair," wrote Michael O'Hearn, lay editor of **Scarboro Missions**: "Mentally we cannot make a judgment until we have walked with the early SFMers — in their shoes and through those initial decades of the Society's existence."

In **The Chinese — Portrait of a People,** John Fraser of the **Globe and Mail** offers a related caution to all would-be evangelizers, religious and secular, and their critics as well:

> *Superimposing Western fantasies on China is a historic fallacy that dates back a long time. When the first Jesuits came to China during the seventeenth century, they saw a land of almost complete perfection, marred only by the absence of Christianity. Today, latter-day, secular Jesuits also see a land of almost complete perfection, marred only by the absence of certain human rights or certain academic standards or certain sociological insights, or whatever their field or expertise or special interest happens to be. I don't mock them because I was among their number until I had my eyes opened by Chinese people themselves.*

* * *

Before following O'Hearn's advice to walk figuratively in the shoes of the Canadian priests and sisters during their years in Chekiang province, we need to situate ourselves in the history and geography of the ancient host culture they entered so confidently.

2 GETTING ON THE MAP

It was never a big operation, let's face it," Bishop Kenneth Turner emphasized as he recalled the Scarboro-Grey Sisters' years in China. "We were neophytes trying to do our best under very difficult circumstances."

Neither the priests' nor the sisters' community had a well-developed missionary background when each group sent members to the Orient. And with few exceptions, the Canadian men and women who went abroad had little or no personal experience as evangelizers on foreign soil.

They did not, however, enter a vacuum. Methodist, Presbyterian, Church of England (now Anglican) and other Protestant missionaries from Canada had preceded them to China. More significantly — since ecumenical co-operation was virtually unknown then, the Roman Catholic missionary pattern had been in place for several generations. Under the watchful supervision of the Vatican's Congregation for the Propagation of the Faith, European clergy and religious had established central churches and outlying mission stations, built up compounds within which most of them lived and started schools, medical dispensaries and hospitals.

When the Canadians arrived in Chekiang province they took up where the French Vincentians (also known as Lazarists), the Jesuits, Dominicans and other European predecessors had left off when most were recalled to their homelands for military service on the outbreak of the First World War in 1914.

The Chinese culture itself was older than any of the Western countries from which first Catholic and then Protestant proselytizers came. While — to use terms in common usage until quite recently — almost all Chinese were "heathens" or "pagans" from a Christian point of view, they had a very old moral and social heritage of their own, along with a bewildering variety of superstitious practices. Foreign missionaries often disagreed in their assessments of the inherent worth of the Chinese tradition but none disputed its longevity.

This vast land once known as "The Middle Kingdom" between

Aged beggar woman.

heaven and earth never had been receptive territory for the message the missionaries wished to announce. China's ethical, quasi-religious customs predated the origins of Buddhism and Hinduism, and also the calling forth of Abraham as "the father of faith" for Jews, Christians and Muslims.

Primitive religion in the form of nature worship and veneration of ancestors was prevalent many centuries before the birth of Christ. The mixed meanings of human life were explained by sages in terms of the feminine-masculine duality known to this day as "yin" and "yang." Each emperor governed by "the mandate of heaven" as the masses under the often harsh rule of the imperial court toiled to survive. Millions perished prematurely in infancy, childhood or early adulthood.

As innumerable spoken dialects developed region by region, a single written language emerged — one that used ideograms (picture symbols) instead of an alphabet. A scholarly elite grew up as custodians of this cultural achievement.

In the sixth century B.C. Lao Tsu fathered the mediative "path of life" known as Taoism. In the same period an even more influential sage, known to us by his Latinized name of Confucius, prepared an exacting code of ethics for rulers, bureaucrats, scholars, landowners and the ruling establishment generally. Meanwhile the black arts of sorcery grew up among the citizenry. Spells to appease or woo the spirits were invoked for all manner of personal and domestic needs, hopes and fears.

By the first century A.D. Buddhist monks had reached China from India, followed soon by Islamic advocates from Arab lands.

Six centuries later we find the first record of a Christian presence when members of the Nestorian sect reached the heart of the Asian kingdom. Seven hundred more years passed before a Franciscan, John of Monte Coromo, founded a church in Peking in the 14th century.

Not until the early nineteenth century did the first Protestant missionaries reach China — beginning with one Robert Morrison in 1807. He was the first of what by late that century had become a Protestant army of missionaries, many of them hailing from Britain, the United States and Canada. Between 1885 and 1925, 350 Canadians served in Methodist, Presbyterian and Church of England mission fields in widely separated areas of China — ranging from Honan in the northwest to Szechwan in central west China, and from Shanghai on the eastern coast to Kwangtung on China's southernmost seaboard. *(See Map)* Over the years this Protestant contingent — which also numbered members of Baptist, Lutheran and other mission societies — included such widely-known Canadian family names as Endicott, Fraser, Hockin, McClure, Ronning and White.

* * *

The first lasting Christian impact in Asia is credited to two Jesuit priests — Francis Xavier, a Spanish compatriot of Ignatius Loyola, founder of the Society of Jesus; and the Italian disciple named Matteo Ricci.

Xavier is said to have been personally responsible for 30,000 baptisms during 10 years of evangelizing in India, Japan and the Malayan peninsula. The principal motivation underlying his zeal was described by the missionary himself in a letter from the Far East, written in 1543:

> *There is now in these parts a very large number who have only one reason for not becoming Christian, and that is because there is no one to make them Christian. It often comes to my mind to go around to all the universities of Europe, and especially that of Paris, crying out everywhere like a madman and saying to all learned men there whose learning is so much greater than their charity, "What a multitude of souls is through your fault shut out of Heaven and falling into Hell."*

Xavier's early death in 1552 at Sangchuan, an island off the coast of China, was a signal to later Jesuits, beckoning them to preach and baptize in "Cathay," still virtually unknown to the European West. No one took up this challenge with more creativity than Matteo Ricci, who first entered China in 1583. Ricci steeped himself in Chinese language, history and culture, then concentrated his attention on the governing elite.

Through a combination of extensive knowledge, influential friendships and the power of preaching, together with his receptive manner, Ricci reached the highest courts. His impact on mandarin rulers and Confucian scholars in Nanking, and later in the capital city of Peking, converted many leading Chinese to Christianity. One of his converts, Michael Yang, founded a Christian mission in Chekiang province three centuries before the first Canadian Catholics would arrive.

Ricci gained the regard of the Chinese elite principally because he demonstrated his respect for their culture. He realized that

Christianity should be as little foreign as possible in order to be acceptable. The Jesuit scholar labored to find a suitable Chinese expression for the word "God." He believed that the traditional rites performed in honor of family ancestors could continue as civil ceremonies, although he hoped that Catholic practices for burial and honoring the dead would gradually supplant the household rites.

Ricci's culturally adaptive approach was comparable to what native prelates in Africa now refer to as "Africanizing Christianity." For a while Ricci's indigenous pioneering flourished in China and enjoyed favor in Rome. Vatican prelates in charge of Propagation of the Faith composed far-seeing instructions to Catholic missionaries in 1659:

> *What could be more absurd than to transport France, Spain, Italy, or some other European country to China? Do not introduce all that to them, but only the Faith, which does not despise or destroy the manners and customs of any people, always supposing that they are not evil . . . . Do your utmost to adapt yourselves to them.*

This enlighted policy was not to prevail, unfortunately. Before long, disputes arose as to whether Mass and other liturgical services could be celebrated in Chinese or in Latin. Latin won out over local tongues. Ritual accommodations to the Chinese culture were condemned and forbidden by Vatican decrees in the first half of the eighteenth century. In retaliation, the insulted Emperor of China and his courtiers revoked the concessions they had granted to visiting missionaries and ordered them to halt all proselytizing activities.

* * *

This crisis saw China return to its traditional isolation — the historic stance that still is symbolized by the Great Wall erected to exclude aliens. But British, French and other Western powers' designs on the rich markets of the Orient were not postponed for long. Throughout the first half of the 1800s the British smuggled opium from India into China for profitable resale in an attempt to offset London's trading deficits. Peking authorities regularly but ineffectively banned such illegal trafficking.

The Opium War that began in 1840 ended four years later with a treaty — the first of several settlements forced upon China over the next 60 years by the much more powerful Western nations. Every so-called agreement extended European privileges on the mainland — and both Catholic and Protestant missionaries from the West were among the beneficiaries. In 1860, for instance, France used its imperial might to negotiate with China's rulers a convention which favored the Paris government's political and economic designs on the Far East. The convention also permitted missionaries with French passports to evangelize freely and to enjoy political protection, not only for themselves but also for their Chinese converts.

Given this situation, coupled with recurring famine, people's motives for becoming Christian could hardly remain uncolored. Hence the origin of the derisive term "rice Christians". As missionary Stephen Neill put it in **A History of Christian Missions**, "a fatal link was being forged between imperialistic penetration and the preaching of the Gospel" — which Protestant and Catholic missionaries zealously pursued in isolation from one another.

Mounting frustration among the Chinese populace was deflected by the ruling empress from her own person towards the "foreign devils" who were exploiting them for commercial gain. A popular uprising occurred in 1899-1900, led by Chinese militants calling themselves the "Society of Righteous and Harmonious Fists". Known in the Western world as the "Boxer Rebellion", this resistance was quelled by foreign troops after large numbers of native Christians had been killed.

Meanwhile, internal reform movements kept failing. The inability or unwillingness of the Manchu rulers to bring about significant improvements in the life of the masses, coupled with the increasingly oppressive presence of foreign powers, spawned the Chinese Revolutionary Movement. Dr. Sun Yat-sen emerged as the most influential of the radical new leaders. During the first decades of the new century he began to lay the foundations for an independent and republican China. He would die prematurely and a long civil war would follow, masterminded by two bitter rivals, both disciples of Sun Yat-sen: Chiang Kai-shek and Mao Tse-tung.

* * *

Mounting Chinese opposition to the Western presence did not deter Protestant and Catholic leaders in Europe and North America from devising ambitious missionary strategies. The same nineteenth century saw the revival or birth of numerous Catholic religious orders with missioning objectives. After years of suppression, the Society of Jesus was reinstated by Pope Pius VII in 1814. The Oblates of Mary Immaculate, who were to play such a major missionary role in Canada, came into existence, as did such related religious associations as the Marists, the Salesians, the Mill Hill Fathers, the Scheut Fathers

Shanghai waterfront, 1937.

and the White Fathers of Africa. Pope Gregory XVI, whose pontificate dated from 1831 to 1846, vigorously encouraged this rapid growth of missionary orders and congregations. He provided a global network for mission when he set up new dioceses in much of the world, including China — headed almost always by European-born prelates.

A popular history of Protestant missions in China between 1860 and 1900 is told in Pat Barr's **To China with Love.** Variations of the "rites controversy" arose for Protestant Communions as it had for Catholics much earlier. A comparative few, among them Baptist and Presbyterian pioneers, attempted with limited success to adapt Westernized Christianity to the Chinese culture. Aside from this imaginative minority, there was much the same general resistance on the part of Protestant leaders as among Catholic prelates to implanting in China anything other than Western modes of Christianity. In the mission fields and home congregations, Canadian Protestants joined their British and American cousins in a global crusade to bring the supposedly superior benefits of Western material progress to pagan peoples, along with the Gospel. Simultaneously, in their own distinctive ways, Western Roman Catholics were "Christianizing and civilizing" in Asia and Africa.

Competitive Catholic and Protestant battle plans in the prolonged missionary invasion of mainland China reached a new peak during the early years of the present century. Protestant missionaries sought to "reach every Chinese with the Christian message" through mass circulation of translated Bibles and by the provision of public health and educational services, Kenneth Scott Latourette noted in his much cited work, **A History of the Expansion of Christianity.** Catholic missioners, on the other hand, "placed their chief emphasis upon winning converts and nourishing a Church".

The combined Catholic-Protestant missionary impact on the Chinese people was meagre on the whole. In her study Mrs. Barr cited one revealing instance in describing the efforts of two Anglican brothers, George and Arthur Moule: "Arthur, making one of his depressingly honest reviews, reckoned that 30 years of missionary effort in Chekiang province had brought a total of 2,000 converts, which was considerably less than one in every 10,000 inhabitants."

* * *

This was the far from promising missionary scene Canadian Catholic evangelizers entered in China. They came as comparative latecomers and in small numbers — French Canadian priests assigned to Manchuria, and the English-speaking followers of John Mary Fraser, who were sent by the Vatican to the central coastal province of Chekiang.

A succession of popes in the first half of the twentieth century — Benedict XV, Pius XI and Pius XII — vigorously promoted the foreign missions in Asia and Africa. While allowing limited adaptations to local cultures and encouraging the gradual development of a native priesthood, resident bishops in China and other mission lands still almost always were European born and trained, and the Mass and other major liturgical celebrations were conducted always in the official Latin of Rome. The presiding missionary bishops in turn were responsible to the Congregation for the Propagation of the Faith ("Propaganda" for short) at Vatican City.

The Chekiang territory to which the Scarboro men were assigned was under the episcopal supervision of a bishop from France, based in the city of Ningpo. The Canadians inherited a missioning system and pattern of practices with which Father Fraser had become conversant during apprenticeship years in the area.

The way to conduct mission had long since been laid down by papal declarations, Vatican instructions and interpretive decisions by the succession of French bishops in Ningpo.

Pagodas — familiar landmarks

Thus when the first Scarboro mission bands took up residence in the 1920s they resumed the evangelizing practices their European predecessors had been carrying out for some generations. In 1929 Dr. John E. McRae, first president of Scarboro's mission college, described the assignment in glowing terms for Canadian supporters of this still new endeavor. Writing in the pages of **China**, McRae said:

> *. . . (Scarboro) efforts have been directed mostly to retrieving the losses caused by the (first) world war, when France, Belgium, Italy and Germany recalled so many of their missionary priests and left the flocks without their shepherds. Now many lapsed Christians have been reclaimed, new churches built, old ones repaired and the schools filled with nurselings of the flock.*

* * *

Between 1926 and 1954 70 more Canadians (i) journeyed to China in the footsteps of J. M. Fraser. Their times there ranged from brief sojourns to extended stays. They were: Dr. John E. McRae as "foster founder," who made two official visits to the Canadian missions; 54 members or associates of the Scarboro community, some of whom subsequently transferred to other ecclesial jurisdictions as priests, while some others returned to the lay state (ii); and 15 Grey Sisters from the Immaculate Conception order. Paul Kam, a priest member of Scarboro born in China, also was very much part of the story. Other native Chinese priests, such as Paul Wong in Kinhwa, worked with the Canadians but did not belong to their Society.

Twenty-five or nearly half of the men Scarboro sent to Chekiang came from Ontario cities, towns and farms. Almost one-third hailed from Atlantic Canada — eight from Nova Scotia, seven from Newfoundland and one each from New Brunswick and Prince

---

(i) Canadian — While exempting the one member born in China, the term Canadian is otherwise used here in a broad sense. It includes a sizeable number of men and women who, while born in other countries, spent all or much of their adulthood in Canada and in serving with Scarboro or the Grey Sisters in Chekiang.

(ii) SFM — Scarboro members in the Society's good standing usually add the initials SFM after their names. While this practice is not followed here, members and associated are clearly distinguished in the text and the Appendices.

Edward Island. Quebec contributed four missionaries to the English-speaking enterprise, and the four Western provinces only two, both of them from Alberta. Another eight came from six other countries. The 15 sisters had similar origins. Eight were born in Ontario, one each in Newfoundland, Quebec and Saskatchewan; two in Ireland and one each in England and the United States.

By the middle of 1980 the geographic origins of all Scarboro members and associates, past to present, had changed very little from the China Years. Again, almost half were Ontarians, and one third were from the Atlantic seaboard, with Nova Scotians numbering 46 of the 76 who had come from that region.(iii)

* * *

Most of the Fraser-Scarboro-Grey Sisters story took place in a comparatively small yet sizeable coastal area. Related to the vast remainder of the Chinese land mass, the location and extent of the Canadian missioning region in the east central province of Chekiang could be likened, very approximately, to New Brunswick and its relationship to the rest of Canada's huge land area.

The portion of Chekiang that became so familiar to the Canadians is made up of hilly and mountainous terrain, interlaced with river valleys and coastal lowlands. The regions which in time were combined into the Diocese of Lishui under an SFM bishop took in about 37,000 square miles (94,000 square kilometers). The estimated population by the late Forties was nearly 3,000,000 (roughly equivalent to that of Metropolitan Toronto and its environs, or British Columbia today), only a fraction of whom called themselves Christian.

The province lies just south of Shanghai, the mighty port city on the Yangtze River. Off Chekiang's coastline is the East China Sea,

---

(iii) This remarkably consistent pattern over a period of six decades raises some intriguing questions. Why, for instance, did the Scarboro Foreign Mission Society attract many more members from the four Atlantic provinces than from the more populous Western ones? Among the probable reasons, two suggest themselves immediately. First, the Catholic Church was historically well established on the Atlantic coast compared to the Prairies and Pacific Coast. Atlantic Canada was exporting clergy when the West was still called "mission territory". Secondly, family names demonstrate that a majority of Scarboro priests came of Irish and Scottish stock, which was notably strong in the Atlantic region but not in the West.

Homes on the water.

and to the southeast lie the islands of Taiwan and Okinawa. Wenchow is the provincial capital and Hangchow is one of the principal centres.

Nearby is Ningpo, the episcopal centre for the Catholic diocese when the Fraser portion of this story begins. Father Fraser served as a curate in the large ornate cathedral of Ningpo from late in 1902 until 1910, and subsequently in the neighboring districts of Taichowfu and Shaohing.

South of Ningpo are Kinhwa and Lishui — the latter known at first as Chuchow, which was field headquarters for Scarboro mission bands. The priests and sisters, and also their thousands of supporters across English-speaking Canada — kept in touch with one another chiefly by the popular Scarboro publication **China** — soon became acquainted with Lishui/Chuchow and the names of numerous mission stations, among them Lungchuan, Sungyang, Pihu, Tsingtien and Dolu. In 1940 the adjoining region of Kinhwa was added to the Chuchow/Lishui area earlier entrusted to the Scarboro priests. The enlarged area remained under the episcopal jurisdiction of the

French-born bishops in Ningpo until 1948. That year Scarboro's own Kenneth Turner became Bishop of Lishui.

Language studies and wartime emergencies in the 1930s and 1940s took Scarboro priests for shorter stays to such major cities as Shanghai, Nanking, Chungking and Peking. Advancing Japanese invaders in 1942 forced most SFM men and Grey Sisters to retreat, some of them trekking thousands of miles into the Chinese interior — to the West central province of Hunan, to Chungking; and also into India. Many of the refugees took up to six months, counting short stops en route, to travel a distance equivalent to a three or four-day car trip from Ottawa to Saskatoon. Shortly before the Second World War was to end in 1945 the Canadians returned to their "home territory" in the Lishui-Kinhwa region of Chekiang. Their return stay was shortlived, however; in less than another 10 years all of them had been expelled. *(See Map)*

* * *

Strange sounding place names on the map tell us little about the typical sights and sounds in pre-Maoist China. First impressions of two new arrivals from Canada convey something of the initial "feel" of this very different land and people.

"The odors peculiar to the Orient were everywhere," John McGoey remembered in describing his arrival in Shanghai early in 1940. Describing his experiences in **Nor Scrip Nor Shoes**, Father McGoey admitted that "odors which can be perfume to those who love China and understand her . . . almost smothered the soul of one who wanted to love her but who was simply appalled by this introduction". This Toronto-raised son of "nice clean Canada," however, soon found the hill city of Lishui and the surrounding territory more to his liking, or at least tolerable.

Harvey Steele also had been appalled by what he saw, smelled and heard on arriving in 1938. For the biographer of **Agent for Change**, Father Steele described a coastal boat trip from Shanghai to Wenchow, from where it would take several days under normal conditions to reach Lishui, only 100 miles further:

> *We had every kind of living creature on board, pigs, chickens, ducks, geese, and — as I knew the morning of the second day — ravenous bedbugs. But most of all — people, for all China was on the move in a frantic, unstructured search for a place untouched by the bombs, the carnage and the starvation. There were hundreds of them, and to my still unaccustomed*

eyes they all looked alike, shrivelled, remote and inscrutable. Yet among themselves the conversation was often animated, the many-toned language adding to the impression of excitement. I felt sure that behind the masks there were human minds that would justify getting to know them.

* * *

Once settled, what was it like each day for these transplanted men and women with a mission? The recollections of several veteran priests ("China Hands" as they called themselves) make up the next chapter.

3 REMEMBERING THE WAY IT WAS

"When it came to confessing imaginary sins he had a terrific imagination," Hugh McGettigan remembered with a chuckle. "He was teaching me the local dialect. Tuning up my ear, you could say."

"He" was Tony Fu, the Chinese catechist who was a right-hand man to the Scarboro priest while Father McGettigan was ministering to one of the outlying missions in Chekiang province. A "born pedagogue," Mr. Fu was introducing the Canadian priest to the tonal inflections of the spoken language in that particular area. And what better way do do so, the native interpreter and instructor reasoned, than to pretend to confess a variety of sins. As Hugh McGettigan told it:

> *Every morning he would be at my desk by eight o'clock. He would kneel down and for the next 10 or 15 minutes go through the Ten Commandments. It was really graphic! You would think he had studied all the moral theology books ever written. It was a very effective way to teach me.*

Like most of the other Canadian missionaries, McGettigan found the written Chinese language difficult and each spoken dialect doubly difficult when he went to the Orient in the Thirties. But he began "hearing confessions in a matter of weeks," thanks to the skilled tutoring of Mr. Fu.

The freshman missionary soon decided to try testing his limited linguistic skills in a brief homily. First he wrote out some reflections in English, then with a dictionary attempted to translate his notes into Mandarin, the written form of expression used for all dialects. Last of all he asked Fu to help him speak the written Mandarin in the local idiom. During many rehearsals McGettigan strove to memorize the strange sounds.

Came the fateful day for this inaugural Chinese sermon on the first Sunday of Advent late in 1936. Encouragingly, the small congregation seemed attentive. After Mass a delegation called on the priest. With great courtesy the several worshippers, led by an elderly woman in bound feet, congratulated him. Father McGettigan was at first delighted, then humbled. "They told me ever so politely that they didn't understand what I said but greatly admired my effort!"

* * *

Hugh McGettigan was one of several veterans of the China Years who shared past recollections and present reflections when asked: "What was it like? Could you describe a typical day and tell us about some high and low points during your time there?"

Other veteran members of the Scarboro Foreign Mission Society who willingly answered these and related questions were Francis Diemert, Alexander MacIntosh, Allan McRae, John Maurice, Harvey Steele and Bishop Ken Turner. Their colorful reminiscences provided most of the raw material for this chapter. Supplementary material was garnered from transcripts of earlier interviews and from past issues of **China** and **Scarboro Missions.**

* * *

The four seasons were among the few realities in the Chuchow/Lishui-Kinhwa regions which reminded the Canadians of their homeland. And even the seasonal highs and lows of Chekiang's semi-tropical climate took "a lot of getting used to":

> *Because the summers were so blessed hot, we had daily Mass by six o'clock in the morning or earlier. You couldn't do much in the real heat of the day. Even the birds were panting like puppies. But the ordinary Chinese had to keep working in the fields and shops for their meagre living. I often wondered how they did it.*

Spring and fall were the most enjoyable seasons of the year, as in much of Canada. The comparatively short winter season could be uncomfortably cold, especially in the months of December through February. While "nothing like a Canadian winter," the coldest months brought some snow to the countryside, and temperatures sometimes fell below freezing. Without central heating churches and priests' residences sometimes were "numbingly cold".

Still the Canadians rarely had to endure what the average peasant family experienced daily. Alex MacIntosh remembered one experience when he was taking emergency medical supplies "up country". As night fell, his bike had a flat tire. Father MacIntosh flagged a rickety bus. The driver readily agreed to deliver the medicines further along the road. Then the priest sought overnight shelter from the winter cold in one of the little houses perched on the edge of a steep hill:

Chuchow/Lishui, after a snowfall.

I asked the family if they could take me in for the night. They would. They didn't even have much rice to share. So the husband went up the hillside and dug out some bamboo shoots to provide a meal for the visitor. They gave me a thin quilt and a little back space that was only partly closed in — the best they had. I slept with my clothes and helmet on, trying to keep from freezing. My hosts had done the best they could. You couldn't help but like people like that.

* * *

Overnight stopovers were unusual for the Canadians. In Chuchow/Lishui and Kinhwa the missionaries lived in enclosed compounds, while the men posted to outlying missions also lived apart from their small groups of parishioners. On an average day the priests spent much of their working time with trained native catechists who in turn instructed prospective converts among their countrymen.

The main mission compound in Chuchow/Lishui had been built by missionaries from France. The nearly half-acre site was surrounded by a high wall. Inside were several major buildings, including the church which one priest said could accommodate between 200 and 300; a residence large enough for clergy stationed there and for several visiting priests, as well as for the native-born domestic staff; a school of several classrooms for male pupils, and a medical dispensary. Several catechists and China-born teachers spent most of each day inside the compound, although their families lived elsewhere in the city.

The Grey Sisters resided in a large convent nearby where each day some conducted school courses for girl pupils, while others in the nursing order ministered to the many sick adults and children who always crowded the dispensary. In the later years there also was a hospital administered by the women of the Pembroke order.

The mission compound at Kinhwa, where J. M. Fraser spent most of his China years, also had been constructed by French Lazarists. Situated on a prominent hillside site, the walls enclosed a large church and residence. Nearby lived the chief catechist and his family.

Nearby Shanghai was a favorite place to visit. In this partly Westernized metropolis the missionaries purchased household and medical supplies, and some prized extras — "good Johnny Walker whiskey once in a while," for example; tobacco, books and periodicals, gramophone records (as disc recordings were called then), batteries and other parts for their radio sets, and on one occasion, a Delco generating unit which Father McGettigan said he helped assemble. This provided the Chuchow/Lishui compound with its own electricity some years before limited power service was available in the city.

Transportation was also limited by today's norms. In the Twenties and Thirties, sedan chairs and rickshaws drawn by Chinese runners, and river boats also operated by the Chinese, were the principal means of conveyance. Bus service was to become more or less reliable when available. And in time the priests acquired bicycles, motorbikes, jeeps or small cars. When all else failed, priests and sisters alike walked. In fact visits to the more remote mission stops in the mountainous areas sometimes called for hours of walking each way.

* * *

"Before I went there, my only impression of the Chinese was that they were guys who worked at corner laundries and in restaurants." The speaker acknowledged that he soon learned otherwise when in China. Here were many millions with numerous ethnic backgrounds, ranging, for example, from the short Cantonese in the South to the tall Northerners in Peking. He found that he had much to learn from these host peoples with whom he wanted to share the Good News of Christianity.

Most of the Scarboro men interviewed spoke favorably of the Chinese people as they had come to know them. Some complimentary reactions:

> *The ordinary Chinese were very lovable people. They would do anything for you if you treated them half well.*

> *I liked them. They were the soul of politeness.*

> *I enjoyed their sense of humor. They always seemed able to laugh along with you. I think their good humor helped keep them alive. Every time you saw an adult Chinese, you could say, "There goes a miracle." In those days it was a miracle to have survived long enough to grow up as an ordinary Chinese.*

> *You could move among them quite freely. They were always very courteous, even the pagans.*

> *The rural way of life was very simple when we were there. It still wasn't complicated by the modern ways of urban life. People were close to nature, close to the cycles of life and death.*

> *The average Chinese had a very hard life. They seemed to take everything as it came. Crying about it wasn't going to solve it. They were stoics, very philosophical about living. They had to be.*

Some of the missionaries' qualified or critical remarks:

> *The people acted very differently after nightfall. They stayed indoors and were suspicious of any callers. No wonder, considering China's long history of raids by bandits, warlords and other marauders.*

> *Farm families lived in village clusters for protection. They walked to their land very early each morning and worked until night time and then went to bed soon after dark.*

> *They're born gamblers and very curious.*

> *The Chinese couldn't believe we were celibates. They thought we were crazy. We couldn't have women on the cooking or housekeeping staffs. The confessionals had to be open so they could keep an eye on the confessor.*

> *It must have been the dirtiest country in the world then.*

Hugh McGettigan, SFM.

> *They had a strong pagan tradition and very many superstitions and superstitious rituals.*
>
> *The Chinese really saw themselves as the centre of the world. We were the barbarians. We didn't realize at first that we were not wanted there. We imposed ourselves and we were tolerated, that's all!*

Mixed feelings were not all retrospective. While still in China, some Scarboro men frankly expressed some critical reactions in print. One of them was Edward Lyons, a native of spacious, uncrowded Alberta. In 1940 he wrote from the missions describing "the unbelievable crowding and congestion in China where one rubs elbows with his neighbor all day long and every day." And Father Lyons, who was not alone in finding the self-effacing courtesies of his hosts sometimes hard to take, continued:

> *Their etiquette demands the constant praising of one's neighbor (to his face only, of course) and on the receiving end it is never lawful to accept a compliment, but every*

John Maurice, SFM.

> *word of praise must be emphatically denied, word for word.*
>
> *If it is hypocrisy with a purpose, it is nevertheless hypocrisy, and does prove very annoying to us at times . . . .*

* * *

"There was no such thing as an average day; each had its own peculiarities," Alex MacIntosh said, adding, "And there were a lot of extraordinary days." Other China veterans agreed, although all spoke of experiences they had shared in common.

"Lousy" or at best indifferent food, for instance, had been a major drawback, most of the men said. Plus water that rarely was palatable or safe to drink. One of the SFMers recalled a joke current at the time:

> *"Is the water safe to drink?"*
>
> *"Yes. First boil it, then filter it and then make beer."*

Another compatriot cheerfully reported that some of his happiest moments came on hot afternoons when he pulled up from an outdoor well chilled bottles of home-made beer. "We got the recipe from some Polish priests. It was the big thrill of the day, worth staying alive to enjoy."

What foods were available and in what forms? Those who were posted to the major missions probably fared better than their colleagues living alone or in twosomes at the mission stations. Craig Strang explained why in a transcribed interview:

> *. . . we lived as closely as we could to the Canadian way. Of course there weren't any of the amenities we have here, like electricity and plumbing . . . . But we had the habit of sending our cooks to the Sisters and the Sisters would teach them how to cook the local food the way we would like it, ... which was mostly staying away from all the oils they put on them which made all the food greasy.*

Two of the main meals on an average day, as recalled by Allan McRae:

> *Breakfast: A kind of gruel made from rice left over from the previous day. Hard bread, rather like a bagel. Coffee, which came from Shanghai, with milk powder. Fruit in season.*
>
> *Evening dinner: Usually a pork dish or a scrawny chicken (which had had to scrounge for food in the streets). More rice and some vegetable such as carrots, potatoes or sweet potatoes. Tender bamboo shoots or fruit for dessert. Usually green tea.*

Potent Chinese wine, made locally, was mentioned by several of the men. Some called it "100 proof", and one thought it "120 proof"; all agreed that "it really burned your gizzard on the way down".

Imported liquor purchased in Shanghai was an occasional bonus — a "real treat" for some of them. And what of their founder when it came to alcohol? "Father Fraser was a total abstainer, like a dyed-in-the-wool Presbyterian," one of the missionaries remarked jovially.

* * *

"When we went over in 1934 there was nothing much organized with regards to learning the Chinese language," said one priest. "The catechist would come in every morning and read something in

Bishop Ken Turner, SFM.

Chinese as fast as possible. We were supposed to pick up the local dialect that way."

This SFMer was not alone in feeling frustrated by the formidable language barrier. John Maurice admitted that he "had to work at the language continually" and still, he felt, he had not been able to speak the Chuchow/Lishui dialect very well. Alex MacIntosh thought those whose mother language was English probably "have the laziest tongue in the world" when it came to speaking another language. Allan McRae found his language studies "extremely difficult". So did Francis Diemert, who was a student at a Jesuit language school in Peking until he and other classmates were interned by Japanese invaders. After a long day of studies plus an evening class he often reached "a saturation point". Father Diemert said he did learn to read a newspaper in Mandarin but found speaking the strange tongue much more demanding.

For one thing there were hundreds of local dialects. Every hundred li or so (about 35 miles distance) meant another mode of speaking Chinese, Father Maurice pointed out. He remembered travelling up river with Aaron Gignac, one of Scarboro's more gifted linguists. "Father Gignac had to act as interpreter between two small groups of Chinese passengers, each from another part of the province."

Francis Diemert observed, as did some others, that perhaps the quickest way to pick up local intonations was "to listen to the youngsters talking on the streets and then try to talk with them". He noted that they were "not afraid to laugh at our mistakes," which custom would not allow adults to do.

* * *

"When I heard the bangs I was scared half to death. I thought it must be a Japanese raid. Instead," Allan McRae said, "it was the people behind me letting off firecrackers at the consecration of the Host."

He was describing one of the unforgettable moments in his missionary career. J. M. Fraser had despatched the newly-arrived priest to a small church far from Kinhwa. There Father McRae was to celebrate Midnight Mass to usher in that Christmas of 1938.

About 100 people came to the service. As was their custom on major feast days the worshippers ignited firecrackers at the most solemn moment in the celebration of the Eucharist. McRae soon learned to take this custom in his stride — as do foreign missionaries in Latin America nowadays.

Daily Mass, usually early each morning, was the religious focal point of the missionary's working day. And Sunday Eucharist initiated another week of trying to witness to the Christian faith in this strange, mostly uncaring land.

"Mass was celebrated in Latin with a native server — sometimes the priest's catechist and sometimes the houseboy," John Maurice explained in describing the usual weekday setting. "And perhaps with a few of our school teachers present as well."

The Sunday congregation was larger, ranging upwards to 20 or 30 at the average mission station, he estimated. As ever, the native catechist played a key role. Before the Mass began the catechist led the people in reciting morning prayers and then conducted the question-and-answer session on the Chinese Catholic catechism in use at the time.

"They would sing out the questions and answers, first the men on one side and then the women on the other," one Scarboro member said. Another recalled the simple, straightforward questions and answers that the people had committed to memory: "Who made the world? God made the world. Why did he make the world? And so on."

The Christian terms had to be repeatedly explained in local idiom to those preparing for possible baptism. Often the Chinese tongue did not have expressions corresponding to the Christian concepts that had originated in the Near East and Europe. More than one SFMer observed that Chinese Catholics in their charge had no difficulty acquiring a "great devotion to the Blessed Virgin Mary".

Those interviewed described native catechists as indispensable collaborators for the foreign missionaries. The catechist was "the go-between," the interpreter who enabled each priest and the people to communicate in meaningful ways — and largely on his own terms, if he so chose. One missionary said:

> *The catechist knew the people and their problems and he also knew our problems. He had learned his religion well and was able to put it across well. We would have been pretty helpless without the catechists.*

Besides instructing candidates for baptism, known as catechumens, the catechist sometimes preached the Sunday sermon, after consulting with the pastor.

Usually catechists were family men who had given up their former means of livelihood to work in the paid employ of the missionaries. The main mission compound conducted a training school for promising native assistants, who were always in demand. As the Scarboro enterprise grew, each parish employed several catechists and each mission station one or two.

Most of the men told of memorable happenings during their evangelizing efforts in China. Father McRae described his monthly walking tour of the outlying mission posts. Each night on the road he would stay with a Christian family. "They always gave you the best they had." Sometimes this would even be "a big spread" — a welcoming banquet by local standards. There would be plenty of wine and sometimes "bottoms up" contests between the Chinese men.

Father Maurice noted that the distance between outlying stops sometimes was 25 miles or more. In walking time this would take up most of two days — one to reach the destination, stay overnight, celebrate Mass and administer Sacraments, and then press on or return to the main mission the next day.

"You had to be in good condition to travel. It was very hot in summer and sometimes quite cold in winter," he observed. In some cases the visiting priest was accompanied by a houseboy who carried the Mass kit and overnight supplies. At each stopping place, he said, the local catechist and his family usually were the main hosts.

Bishop Ken Turner praised the effectiveness of the Grey Sisters' "indirect evangelization" in Chekiang. Their nursing and para-medical skills, applied with tireless dedication, attracted thousands of Chinese to the Canadian dispensaries. Face to face the women skilfully administered "foreign medicine", which often prepared the way for instruction and sometimes conversion.

The SFM bishop, by 1981 serving as chaplain at the Grey Sisters' motherhouse in Pembroke, recalled that a missionary's life at an isolated station was "sometimes lonely but not frightening".

"The Bible came to life in China," Alex MacIntosh said. "You could see the parables being lived out before your eyes." And as he made his way over the stony paths of the mountains and sometimes could look out over a city or town lying below, he understood as never before "why Jesus wept over Jerusalem when he saw it."

* * *

When asked what they did for recreation, these Scarboro elders listed a wide variety of pastimes. These ranged from brisk walks back and forth while in conversation with Monsignor Fraser (more or less a prescribed activity in Kinhwa) to reading books and periodicals, playing Scottish and Irish records, listening to English-language newscasts on shortwave radio, keeping a small garden, "sawing away on the fiddle by myself," playing auction bridge or other games of skill, taking part in sporting contests and, of course, visiting with one another.

Letters from home were an obvious highlight when mails were received. So were periodic furloughs in Canada or even a few days away in Shanghai.

* * *

"There was many a time when I said a good Act of Contrition," one of the priests admitted in describing the bombing and strafing raids which Japanese planes carried out over Lishui and Kinhwa in the early 1940s. While only a few planes were involved in most raids, the forays were frequent, and often the planes would spray the countryside with machine-gun fire. "It was touch and go more than once."

Fearful experiences were almost commonplace for several years. The hazards and disruptions were summarized by Kenneth Turner in a letter written from Lishui as the Second World War ended:

> *The last few years in Chekiang have almost made our veteran missionaries forget what life was like in peacetime. The invasions, bombings and epidemics; the ebb and flow of refugees in a sea of confusion, seeking sanctuary from the storm of fire and steel that rained down on them; the uprooting and tearing apart of families; the terror-filled cries of children and the mute agony of the aged . . . . and we were powerless but for prayer. From the withdrawal of enemy armies, many local families, impoverished and homeless, presented a pitiful problem. Rice was scarce and I mean scarce! Drainage was clogged with the ruins of buildings, and wells were filled up. Bubonic plague struck viciously, dropping victims in the streets where they writhed in pain and died. We did what we could with the supplies international relief could allocate to us. And inflation! Indescribable!*

Several of those interviewed said recurring illness from communicable diseases was the main danger they encountered in China. Cholera, malaria and dysentry were among the most feared. Some of the missionaries had repeated bouts of serious illness abroad, and three Canadians died of disease or surgical complications while in China, including a Grey Sister.

* * *

What about high and low moments while in Chekiang? Boredom was a frequent problem, some of the men said. Especially when trying to concentrate on their language studies.

The loneliness a person felt in an isolated mission station, far from one's native land and family and even hours of walking distance from fellow priests, could be excruciating. And with loneliness, a few said, sometimes came the fear of death or injury while alone in a foreign place.

Add a lurking sense of hopelessness; the feeling that no matter what they tried to do it would not make much difference in the end. Harvey Steele quoted the rather cynical advice an old French missionary offered newly arrived Canadians: "Everything in China is hopeless but don't take it to heart. It's not serious."

Father Steele said he had tried to follow another maxim: "Keep your mind open and your bowels open." In China, he said, the first was much harder than the second.

Hugh McGettigan recalled a touching experience while he was missioning in Dolu:

> *The people more or less adopted me there. One old man with quite a lot of property was going to make out his will so as to leave everything to me. I asked this old pagan, "What's this? Why leave your wealth in the hands of a Christian?" "Because you're the only honest man around here," he said. He wanted the income from his lands put to good use to help pay for a good school and a home for teachers.*

Absence of any mail from Scarboro, family and friends in Canada was one of the worst hardships, Allan McRae stated. When Japan occupied much of coastal China and was at war with the allied powers, including Canada, little or no mail reached the missionaries in Chekiang for over a year.

Father McGettigan summed up his China years in a reflective mood:

> *There were times when I was miserable and times when I was very happy and there were a lot of times in between. It's just the same as anywhere else. Wherever I am I try to make a go of it.*

Most of his colleagues in China could have said the same.

* * *

What might have been? What might be achieved in future?

With few exceptions, these missionaries to the Old China insisted that, even though conversions had been very slow in the first decades of Scarboro's efforts in Chekiang, eventually they would have made substantial gains under stable conditions. And most predicted that Christianity, if given a fair chance in future, would multiply in the now Marxist republic.

As to what might have been, these comments were typical:

If there had been normal times, I think we could have made a lot of headway.

While it was very slow at first, it was just beginning to come along when the Commies came in and spoiled everything.

Foreign priests were only there temporarily until native clergy were ready to take over. That was beginning to happen when we had to leave.

We didn't break into the culture because we still had that superiority feeling. But if we had stayed there that attitude would have eroded gradually. It would have gone easier in this day and age.

Another Scarboro member expressed sharp disappointment that the Society's leaders had not called together the men who had served in China so as to hear their shared insights and recommendations for future missions. This was unfair, he felt, and also a great opportunity lost.

Other veterans were confident that new opportunities would come in time:

It would be wonderful if before the turn of the century the Church could go back to pick up where we left off. Even China may be ready to receive the Gospel.

In those days I often said the Chinese would not be ready to hear the Gospel until they had become a united country instead of a collection of warring provinces. Mao Tse-tung turned out to be the instrument for bringing about this unification. The discipline and order brought about by the Communist government could well serve as the base for accepting Christianity without capitalism.

If the Communists would get out tomorrow, there wouldn't be enough churches in China to hold all the people who would come.

4 THE FOUNDER'S FIRST YEARS IN CHINA

In 1902 two priests — one a Belgian Lazarist, the other a Canadian diocesan clergyman trained by the Vincentians in Italy — arrived in China. Both were 25. Both were destined to begin their notable missionary careers in the same Diocese of Ningpo of Chekiang province. Vincent Lebbé was assigned by Bishop Reynaud to Shaohing, an important centre of 700,000 people. During most of his first term in the Orient, John Mary Fraser served as a curate on the cathedral staff. The Belgian and Canadian probably met, but if so, there is no known record of how they regarded one another.

Both looked forward to the day when native clergy would replace all foreign missionaries. Otherwise, their ways of thinking and acting mostly diverged. Pere Lebbé openly questioned ecclesial policies and politics when he disagreed; Father Fraser rarely if ever did so, not publicly at least.

* * *

Soon Lebbé was asking awkward questions. Why, for example, were there so few native-born bishops even though there was a growing number of Chinese clergy? The Belgian's opinions eventually came to the attention of Cardinal Van Rossum, prefect of Propaganda at the Vatican from 1918 to 1932. This gruff, forward-looking Dutch prelate (with whom Father Fraser would later negotiate a mission territory for Scarboro men) was to set in motion the first steps that led to the naming of six China-born bishops in 1926 — the episcopal breakthrough Lebbé had envisaged a quarter century earlier.

In **Thunder in the Distance** Jacques Leclercq called Pere Lebbé "one of the great figures of modern Catholicism". The influential French writer described the Lazarist's distress on seeing prominent symbols of Western, and especially of French domination in the Chinese Christian community where he was stationed:

> *. . . . when Pentecost came along the Shaohing church, like the others, was hung with the tricolor, and one even flew over the residence. Pere Lebbé was haunted by the thought of these flags, symbols of what a foreign thing*

> *Christianity still remained in China. The fundamental need before there could be any real conversion in the country as a whole was for the Church to become as Chinese in China as it was French in France and Belgian in Belgium . . . .*

Stephen Neill, the Anglican missionary and historian, gave a similar account of Lebbé's outlook in describing the young European's reactions to the privileged convention France had imposed on Chinese rulers some decades earlier:

> *Why should missionaries be protected? If the answer is "from the Chinese", how will it ever be possible to win over a man from whom you need to be protected? The only method is the total self-identification of oneself in love with those whom one desires to win . . . . Lebbé saw the extent to which the Church in China was foreign; he was convinced that, if it was to do great things, it must become completely Chinese.*

Lebbé felt so strongly about this that he became a naturalized citizen of China.

* * *

J. M. Fraser saw the situation with different eyes. For one thing he had some reservations about the indigenous innovations favored by Vincent Lebbé, and long before him by Matteo Ricci. According to Scarboro's Hugh F. X. Sharkey, in time Fraser would challenge the assumption that conversion of "the literati and the upper strata" would lead the masses to become Christian. During an interview Father Sharkey recalled:

> *Monsignor Fraser didn't feel that way about it at all. He said . . . . that it's very definite in the Gospel where Christ said, "I have come to preach the Gospel to the poor" . . . . Monsignor Fraser thought that we should learn the dialect of the people we were working among, and maybe later there might be the odd person who had the gift of languages who might take up Mandarin, the language of educated Chinese.*

However, the Scottish-Canadian did not have much patience with any "indirect approach" to evangelization through social action, although he regularly provided such "corporal works" as schools and orphanages in his pastoral programs. Fraser said he wanted to come "straight on like St. Paul." There were so many souls to save and so little time before millions more of them would die! This was the constant preoccupation of the young Torontonian.

Some years later this same sense of urgency was visually expressed in bold headlines on the covers of **China**, the mission magazine Father Fraser would found and edit. Month after month for several years the cover was the same. In vertical type down the left-hand side readers across Canada saw the stark statement: THERE ARE 400,000,000 PAGANS IN CHINA. And in the right-hand column on the other side of some appropriate photograph, headlines read, IN CHINA 33,000 PEOPLE DIE DAILY UNBAPTIZED. (iv)

* * *

The same compelling motivation is very clear in one of the earliest Fraser letters now in the Scarboro archives. Writing from Ningpo to a priest friend on January 6, 1906, feast of the Epiphany, J. M. Fraser described some lasting impressions and convictions after three years there. In Ningpo and in the surrounding districts he daily saw millions following pagan ways. He spoke too of the desperate need for more orphanages "to save the souls of myriads of little girls who are now being done away with on account of the poverty of the inhabitants". He continued:

> *It was in Ningpo that I saw for the first time a person committing the sin of idolatry. It was an old woman prostrating herself before an idol. I'll never forget the feeling that came over me — I felt like vomiting; but now it no longer makes any impression on me as it is an everyday occurrence. China could be described as a great sea or ocean of idolatry. It is full of it from top to bottom. High and low from the Emperor to the peasant, men, women and children — all are sunk in the darkest idolatry. The land is swarming with pagan temples . . . Idolatry and superstition is rife in all walks of life and all circumstances . . . .*
>
> *How sad! Four hundred million rational beings . . . . When will missionaries come in sufficient numbers and with*

(iv) Such dramatic presentation was not original. Decades before Protestant missionaries, led by Evangelicals, began using statistics in this graphic fashion. One nineteenth century example called "Every Stitch Represents One Million Souls" portrayed several rows each of brightly colored stitching for Roman Catholic, Protestant, Orthodox, Mohammedan and Jewish believers, and many more rows of dark black stitching to represent the world's unbaptized majority. This fund-raising poster was entitled A PLEA FOR MISSIONS.

Scarboro's founder — John Andrew Mary Fraser.

> *adequate zeal to redeem these people from folly during life and hell after death?*

Millions of souls to be saved — through Baptism into membership in the Catholic Church: this was the compelling imperative that drove John Mary Fraser. What had taken place in earlier years to persuade him that he should embrace so awesome and, some would say so presumptuous an undertaking on the other side of the world from his home? What clues are to be found in his family background, childhood experiences, parish and school life and higher education? Or was he mysteriously "called forth" from quite unexceptional circumstances?

* * *

On June 28, 1877 at 19 Clinton Street, Toronto, the ninth of 11 children was born to William and Joanna (nee Chisholm) Fraser, who had migrated from Scotland some years before. This son was baptized John Andrew.

Catholics were a small minority in what was then a mostly Protestant, Anglo-Saxon city. William Fraser, by trade a builder, instructed in Toronto Technical School and for a time served as a Separate School Board trustee.

The large family lived frugally, from necessity and perhaps also by preference, in the dwelling built by the father and later expanded to a two-storey dwelling at 21 Clinton Street. Years later Monsignor Fraser would write in his memoirs:

> *Mother would heat a blanket and wrap it around our feet. She was very thrifty, and had to be to feed her large family. Father was earning only 20 cents an hour; later on becoming foreman, he got a raise to 25 cents. How they ever managed to get along I do not know. Things were cheaper then, it is true, but even then bread was six cents a loaf, milk six cents a quart and meat 10 cents a pound. Mother made our clothes and knitted our stockings and mitts.*

Although he spent most of his life thousands of miles from his family, Fraser remained close to them in thought and prayer. "I was blessed with good parents and good brothers and sisters", he wrote as he approached 80. Apparently he was closest to the brother born next after him: "Charlie and I were chums. We went to school and church together and to Sunnyside to swim."

The Fraser children received an upbringing typical of a devout

Catholic household of that time and place. John Andrew found the pattern of family worship and parish activities at St. Mary's Church much to his liking. There he made his First Communion, was confirmed and became a very active altar boy:

> *Sunday was a busy day. First, I went to early Mass and Communion. Then home a mile for breakfast. Then back again for High Mass and sermon. Home for dinner. Then at 3 p.m. Sunday school and in the evening another long walk for Vespers, sermon and Benediction.*

The curate at St. Mary's was to have a lasting influence on the impressionable youngster. John Mary Cruise asked the 14 year-old lad when they first met, "Would you like to be a priest?" Not an unusual question to ask altar boys in those days. Yes, John Andrew said he was interested. "I was overjoyed and raced home to tell them the good news. I was to be a priest!" Immediately Father Cruise began Latin lessons with his protégé. Studies followed at De La Salle School and later at St. Michael's College.

Candidates for the diocesan priesthood in Toronto were sent for studies to the Grand Seminary in Montreal or abroad to the Collegio, Brignole Sale, in Genoa, Italy. Here again Father Cruise played a decisive role; he had taken his priestly studies in Genoa and he advised John Fraser to do the same. In 1896, not yet 20, Fraser sailed from New York for the Italian city where he enrolled at the institution managed by the Vincentian Order under the watchful supervision of Propaganda in Rome.

Although he did not enter the seminary with the intention of becoming a missionary priest, it is not surprising that John Andrew chose that apostolate. The Genoan college was a mission seminary with students enrolled from many countries. Fraser's interest in the missions soon was aroused by the stirring tales and exhortations of visiting missioners. He decided to become one of them.

On July 14, 1901 he was ordained a priest by the archbishop of Genoa. According to custom the ordinand took another name on receiving Holy Orders. John Andrew Fraser chose the name "Maria." Henceforth the Canadian missionary called himself John Mary, not John Andrew, and regularly signed his correspondence "J. M. Fraser." Toronto's Father Cruise had left a lasting mark; this mentor's name also was John Mary.

Although ordained a diocesan priest of Toronto, Father Fraser was designated a "missionary at large" under the direction of the

Holy See's Propagation of the Faith, and assigned by Rome to Ningpo, China. Arrangements for his stationing there took months, given communications by sea mail and the Vatican's working pace. Consequently, for more than a year Fraser waited in Toronto to begin his foreign service. Not that he was idle; it is impossible to imagine that he ever was. He worked diligently on the clerical staff of his home parish, St. Mary's; then at St. Michael's Cathedral, and in St. Joseph's parish.

Father Fraser's first communion class, 1905.

By late December 1902 he was in Shanghai — the port city of China then infamous for its international drug trafficking and gambling, and for its segregated, highly privileged foreign quarter. J. M. Fraser's arrival in China later was hailed by a Scarboro editor as "an historic event, for he was the first English-speaking secular priest from the continent of North America to set foot in that vast land as a missionary". But not by any means was he the first Canadian missioner to arrive there. The first Protestant evangelizers from Canada had preceded him by nearly 20 years.

Father Fraser, seemingly unaware that he might be making history as a Canadian Catholic, was impressed with the Western nations' segregated-quarters in Shanghai and heartened by his welcome in Ningpo:

> *The foreign concession . . . has handsome buildings and well-paved avenues. Here everything is up to date — everything, of course, except the spiritual life which is in a sorry plight . . .*
>
> *From there I sailed . . . to Ningpo, 90 miles further south on a beeline. We landed in front of Bishop Reynaud's residence, who received me with indescribable kindness. It being early on the Feast of St. Thomas, Apostle and patron of China, I immediately proceeded to say Mass in the Cathedral.*

The first day the new missionary was probably impressed most when he heard a sermon in the local Chinese dialect. Fraser realized as never before that some facility in the native tongue was indispensable if he were to be an effective missioner. But how long might it take him to acquire this strange language? He was determined to make every effort and he did. This undertaking — so indicative of Fraser's resolute pursuit of his goal — was also described in his 1906 letter to a priest friend:

> *A Chinese priest preached that day and I was amazed at the queer sound of the Chinese language. I was impressed however by the force and ringing-clear tone of my adopted tongue. How I longed to be able to preach! I imagined there were five long years of hard labor ahead of me before performing that feat.*
>
> *Little did I think at that time that in less than five months I would be making the vaults of that same church ring in that strange tongue.*

Ningpo steamer near Taichowfu, 1902-10.

Neither then nor later did the Canadian missionary have much to record about political and economic conditions in his host country. There were a few exceptions — two of them pertaining to the Boxer Rebellion, that turn-of-the-century effort by the often exploited Chinese to drive out the "foreign devils," missionaries included. When he was leaving Toronto for "the great unknown" in 1902, Fraser noted in his memoirs, the "anti-foreign Boxer uprising . . . had barely been quelled". Then the author added this surprising admission: "I did not expect to last more than a year." In fact he was to stay nearly eight years on the first occasion and was to spend almost all of his long adult life in the Orient.

"During my first year in Ningpo, when walking through the narrow streets, I often expected to be run through by a Boxer's lance upon turning a corner," Fraser remembered, "but nothing happened." However, he said a fellow curate named Andrew Tsu was "captured and put to death by the Boxers" in 1903.

Later the Canadian newcomer was assigned part-time to his first mission field outside Ningpo — the district of Fenghwa, about 500 square miles in extent and densely populated. One of its native sons was Chiang Kai-shek, who would become the Nationalist leader. Whenever time allowed Father Fraser travelled to Fenghwa "to propagate the Faith, opening chapels here and there and finally building the Sacred Heart Church in the central city of 1908". It was the first of nearly 20 churches and residences he would supervise during his missionary career.

Father Fraser had a shrewd eye when it came to appraising Chinese social conditions in terms of the potential for conversions. In an early letter to his family, he shared some observations:

> *The inhabitants of Ningpo are nearly all pagan and they do not seem much inclined to become Catholic, on account of their minds being engrossed with business and worldly matters. In country places it is not so. The people there are very simple, often leading a life free from sin and observing the law of nature which God has stamped on their hearts. The country folk are therefore more disposed to receive the light of faith and eternal salvation. For that reason the greater number of our converts in Chekiang are among the farmers. . . .*

He also looked forward to "a speedy increase" in the number of catechumens — persons learning Catholic teaching prior to Baptism — in the smaller villages. As he explained, "They are hemmed in by the mountains and thus shut off from the busy world."

* * *

John Mary Fraser was doing his utmost to live up to an honorary Chinese title conferred on him by Bishop Reynaud — one that meant "Pillar of the Kingdom". Soon the limitations of one man's labors, no matter how strenuous, dawned on the idealistic, yet also practical young missionary. The question he had raised in an earlier letter continued to haunt him: "When will missionaries come in sufficient numbers and with adequate zeal to redeem this people from folly during life, and hell after death?"

By 1910 the lone Canadian decided that he should return to the Western world in quest of more laborers for this crowded corner of God's vineyard. That November Father Fraser sailed from Shanghai bound for North America and later Europe. He had "a double object in view, to collect funds and to found, if possible, a seminary for the training of missionaries".

5 CRUSADER ON THREE CONTINENTS

In 1911 and 1912 John Mary Fraser was busy on three continents. He campaigned tirelessly in the United States, Italy, Ireland and briefly in Scotland and England during 1911, seeking episcopal approval and funding to open a missionary college in Canada.

This dream remained uppermost in his mind when he returned to China early in 1912, accompanied by the Irish priest who was to become a founder of a large missionary society in his homeland. Father Fraser remained in Chekiang province until the middle of 1918, continually promoting his college proposal by letters and articles for the religious press.

* * *

From the day he first set out in pursuit of his college dream, it took Father Fraser exactly eight years to establish a mission seminary. Despite delays and disappointments, evasions and refusals, he pursued this objective with determined hopefulness. Like the proverbial salesman, he never took "No" for a final answer. He achieved what he aimed for — if not as soon or as fully as first intended.

After spending Christmas of 1910 with family and priest friends, Fraser began his long campaign to persuade thousands more Catholics to become "mission minded" towards the faraway Chinese. For reasons that are not clear now, he did not begin his crusade in Canada, but in the northeastern United States. Perhaps because this was the heartland of American Catholicism; it was potentially the best territory in which to find influential support and substantial funds.

For five months Father Fraser advocated his "mission propaganda" in and around New York, presenting his cause to prelates, clergy and laity alike. American bishops who heard the Canadian were generally receptive. However, they also were considering a similar appeal from two American priests — James Anthony Walsh and Frederick Price. In April that year the U.S. hierarchy approved a Walsh-Price proposal that led to the opening of a national mission seminary at Maryknoll, New York. Thus began one of the best known, and nowadays also one of the most socially active and controversial mission societies.

Transportation: "labor intensive".

Fraser, whose name is listed as an associate priest on some early Maryknoll records, was said to have been pleased by this parallel development, even though it meant rejection of his particular appeal. Several years later he would travel with Father Walsh during the Maryknoll leader's first visit to the Orient. (v)

J. M. Fraser's next stopping place was Rome. Propaganda officials were not prepared, as he had hoped, to direct the bishops of Canada to found a national missionary seminary as the Americans were doing. Vatican authorities did promise every encouragement for any Canadian prelate who initiated such a project. Seven more years were to pass before Father Fraser found his man in the person of the archbishop of Ottawa.

On to Genoa. There the Canadian priest visited the seminary he had attended in 1896-1901. Irish students urged him to visit their homeland. In Ireland he received his warmest reception from church

---

(v) In time two Walsh names became prominent in the Maryknoll story: that of James A. Walsh, co-founder and first superior-general of the American missionary society; and James E. Walsh, veteran missionary to China, influential missiologist, superior-general and for 12 years a prisoner of the Chinese Communist government.

leaders and aspiring candidates for the missions — at Maynooth and All Hallows seminaries, in Dublin and Cork, and wherever else he visited. Cardinal Logue of Armagh reportedly offered buildings and land if the Canadian priest would stay to establish a mission college in Ireland. Fraser declined, seeing this as a responsibility for Irish clergy. There were other encouragements, although none involved immediate help. These included an offer by All Hallows to educate two future mission students for China without charge. And Father Fraser received promises from two men to join his seminary project once established, as in time they did.

The first commitment came from a priest named William O'Toole, who later would join Fraser as a faculty member. And there was Daniel Carey, then an altar boy who had expressed great interest in becoming a missionary. When he heard about this youth, Father Fraser with typical thoroughness sought out the boy and his family in Cork. As a result, Carey would migrate to Canada in 1919 to join Fraser's new enterprise.

The Canadian's single-minded crusade was to inspire a third Irishman, with notable results. In October 1911, by then back in the United States, Fraser met Edward Galvin, a visiting curate

Chapel in an outlying mission.

in a Brooklyn parish. The next year Galvin accompanied Fraser to China. Later Edward Galvin was instrumental in founding St. Columban's the Irish Foreign Mission Society that would despatch numerous priests to many nations.

But these were fruits yet to come. Early in 1912 the outlook seemed discouraging, if never hopeless, to Father Fraser. He had spent more than a year campaigning in the U.S., Italy, Ireland, briefly in Scotland and northern England, all without tangible results except for promises and some donations. And as yet he had not made any significant impact in his own country.

Fraser decided to return to Ningpo and conduct his crusade from there as best he could. When he and Father Galvin sailed for the Far East in March 1912 there seemed little likelihood that a missionary seminary could be opened in English-speaking Canada in the foreseeable future.

* * *

Father Fraser returned to a China undergoing radical change. The Manchu dynasty had been overthrown and a new republic proclaimed by Sun Yat-sen. The Canadian missionary, however, was too preoccupied by his own aspirations and a regional emergency to pay much heed to these major political developments. J. M. Fraser found much of the region around Ningpo ravaged by floods and famine.

"The people had eaten up every bit of vegetation, even the leaves and roots of trees," he would recall. He saw small children begging a carpenter for sawdust "to put in their rice to make it go further". With money collected mostly from American donors for his prized seminary dream, Fraser arranged for the purchase of emergency rice supplies. Bishop Reynaud distributed the food to those judged in most desperate need.

Soon J. M. Fraser also attempted to contend with the desperate custom that saw many impoverished parents allow their infant daughters to perish:

> *Hearing that infanticide was rife in the (Taichowfu) district, I announced to the inhabitants that rather than destroy their offspring, they could bring them to me. I was soon inundated, with a hundred babies on my hands . . . I hired nurses, built a convent and begged the Bishop to send me some foreign Sisters . . .*

I saw I would have to change my plans or else I would be overwhelmed with foundlings to support. I sent three women to Ningpo to take a course in the medical treatment of infants. On returning, bringing a supply of pills, medicines and such, I placed them in my three principal cities to baptize dying infants. By this means we saved more souls than if we had taken them into the orphanage.

* * *

Family washings at the river.

For most of the next six years J. M. Fraser gave all his waking hours to two tasks: ministering to the Chinese committed to his pastoral charge, and using his facile pen to muster support overseas for a Canadian mission college. From Taichowfu he oversaw the building of churches, rectories, schools and a convent in his large mission district, while also preaching, instructing, baptizing, absolving, celebrating Mass and otherwise dispensing the sacraments.

Probably Fraser had more pastoral duties than before. These were the years of the First World War which had seen most European missionaries called home for military service — some with the Allies, some with the forces of Kaiser Wilhelm and his alliance. Canadian missioners evidently were exempted by Ottawa.

He still found time to write innumerable letters to people across Canada and to compose articles, mostly for publication in the **Catholic Record** of London, Ontario, whose editor had agreed to publish Fraser letters and photographs. The weekly also opened a special column for mission reports, and eventually set up a fund for readers' donations to the cause. Through this medium, which reached a reputed 30,000 homes, Father Fraser's descriptive and persuasive powers gradually brought about a popular awareness of the China missions among many more English-speaking Canadian Catholics. The continuous stream of material when published was said to have elicited $12,000 in contributions in four years.

* * *

In June 1918 Fraser crossed the Pacific once more, this time to launch a personal offensive in Canada. He brought with him a native Chinese student named Paul Kam whom he had trained as a catechist and who wanted to become a missionary priest and then return to his homeland. The two men travelled to Antigonish where young Kam was enrolled for classes at St. Francis Xavier University, at this institution's expense.

In October a decisive breakthrough came. Fraser accepted an invitation to help conduct devotional services in the parish church at Almonte, 30 miles northwest of Ottawa. The pastor, Father Cavanagh, wondered out loud if his visitor might be interested in buying a large local building for his proposed seminary. Fraser definitely was interested. His request to purchase the land and building, then in the custody of religious sisters, was sent to Archbishop Gauthier of Ottawa, who was in Boston for medical treatment.

The archbishop's reply came on November 9, 1918 — two days before the Armistice that was to terminate the First World War. Archbishop Gauthier's reply contained its own good news for Father Fraser. Permission was granted to purchase the property from the Sisters of St. Joseph for $5,000. Best of all, the archbishop authorized Fraser to establish a mission college at Almonte.

This date — November 9, 1918 — is officially designated as "Foundation Day" by the Scarboro Foreign Mission Society. Not that all plans and programs unfolded serenely and on schedule thereafter. New struggles and crises lay ahead. But now the potential promise was to become tangible, as the Catholic journal **America** would observe in an editorial note in 1919:

> *The well-known missioner, Rev. J. M. Fraser, has founded a college in Almonte, Ontario, Canada for the preparation*

of priests destined for the Chinese missions. It is a hopeful sign that Canada is about to compete with Ireland and the United States in supplying evangelists for this far-away land teeming with souls untouched by the light of the Gospel. The more colleges of this kind the better; and they need never fear that resources will be lacking. He who provided for the birds of the air will not forget the men who leave kith and kin to make His name known in the land of idols.

Sixty years after this founding date, the Scarboro Foreign Mission Society counted a three-generation total of more than 225 members and associates — including priests who were deceased, and resigned or transferred. Its French-speaking counterpart, the Societé des Missions-Étrangères, established by the bishops of Quebec on February 2, 1921, had some 400 members and associates listed on its rolls by the time of its golden anniversary year of 1981.

6 A NEW COLLEGE AND ITS MONTHLY VOICE

Less than a year after he founded the China Mission College in Almonte, John Mary Fraser gave it a public voice. Thereafter the histories of the society-to-be and its publication were almost as one. The monthly periodical provided selective accounts and more or less official interpretations of the mission enterprise's developing story.

Called **China** until it became the present **Scarboro Missions**, the journal was a narrowly focused house organ in its first decades. Like contemporary Protestant mission journals in those times, the new Scarboro periodical proclaimed what some later critics would describe as an "imperialist righteousness" — one that saw Christianity and Western culture as an inseparable package deal for global export. In recent decades, however, **Scarboro Missions** has reached out to a wider public, as can be seen in its numerous articles on contemporary public issues involving faith and justice.

The prompt founding of the periodical followed Father Fraser's fruitful collaboration with the **Catholic Record** of London, Ontario. When the priest was attempting to rally Canadian support for his mission-college dream, the editor of the London weekly, Dr. G. T. Foley, gave an invaluable helping hand. Through the pages of the **Record**, as Monsignor Fraser was to note in his memoirs, thousands more Canadians "came to know of my work in China." Thus the "task of founding the Scarboro Foreign Mission Society was facilitated".

This support persuaded Fraser — always publicity conscious when it came to his cause — to start a monthly journal as soon as possible. He regarded this undertaking so vital, in fact, that he served as first editor and himself wrote much of the contents, beginning in October 1919.

CHINA MISSION COLLEGE MEETS WITH UNIVERSAL APPROVAL was the proud headline on the leading article in the first issue. Buoyant optimism and flowery praises characterized the tone of this initial story — a harbinger of what readers would often find in future issues. Since July 1918, the lead article said, Fraser had "traversed the length and breadth of Canada, preaching in the churches and lecturing in the seminaries, colleges and schools; and everywhere finds the people prepared and eager for the work he is inaugurating . . . ." Some pastors and parents of prospective missionaries were not of the same mind, as it turned out.

* * *

The November, 1918 acquisition of a 25-room building in Almonte as a site for the long cherished mission college delighted Father Fraser. He would write in his 1955 memoirs:

> *I will never forget the self-sacrificing spirit of those good Sisters of St. Joseph. Imagine making a novena in order to be evicted from the convent they loved! What a heroic sacrifice for the conversion of China. With the money ($5,000) I gave Father Cavanagh he purchased a house for the Sisters. I remember the day they moved out . . . I slept in the empty house that night. The only piece of furniture I had was the bed Father Cavanagh gave me.*

Immediately the founder called together the first two of his associates — Paul Kam, the young Chinese who had been studying in Antigonish, and a Spanish-born priest named Michael de Sanctis Caralt, then trying to learn English in Toronto and about to become the first teacher at the mission college. In Fraser's words: "After Paul got settled down he wanted to know when I was going to open the new college. It is opened already, I said. We have a superior, a professor and a student."

Fathers Fraser and Caralt soon were joined on the fledgling faculty by three other priests: Joseph Basso, who had been an Italian classmate with Fraser in Genoa; John Joseph Sammon, a diocesan clergyman and former war chaplain, from Pembroke; and William O'Toole, whom Fraser had recruited in Ireland.

As superior, J. M. Fraser sent soliciting letters to Catholic bishops and hundreds of clergy across Canada. Many laudatory replies were received — and some donations. Bishop Ryan of Pembroke promised $1,000 and granted Fraser permission to preach and collect funds in diocesan parishes. Archbishop Sinnott of Winnipeg wrote that any of his clergy or seminarians were free to become missionaries to China, and he invited the college founder to preach in the Manitoba archdiocese. Henry Carr, Basilian superior of St. Michael's College in Toronto, wrote: "You are quite right that the need of such an institution is very great." Appeals by mail and in person, and later collections from "mite boxes" distributed to thousands of schools and subscribers to **China**, brought in sufficient money for the beginning years.

Scarboro's new seminary on Kingston Road, opening day, 1924.

However, not all English-speaking Catholics were persuaded that the missionary college was a sensible undertaking. William Amyot would recall that the Almonte College "was in disrepute amongst most of the pastors" he knew when, as a young Torontonian, he became interested in joining the new Fraser company:

> *It was a brand new venture as far as the Church in Canada went, and they (the pastors) couldn't believe it had any possibility of success. This didn't worry me. I wanted to go to "the missions" and for me "the missions" was China.*

Daniel Carey was Scarboro's first ordained member.

A classmate at Almonte, Lawrence Beal, encountered the most opposition in his family when he announced that he had been accepted as a candidate:

> *The Beal roof just about caved in. "Why pick China so far away?" This time my father started to talk. "Do you realize that you are the hardest one to please at table? If you go to China, you will starve. You don't like rice — their staple food. They have pork twice a month and other days they fill in the menu with snakes and fat rats."*

* * *

J. M. Fraser was not in the least deterred by clerical criticisms and parental objections. He sailed for Rome in 1919 where he reported the college founding to Propaganda officials and then secured a private audience with Pope Benedict XV. He left with a much prized papal document in hand. It read:

> *We bless with all Our heart beloved son John Mary Fraser, Missionary Apostolic, wishing that the College founded by him in Canada for the education of future missionaries to China be a school of good doctrine and training ground of true virture in order that the Holy Name of God may be more easily spread among those who do not yet know Its power and sweetness.*

By December 1920 the Congregation for the Propagation of the Faith had authorized the Canadian college to ordain its priests as missionaries. That month Daniel Carey became the first priest so designated when he was ordained in Ottawa's basilica. Father Carey had completed initial studies at a new missionary college in Ireland before migrating to Canada in 1919, as he had promised to do years before. Seemingly ever cheerful, Carey was to enjoy a long and diverse life, serving briefly in China and then back in Canada in various capacities. He was, for example, the founding editor of the **B.C. Catholic** in Vancouver. Among Monsignor Carey's memories of his college days at Almonte:

> *The student body numbered about 10 in September 1919. These were in all grades, from junior high to fourth year theology. We were of many races and tongues — Chinese, Dutch, French, English, Irish, yet we were one happy family. As prefect, professor of Latin and student of theology, I had not many idle moments . . .*

* * *

Like Carey, other members of the original faculty had comparatively short associations with Almonte. After leaving the college, Father Basso taught at St. Augustine's Seminary in Scarborough before returning to his native Italy in 1932. Father O'Toole died in a car accident when visiting friends in the United States. Father Sammon went to China as early as September 1920. Detailed accounts of his long journey into the Chinese interior were featured in the seminary monthly, but little was published about his brief missionary efforts there before his early return to Canada.

And what of Michael de Sanctis Caralt, the Spanish priest whom Fraser had met in Hong Kong and invited to Canada? Despite his limited abilities in English, Father Caralt worked diligently in the new college until August 1920 when he departed for Spain with the declared intention of founding a mission seminary in his homeland.

His leavetaking was described with enthusiasm in the September 1920 issue of **China**, under large headlines: FATHER CARALT SETS SAIL FOR SPAIN. MEMBER OF CHINA MISSION COLLEGE TO LAUNCH GREAT ENTERPRISE. A photograph of Fraser and Caralt, each looking quietly confident, accompanied the news report, which read in part:

> *Father Caralt, of a most amiable disposition and full of zeal for the conversion of the poor Chinese, sunk in idolatry, is sure to be received with open arms by his noble-hearted countrymen.*

The following February the house organ featured a full-page report based on a letter from Caralt to Fraser. Again blazing headlines: GREAT TRIUMPH FOR CHINA MISSION COLLEGE. SEMINARY IN SPAIN STARTED. INAUGURATION DESCRIBED BY FATHER CARALT IN A LETTER TO FATHER FRASER. Something happened or failed to happen, however. The promised college seems never to have materialized; not at least under Michael Caralt's auspices.

Thirty some years later, writing from Fatima in Portugal, Father Caralt would ask Dr. John McRae, then Scarboro's superior general, for "the blessing of my Superior" before undertaking some other pastoral adventure. This request was taken as evidence that Caralt considered himself a member of the Canadian missionary society, although there was no official record to confirm this. Furthermore, Caralt appeared to imply that he was a co-founder of the Scarboro Missions. Any such claim was brusquely denied by Monsignor Fraser.

As for Almonte's first student, Paul Kam was to have an eventful and perhaps tragic missionary career in his homeland. In June 1925 he was ordained, reputedly the first native Chinese to receive Catholic orders in Canada. Father Kam reached China as a Scarboro missionary in 1926. Many years later he would experience imprisonment in his native country.

* * *

When the Almonte college opened for its third term in the fall of 1920 the increased number of applicants meant that cubicles had to be built in the auditorium. Not only was the college overcrowded, but Almonte was considered "out of the way" in relation to Canada's major cities and senior educational institutions.

After campaigns of prayers, ecclesial politicking and shrewd business probes, J. M. Fraser in November 1921 negotiated the purchase of a well-known mansion in Scarborough, close to the educational centres of Toronto. The building was known later as the Guild of All Arts and subsequently as the Guild Inn. In 1921 its owner was a Colonel Bickford. His asking price was $35,000. Fraser bought.

At "Stop 40" along Kingston Road street car passengers bound for the new college site disembarked and then walked approximately one mile to their destination. Distances soon became an institutional problem, judging by this appeal in **China** the following October:

A CAR PLEASE!

> *St. Francis Xavier, China Mission Seminary, Scarboro is greatly in need of an automobile, it being over a mile to the nearest flag station and Post Office, to which we have to go twice daily; about four miles from a station with freight and express offices, and nearly a mile from the street car. The gift of any sort of motor car or truck would be very gratefully received. Our 'phone number is Beach 1124.*

This inconvenience and more serious problems, such as having to house the student body in more than one place and overcrowding as the mission population grew, compelled more improvisations and advance planning. Archbishop Neil MacNeil of Toronto recommended that the mission college construct a new building near St. Augustine's Seminary and along Kingston Road. Father Fraser agreed. Business negotiations and prayer novenas were begun so as to sell the former Bickford property. An account of this capital venture, as recorded in the founder's autobiography:

Early promotion!

A holy Magdalen at Good Shepherd Convent . . . undertook to pray that we might sell the property. She even announced the exact day we would sell it. On that day I was called to the office of the millionaire, Mr. Look.

"I learn," he said, "that you only paid $35,000 for the property. I will give you $42,000. You will be making $7,000."

"No," I said. "Take it or leave it for $50,000. If you do not buy it I intend to do just what you said; spend $5,000 on repairs and sell it for $75,000. That is what Colonel Bickford told me it is worth."

"Oh, you can't do that. I'll take it for $50,000. Will you come across the road to the lawyer and sign the deed?"

I did so and he gave me one cheque for $25,000 and assumed mortgages for the rest. I made $15,000 on the deal.

It was late that evening before I could 'phone the Good Shepherd Sisters . . . I announced to the Sisters the good news. They went into the chapel and chanted a Te Deum.

The first sod was turned on a new building site along Kingston Road in July 1923 and the cornerstone laid later that summer. This original portion of the present SFM seminary-residence-workshops complex was completed without any mortgage financing.

Confusion and something of a crisis developed, however, as to how the new seminary structure was to be administered. For a while Father Fraser entertained the idea of asking the Basilian teaching congregation at St. Michael's College to take charge. Then three bishops intervened: Archbishop Neil MacNeil of Toronto, Bishop Michael F. Fallon of London and Bishop Michael J. O'Brien of Peterborough. They took the missionary enterprise under their episcopal care. Fathers Fraser and William McGrath, recently arrived from St. John's, Newfoundland, were appointed to the Board of Control along with the three prelates. Father John E. McRae of Alexandria was named president of the college in August 1924. On September 21 that year the new St. Francis Xavier China Mission Seminary was formally opened and blessed.

In 1925 the Vactican's Propagation office gave provisional approval to draft constitutions for a mission society. The seminary was renamed as St. Francis Xavier China Mission Institute.

* * *

Earlier in the Twenties J. M. Fraser had recruited Father McGrath for the college faculty. This gifted, emotional man would have a marked influence on the missionary society — as a teacher and administrator and particularly as a forceful preacher and colorful journalist.

When he became editor of **China**, William McGrath undertook his new duties with typical ardor. Like Fraser before him, he used the pages of **China** for the propagation of the Catholic faith in general and for zealous promotion of the Scarboro mission in particular. This twofold motivation shaped and colored countless reports and features, sometimes to the exclusion of almost everything else in the publication.

Father Fraser continued to contribute his own pieces. Typical was a 1922 appeal to prospective candidates for the missionary team. He recalled an early desire of St. Therese of Lisieux, the popular

19th century saint, to become a missionary. Later "The Little Flower of the Child Jesus" acknowledged that her dream was not God's will for her. She decided instead to "send Missionaries to China by her prayers," Fraser wrote. Then he asked:

Does not the ardent thirst for souls with which the Little Flower burned, kindle in the heart of some generous young man a like desire to co-operate in the great work of evangelization of the heathen?

* * *

As noted, the contents and tone of **China** in earlier decades were dramatically different from the flavor and scope of present day issues of **Scarboro Missions,** the periodical's name since April 1950. (The name change came about after the Society had broadened its missionary outreach to Latin America, Japan and the Philippines.)

SALVATION OF FOUR MILLION CHINESE DEPENDS ON CANADA! So readers were advised in 1923 when the mission magazine solicited prayers and donations for Oriental conversions:

Religion is not strange to the Chinaman . . . But their faith is a faith of fear. And when they hear of the Religion of Love they bend forward to listen eagerly to this strange Good News . . . (which) fills their hearts with a new hope. The poor and the outcast have something to live for still.

Later that year, a lengthy Editorial Note, probably written by Father McGrath, examined "The Pagan's Chances and Our Own":

If the pagan does not co-operate with the grace of God, if he does not rise from the mire of his idolatries and only too often devilish surroundings, he will forfeit not only his hope of sanctity but his very possibilities of salvation. . . .

For the Christian the strongest motive for concern for the pagan lies in the fact that Christ Himself has spoken in no uncertain terms. "Teach all nations": "Preach the Gospel to every creature"; by what authority do men presume to say that the pagan is very well left alone?

Early issues of **China** had promoted only one point of view on the China missions — the official policy decreed by the Holy See, as interpreted by Fraser, McGrath, McRae and their associates. But the perceptions of Scarboro editors gradually evolved — thanks to the Society's chastening experiences in later decades, coupled with the

Catholic renewal after Vatican II and mission experiences elsewhere. For example, the November 1978 issue of **Scarboro Missions** offered readers a variety of viewpoints on the China theme: SFMers Gerald Kelly's appreciation of Monsignor Fraser and Clair Yaeck's mixed impressions of the New China, Paul Ferner's account of a recent visit to the People's Republic, plus Raymond Whitehead's generally favorable interpretation of Maoist society, which he wrote as director of the Canada-China Programme of the Canadian Council of Churches.

Strikingly different perceptions by believers living in very different decades! As Michael O'Hearn wrote after he had assumed the editorship of **Scarboro Missions**: each of the magazine's 15 editors over a span of some six decades "had had his own way of doing and saying things." O'Hearn continued:

> *Indeed, the 670 issues (to February, 1981) of **Scarboro Missions** and its predecessor, **China**, faithfully reflect the personality traits — some would say "quirks" — along with the interests, concerns and views of the various editors. More important, perhaps, the magazine reflects the changing emphases and orientations in the mission endeavor.*

Whatever its shortcomings over the years (and shortcomings are largely a matter of each reader's taste and preference), the Scarboro periodical is an invaluable and fascinating source of facts, dreams and opinions concerning the Canadian-born missionary enterprise. Through the Society's journal we hear hundreds of diverse voices speaking through the pages of time.

One of the most significant belonged to another tall, austere Scottish-Canadian, whose story we turn to now.

7 SCARBORO'S FOSTER FOUNDER

When the Society observed its 50th anniversary in 1968 **Scarboro Missions** likened the Canadian creation to a baby that had reached mature manhood after a precarious childhood and many adolescent struggles. Of course J. M. Fraser was credited with parenthood; he "gave birth to a dream." And John E. McRae was seen as a foster parent who had fed and clothed the Society in the difficult first decades of its life.

Left to right: Mgr. J. M. Fraser, Fr. Thomas McQuaid, SFM's second Superior General, and Dr. J. E. McRae, Scarboro's foster founder, 1949.

Later Rogers Pelow would sum up the uneasy Fraser-McRae partnership in a memorable sentence: "Fraser's dream needed a McRae to come true."

* * *

Year by class year, framed photographs of graduating seminarians — so youthful and expectant in appearance — hang in a long, dim corridor of the Scarboro Foreign Mission Society complex along Kingston Road. In many of the frames an older face is prominently featured. It is not that of John Mary Fraser, but the likeness of John E. McRae. He was "Doc" to his many students, the first rector of the reorganized mission college and later first Superior General of the Society.

While his leadership involved some decisions that remain controversial to this day, there is general agreement that (to cite one researcher's assessment) "In terms of organizational survival, McRae is far more important than Fraser."

Still, it was not until 1968 that a General Chapter accepted a committee report designating McRae as "the foster father of our Society." Comparatively little has been written about his administrative contributions and managerial shortcomings during the critical first quarter century in the SFM story, especially regarding decisions around the the troubled mission in Chekiang province. Also, McRae, unlike Fraser, was not given to recording his aspirations and experiences, and his side of an often contentious story.

* * *

John Edward McRae was born April 9, 1875 at Moulinette, Ontario. After schooling and further studies in Cornwall, St. Michael's College in Toronto and at Montreal's Grand Seminary, he was ordained July 17, 1898. Once he had acquired a Roman doctorate in canon law, Father McRae served first as an assistant and later as pastor of parishes in the Diocese of Alexandria, Ontario. In 1922 he became rector of St. Finnan's Cathedral in Alexandria and chancellor of the diocese bearing the same name.

In August of 1924 he accepted an invitation from the governing Ontario bishops to assume the post of president of the China mission college in Scarborough. That September the newly relocated seminary was formally opened with McRae in charge. For the next 17, often trying, years he remained in this position until his election as Superior General. Eight years later he retired.

* * *

For much of his 25 years with the Scarboro missionaries, what he called "The Chinese Puzzle" complicated and sometimes confounded the life of Dr. McRae, and the lives of the men and women directly affected by his decisions. After his first official visit to the fledgling Scarboro beachhead in the Orient, he shared some impressions with readers of **China:**

> *That there is a "Chinese Puzzle" is my firm conviction after completing a visitation to our missions in China. China, its people, its civilization, its customs and traditions are more of a puzzle to the Western mind than the world has ever attempted to imagine. The explanation may lie in the fact that Oriental life in all its aspects is entirely different from that of the West, and that the latter, taking too much for granted, is led into the error of judging the former by its own standards. The East is a world as different from the West as is night from day.*

Here he may also have been reminding himself that wise judgments were doubly difficult when it came to the new mission in the Chuchow/Lishui region. Difficult first of all because of the cultural gulf he described. And difficult also because of the gaps between his perceptions and administrative decisions and those of at least some of the men serving in China under his direction.

Unknown to the Society's many supporters, the mission in Chekiang soon became and was to remain a recurring headache. Dr. McRae's relations with Father Fraser and successive regional superiors, and in turn the superiors' relationships with at least some of the missionaries under their field direction were often strained and sometimes stormy. Long after his death, McRae continued to have his advocates and critics within the Society concerning this complex, very human issue of relationships between the home office and the mission field.

Evidence at hand seems to weigh definitely in favor of McRae in his long struggle of wills with Fraser in a dispute that began in the late 1920s and continued into the early 1930s. However, McRae's later choices of superiors in China were widely faulted, for what now appear to have been valid reasons. Still, such criticisms probably were inevitable, given the external crises and internal tensions which often plagued the Scarboro endeavor.

* * *

Early in 1926 the first mission band led by J. M. Fraser established a Canadian presence in the mountainous Chuchow/Lishui region assigned to Scarboro by the Vatican. Concurrently, Dr. McRae was supervising an expanding family of seminarians at the Society's headquarters in Canada. Ordinations took place every year. The new priests, usually in annual groups of three or more, were assigned to join their brothers overseas.

In 1928 John E. McRae accompanied two of the China-bound missionaries, Lawrence Beal and William Amyot. The seminary's Board of Control — three bishops and two senior staff, including McRae himself — had mandated the college rector to assess the overseas mission at first hand and report back concerning complaints which had been received from some of the men.

On returning Dr. McRae presented his findings to fellow members of the Board. As feared, he had found that major differences in age, temperament and outlook between Father Fraser and his colleagues were hindering mission work. The "loner" qualities that enabled Fraser to excel as trail-blazing pioneer were not the gifts needed to cultivate community spirit among the priests or to make administrative decisions with an even hand.

As a result the Board of Control decided to recall the institute's founder — obviously no easy matter for them or for him. The board then appointed Ramon Serra as "temporary administrator" in China. However, Father Fraser was to delay his return by almost a year, all the while protesting the board's decision and adding to the tensions among the men in the field.

Reasons for the recall were set out by McRae in an exchange of letters with Fraser. For one thing, the Scarboro rector wrote, "Bishop Defebvre (of Ningpo, who exercised episcopal authority over the Scarboro team) has advised your recall and the Board, acting on his advice, decided to recall you and in the meantime is awaiting confirmation of its action from Propaganda (in Rome)." Father Fraser protested that the board was "contravening the seminary constitutions." Dr. McRae pointed out that these provisions authorized recalls based on unanimous decisions of the Board of Control, the presiding bishop in Canada and by Vatican authorities.

Then the rector went on to emphasize that there were reasons for the recall beyond the publicly stated one that Fraser's campaigning skills were required in Canada to drum up more support for the Society's mission. Stating that "no one knows better than we that in this particular phase of our work you have been singularly successful and are thoroughly qualified for it," McRae continued in a letter he wrote October 17, 1929:

> *For obvious reasons . . . the chief and underlying reason for your recall is not mentioned. It is the constant state of discontent and dissatisfaction of the priests under your charge. So persistent were the complaints that we could remain silent no longer. My visit to Chuchow was the outcome. It was to ascertain from observation and information the grounds, if any, for the complaints. From correspondence it appeared that discord and lack of Christain harmony were rife in Chuchow and it was in order to be certain of this before any action could be taken that I was sent to Chuchow by the Board.*

Ramon Serra's appointment as temporary superior while J. M. Fraser remained there, protesting the decision, put the Spanish-born priest in a delicate position. He referred to this situation in letters to Scarboro authorities. Late in November 1929, for example, he reported that Father Fraser still was ignoring his recall, while sometimes undercutting Serra's rulings as temporary head. Given the controversial situation, Serra's letters were restrained. And, even though his limited abilities in English somewhat complicated matters, Father Serra was earning the respect and helpful support of other priests in the mission.

Father Fraser, meanwhile, went about his chosen tasks in his own way. Not until September 1930 did he return to Canada, and then only briefly. Years later, when composing his memoirs, he passed quickly over this unpleasant episode in his long and noteworthy career. In a single sentence, actually: "I returned to Canada in 1930 to campaign for funds for the upkeep of the seminary and for vocations." By 1932 the founder of Scarboro had returned to China where he worked for some years under the bishop of Wenchow.

It is not surprising that the Scarboro house organ never so much as hinted that there was dissension within the Society during these trying early years. Fraser's name did disappear from **China's** masthead after June 1929, although there was no corresponding mention that Ramon Serra had succeeded him as temporary administrator of the China missions.

* * *

Not long afterwards it was Dr. McRae who came in for the main brunt of criticism, although the appointment in question was one for which the whole Board of Control must have shared responsibility. Again, leadership of the China mission was the sore point. Before he had gained a single day of experience in the Orient, William

Very old and very young in China.

McGrath, until then vice rector at Scarboro, was named as the first Prefect-Apostolic (next in ecclesial rank to that of a governing bishop) of Chuchow/Lishui in 1932. Father Serra stepped down as temporary superior, evidently with relief. "Who was the goat to carry on?" Serra would ask rhetorically in a letter years later. On his part, Father McGrath paid his predecessor a generous tribute: "Only for the fact that you were the superman, I don't know what we should have done." Serra would be called upon again to fill in as a temporary "superman" in China.

* * *

Monsignor McRae weathered these and other crises abroad and at home. Along with his colleagues, first on the Board of Control and later on the self-governing General Council of the Society, he tried to make the best of each complicated situation. Internal relations within the Society reportedly worsened under the trying conditions of the Second World War, when communications to and from headquarters were cut off, along with needed funding, for months at a time.

There also were some positive developments in the Forties under McRae's leadership. On returning from China some of the missioners accepted assignments to the Society's Canadian mission among Chinese living in Vancouver, Victoria and Toronto. As well John McRae and his councillors looked for new missionary challenges outside Canada. In October 1942 the superior general wrote Archbishop Richard Pittini of Santo Domingo in the Dominican Republic to say that a number of Scarboro priests were ready for mission service. Archbishop Pittini replied with enthusiasm: "Your offer . . . fell on my soul like a drop of water on the thirsty tongue of Dives, in the Gospel parable. We are here in an extreme need of good priests." So began the Latin American chapter of the Scarboro story in what was to become a major theatre of the Society's endeavors.

In 1939, in recognition of his long, often unseen and usually thankless labor, Dr. McRae had been named a "domestic prelate" by Rome, with the title of Monsignor. And at the first General Chapter of the newly autonomous Society in 1941 he was elected by his peers as the initial superior general, a position he occupied until his retirement from active ministry eight years later.

"It is not easy to put into words how much the personal influence of Monsignor McRae has meant," **China** magazine commented in its September 1949 issue. The editor settled for a homey compliment: "His fatherly kindness to all has won our deep affection."

The rickshaw man with unusual "fares."

From then on McRae lived in quiet retirement at Scarboro. Towards the end he was blind. Still, he continued to celebrate Mass until his death February 5, 1955 in his eightieth year.

An appreciation of the man and his works appeared in the next issue of **Scarboro Missions**. Alphonsus Chafe, who had been McRae's assistant for some years, recalled that "Old Doc" as he was popularly nicknamed (it is hard to imagine anyone giving a nickname to Monsignor Fraser) had a "brusque Scotch way" and undertook every task "with gusto." Chafe continued:

> *He taught us well, and he expected us to live up to his teachings. He wasn't "soft." That, indeed, was the last thing anyone would accuse him of. He knew how to temper strict discipline with a rare understanding . . .*
>
> *It was the heart of the man that made us love him. He shared with us his vast scholarship and his sane appreciation of the priesthood. He knew what he was training us for, and he followed with personal interest the lives of each of his*

spiritual sons . . . Monsignor McRae was the Heart of Scarboro and he will have his place in the hearts of Scarboro men who owe him their priesthood and their missionary accomplishments.

General affirmation of this flowery tribute came years later from a younger contemporary of John E. McRae. Rogers Pelow said: "He had a big gruff exterior but inside him was a heart of gold." Father Pelow had been seminary rector while McRae was superior general. "He was a big man, physically and in every other way too." Other of his insights into the foster founder's personality and career, based on interview notes:

He always emphasized the family spirit. He tried to drill in this spirit because we did not have the bond of vows that a religious order has . . .

He was strict by today's standards but the kindness was there underneath. He inspired a reverential fear among the seminarians but he also emphasized that responsibility was up to each man's conscience.

He had a quality like all the other Scottish Canadians I have known, and that I couldn't believe at first. No matter how much he disagreed with you in an argument, and he could be fiery, he never carried a grudge . . .

Fraser and McRae were very different types. Father Fraser had only one interest in life — the missions. McRae had a great interest in sports and in many other things. He was a man for all seasons.

* * *

More than 13 years after his death the Fourth General Chapter in 1968 recognized "the very large role played by the late Monsignor John E. McRae during half of the Society's first 50 years." A portion of the special report prepared for the Chapter:

. . . whatever growth the Society made between 1924 and 1949 must in very large measure be attributed to him. It must be said that under Providence he saved the Society in its early years and led in its growth for a quarter century and so in effect became the foster founder of our Society.

8 EXPECTATIONS AT HEADQUARTERS

Surely the time would come, and soon, when there would be hundreds of conversions each year, then thousands and eventually tens of thousands. Some day not far distant Scarboro could be sending to Rome an annual report that recorded 150,000 or more baptisms in the Chekiang districts entrusted to the Canadian missionaries.

For a while an expectation along these lines was the beckoning dream that motivated Fraser, McRae, McGrath and other teachers at the mission college and writers in the editorial offices of **China**. The same heady vision animated most young protégés who sailed to the Orient as newly-ordained members, beginning in the 1920s.

This expectation of mass conversions — the lessons of history notwithstanding — was by no means confined to the mission institute along Kingston Road. The same aspiration was fully shared and formally encouraged by successive pontiffs in the Holy See, by their Vatican advisers, by many local bishops, and by numerous Catholic writers and journalists.

Philip Hughes, author of **A Popular History of the Catholic Church**, described the optimistic outlook that prevailed as the last century gave way to the present one.

> *The 19th century, the century of Catholic losses and trials in all the Catholic countries of Europe, is then, at the same time, the century in which the Faith has at last been carried to every part of the earth. Everywhere, now, it has at least made its appearance, and everywhere the immense work is at hand to convert the two-thirds of the peoples of the world who as yet remain pagan.*

In 1933, when the Scarboro mission college reached its fifteenth year, the editor of **China** echoed this ambitious outlook. Alphonsus Chafe declared:

> *Those who now favor a policy of "There's China enough at home" are out of step with the policy of the great leader at the Vatican (Pius XI), and they would feel considerably*

> *abashed if they were told they were denying their right to the name "Catholic," for as it belongs to the nature of light to illumine, and to the nature of the plant to develop, so is it essential to the Church to be active in missions. As long as the Catholic Church claims to be animated by the spirit of God; as long as she claims to be the exemplification of God's plan upon earth; as long as she will obey her Divine Founder and remain faithful to her ancient traditional customs; as long as she is the one Church outside of which there is no salvation, so long, too, must she devote herself to the missions.*

Some 20 years later, despite almost continuous warfare in China and looming Communist domination, the second superior general of the Scarboro Foreign Mission Society sounded serenely confident that Canadian Catholicism's "missionary destiny" would be fulfilled in due time. In paying tribute to Monsignor J. M. Fraser on his golden jubilee as a priest, Thomas McQuaid said all should know and honor the founder of Scarboro missions:

> *For under God, he is the man who has awakened Catholic Canada to its wonderful missionary destiny. Until, by his efforts, the Church took an active interest in the propagation of the Faith outside its own borders the Canadian Church could not rightly be said to be a fully formed and efficiently functioning Church. It lacked the character of "missionary."*

In the mission college, meanwhile, seminary teachers imbued candidates for the priesthood with the traditional Catholic teaching that ordination was the highest of all vocations. It was a calling to become "another Christ," a person "called apart to serve the altar and save souls".

Missionary priesthood was seen as the finest expression of this prized vocation. Indeed "the desire to be one of God's Holy Missionary priests" was regarded as "the noblest ambition which can fill the heart of a boy". Candidates for this exalted office could, in their turn, look forward to the missionary experience J. M. Fraser had described as his greatest joy: "There is no delight compared with that of saving souls single-handed, baptizing them with one's own hand, and personally leading them to their Father's house."

Given these great expectations on the part of their mentors, most of the young men Scarboro sent to China must have set off with lofty ideals and a commitment to sacrifice themselves if necessary in saving souls overseas. One of the new missionaries in the 1929

Shortwave radio brought live reports from the Western world.

mission band, in fact, composed a poem which extolled the aspirations of "Scarboro Missioners" as they set out for the pagan lands. Three of the verses penned by Hugh F. X. Sharkey:

They are the chevaliers of Christ
Knights of the Holy Grail,
They are legionnaires of God
In a cause that can never fail . . .

They stake their claims in the hearts of men,
Be they yellow, or black, or brown
And they pitch their tents on a hundred hills,
Where the Christ on the Cross looks down . . .

Say your goodbyes and break your hearts
On your Calvary of sacrifice,
Canada sends you forth with pride,
Go — win the world for Christ.

* * *

A few of China's "teeming millions".

Jolting realities on the far side of the Pacific soon challenged the ambitious dreams and fond hopes cherished at Scarboro headquarters. The daunting situation arriving missionaries encountered in the Lishui-Kinhwa regions tested the Canadians' idealism more than any of them reasonably could have anticipated.

While living in sometimes dangerous and always strange and trying circumstances, they had to face yet another unexpected difficulty within their own ranks: the difficulty of getting along with one another under such taxing conditions. Plus the related problem of having their complaints, suggestions and urgent requests understood and acted upon by the SFM leadership in Canada.

Craig Strang was one among many of the Scarboro men in China who discovered that evangelizing was a frustrating process, compared to expectations on arrival. Strang shared his mixed reactions with a colleague in a letter he wrote in December, 1937:

> *A year ago I was dreaming what I might have to tell you in this letter — hoping that it would be taken from a glorious page in the history of the Mission here, yet fearing that it might be but the record of another failure, and now that it has come to pass I hardly know how to classify it. It seems just another ordinary page of progress, and it is probably better that way.*
>
> *It is the first result of the new mission in Liu Ts'un where over 60 signed up last year, with an increase of 30 during the twelve months. One half of them are now baptized and are good practising Christians. Of the other half, some were not quite ready for baptism. Others have not fully rejected their family idols, or still cling to ancestor worship. A few are out and out antagonistic.*

These and later experiences persuaded Craig Strang to have second thoughts, some of which he shared during an interview in Canada many years later. For example, he wondered aloud about the divided loyalties that confronted Chinese Catholics when obligatory attendance at Mass on Sundays was in conflict with traditional marketing days. In Strang's words:

> *. . . the people did not have any weeks as in our calendar. They just went by the lunar month . . . They knew exactly the day of the lunar month; that is, how old the moon was, and they regulated their lives by that. And what made me think about Sunday were their market days. Every 10 days*

was a big market day and the fifth was a small market day. These would often come right on a Sunday.

We tried to tell them they must not buy or sell on Sunday. Some of them, I must say, were very good at that. Although I think that non-Catholic Christians were much more conscientious than we were. They would not open their doors or sell or buy anything or work in the fields on Sunday.

This was only one instance of the contending claims between local culture and a "foreign" religion which, in retrospect, gave rise to reservations for some missionaries. And not just to second thoughts. Given broad agreement on the goals of evangelization, there could be and often were sincere and vigorous disagreements as to the best means of pursuing these objectives.

In time, another veteran would recall, the men in the field "questioned everything." "If they had not, why would there be all the prose in the archives about discontent, acrimony and dissension? . . . But they did not just quit . . .

"Having committed themselves to a task in which they believed," this veteran continued, "these men were willing to go to China for life. Not one of them actually guessed that they would be back in Canada in a few years, due to events over which they had no control and of which they had little or no expectation."

* * *

After the Vatican formally approved Scarboro's status as a full-fledged missionary body, Dr. John E. McRae in 1941 convened the First General Chapter or assembly of delegated members to shape policy directions and make by-laws for the Society. By then Canada, like so many other nations, was deeply involved in the Second World War. Restrictions on the export of currency meant that the beleaguered mission in China was not able to receive its "full quota of funds". The Chapter recorded in its official Annals that but for $11,000 which W. C. McGrath had raised during "valuable work" in the United States (which presumably he sent to the Canadians in Chekiang through American channels before the U.S. was at war with Japan), the missioners "would be in a precarious position".

Nor were the men in China in a position to send back regular reports of their activities, needs and proposals, on account of the spreading Japanese invasion of the eastern provinces. Does this

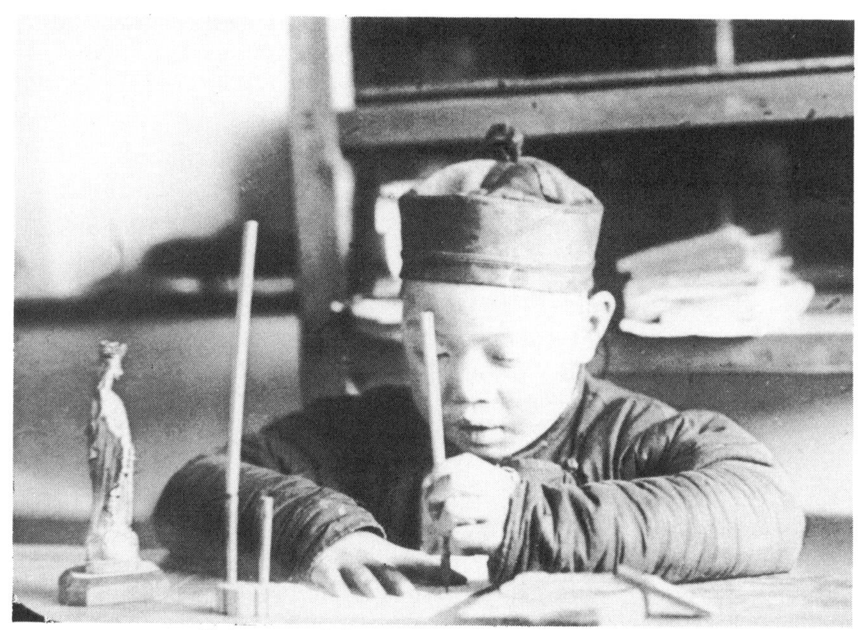

Chinese culture meets Catholic symbol.

added communications difficulty explain why the documents of the inaugural SFM Chapter contain so few clues as to what the Scarboro priests overseas were experiencing and recommending to their superiors in Canada? Possibly so.

Still, a Grey Sister who served in Chekiang at that time has suggested it would be a major error to suppose that the missionaries failed to make their views known in Scarboro, by one means or another. She remembered that they had had strong views on how to bring Christianity to the people, including some cultural adaptations in liturgical ceremonies so as to make these more intelligible for the Chinese.

But there is no evidence in the records of the 1941 Chapter of any decisions having to do with how the Mass and other liturgical events were to be celebrated in Chekiang. This is hardly surprising. The Vatican at the time undoubtedly would not have granted permission for any significant changes in the modes of Catholic worship, which had remained essentially unchanged for some centuries.

* * *

What we do find in the Annals of the 1941 General Chapter and those of the two Chapters following are indications of a gradual loosening up or democratization of Scarboro procedures and structures.

Among the decisions of the 1941 SFM legislative body: A "spiritual year" should be established "for aspirants to membership in our Society". Canada's and Newfoundland's bishops were urged to "continue their paternal interest in the welfare of our mission work" in view of "the tremendous needs of the Church in China if it is to make constant progress in the work of evangelization." The incoming General Council was asked to negotiate "some definite arrangements re the financing of the (Grey) Sisters' work in China". The Chapter recommended that "in the training of seminarians consideration should be given to subjects practical for mission work, such as photography and journalism".

The Chapter confirmed Monsignor McRae's temporary position as Superior General and named four assistants to the General Council: Monsignor McGrath, who had been regional superior in Chuchow/Lishui and who was about to be named SFM director of campaigns and publicity; Hugh Sharkey, who was appointed seminary rector and editor of **China**; Alex J. MacDonald, treasurer-general and seminary bursar; and Leo Curtin, secretary general and spiritual director. Lawrence Beal was named regional superior in China.

* * *

Dr. McRae convened the Second General Chapter in 1949, only several weeks before Mao Tse-tung would proclaim mainland China a People's Republic. Representatives from the soon-to-be restricted mission in Chekiang and from a new Scarboro assignment in the Dominican Republic were among delegates to the Chapter. Participants recorded their apprehension about the future of the China mission and paid tribute to "our valiant priests . . . whose actual conditions are unknown to us". Belatedly, the Chapter enacted that "the General Council in making appointments or reappointments (of regional superiors) should as far as possible avail itself of the opinion of missionaries in the field to which the regional superior is to be assigned".

Concerning formation of missioners, the 1949 Chapter stressed adequate language training — "at least one year in the case of non-European languages and six months in European languages". Also, missionaries "shall be given a course in the history and the customs of the people and the best mission methods in use in the mission". This expression of cultural sensitivity came as the China experience was entering its last phase before expulsion.

As for missionary conduct, the Chapter decreed: "Priests shall be careful at all times to appear in public garbed in a manner befitting their status and dignity as priests, exception being made for participation in athletics, etc."

With Monsignor McRae retiring as superior, Thomas McQuaid, recently returned from Japanese internment in China, was elected as the Society's leader. Other choices: Alphonsus Chafe, first assistant; John McGoey, then still in Shanghai, second assistant; William J. Cox, third assistant; and A. J. MacDonald as fourth. John P. Kelly was appointed regional superior in Lishui.

* * *

The Third General Chapter of the Scarboro Foreign Mission Society did not convene until 1959, five years after the last Scarboro member had been expelled from China. Few changes in the Acts were made by the delegates, except for legislation governing new mission assignments in Japan and the Philippines. By then other missions also were operating in the Bahamas, British Guiana and on St. Vincent Island.

Francis M. Diemert was elected Superior General. Four others were chosen to assist him on the General Council: John Fullerton, Alexander MacIntosh, Lorne McFarland and John J. McIver. Three of the five — Fathers Diemert, MacIntosh and McFarland — had been in China.

Except for the brief regret expressed concerning the closing down of the China mission, the Annals of the Third Chapter reflected the confident mood that prevailed during this period of expansion for Canadian society in general and the Catholic Church in particular. "Business was booming," ecclesially as well as civilly. Few if any Catholic leaders in 1959 foresaw the internal turmoil that would come not many years hence as a result of the Ecumenical Council Pope John XXIII had just announced he would convene in 1962.

9 PIONEERING IN THE TWENTIES

The Chinese see the devil everywhere," Joseph Venini wrote from Chekiang late in the 1920s. He described for readers of **China** some of the examples he had encountered on each journey to the outlying mission stations in his charge:

A freehand map of Scarboro's first mission territory in Chekiang.

If anyone takes sick, it is the devil; they hear a strange noise at night, it is the devil; a youngster fails to return home, the devil has surely taken him; so the stock of holy water must be kept ready for all these occasions.

Add still another use: "Has baby a tummy ache? A gulp of holy water will soon quiet him."

Father Venini described what usually happened at each mission stop:

We say Mass and receive the scattered flock in the home of one of the Christians. There is a great hustle and excitement upon the arrival of the priest, and willing arms soon have the central room cleared of all the rubbish it has collected since the last visit . . . .

The routine at each of the stations is the same. Confessions and Communions, perhaps a soul to prepare for its last journey, or it may be a marriage to regulate. There is usually a baby or two, born during the absence of the priest and baptized privately by the catechist or one of the Christians. They are brought to the chapel . . . . to be "supplied"; that is, having the ceremonies of the Sacrament supplied.

Joseph Venini was one of the most perceptive of the early Scarboro arrivals in Chekiang. He reminded readers that "when we say China we simply mean our little district of Chuchow" — a very small vineyard in "the vast extent of the Flowery Kingdom." Unlike some of his colleagues, he was not so intent on his missionary duties as to almost ignore the social realities around him.

* * *

The pioneers of the Twenties arrived in a China where mass deprivation in the midst of privilege had been a centuries-old way of life. Now this ancient culture was in a state of chaotic transition. There was spreading conflict between "Southerners" and "Northerners" with each side claiming to be the authentic keeper of the revolutionary dream of an independent republic. When the recognized "Father of the Revolution," Dr. Sun Yat-sen, died of stomach cancer in 1925, a major left-right split occurred in the reformist ranks. By 1928 Chiang Kai-shek, a key disciple of Sun, had wrested control of the Nationalist Party (Kuomintang) and also controlled much of the divided nation. Even though he had trained in Moscow, Chiang launched a campaign to exterminate the Chinese Communist Party, which had been founded shortly after the success of Lenin's Russian Revolution in 1917. Mao Tse-tung, another favored disciple of Dr. Sun, later would emerge as the principal Marxist leader.

This was the disruptive context for the Canadian mission. From its beginning there were predictable differences and some understandable dissension among these Christians who had journeyed from the safe and familiar comforts of Canada to the unknown hazards of a far from peaceful China.

* * *

Father Fraser (right) supervises another building project. In the background is a pagoda.

The first three men to travel from the mission college to China went as individuals: John Joseph Sammon in 1920, Daniel Carey, first ordained member of the Society-to-be, in 1921, and Joseph Lachapelle in 1923. For various reasons all three soon returned to Canada. Thereafter mission bands of two, three or more set out together across the Pacific. The first of these small mission bands was headed — at his insistence — by John Mary Fraser himself, then approaching his fifties.

Although he later transferred to another ecclesial jurisdiction, Monsignor Daniel Carey maintained a brotherly bond with former Scarboro colleagues across the years and miles between Vancouver and the Kingston Road headquarters. When he took part in SFM's 50th anniversary observances in 1968, the first graduate of the mission college sketched for his listeners a revealing word picture of the conditions he had found in 1921. That year he had to make his way into the Chinese interior to the remote western Province of Kweichow:

> *At that time China was in travail, striving to bring forth a new republican democratic way of life. Local warlords were in constant conflict. Bandits, often recruited from the ranks of discontented, unpaid soldiers, reigned supreme. Crop failures meant famine and starvation. Trade and travel between the provinces were almost at a standstill. Missionary activity was greatly curtailed. Travel in our mission territory, whenever possible, was by pony or mule, palanquin or sedan-chair.*
>
> *Personally, I preferred "shank's mare" and could manage about 25 miles a day. Incidentally, during my stay in the rural areas of Kweichow, I never saw anything on wheels — not even a wheelbarrow.*

There was no hint of China's "travail" in Daniel Carey's initial letters to Canada once he arrived in Kweichow. With an enthusiasm rivalling that of Father Fraser, his mentor, the young Irish priest described his first impressions and experiences, while always adding exhortations and encouragements to the candidates then preparing in Almonte. Two examples indicate the content and flavor of Carey's correspondence early in the Twenties.

Writing in the summer of 1921:

> *Pagans, as well as Christians, have shown themselves to me as kindly, patient, simple, honest, very hardworking people. My heart has gone out to them . . . .*
>
> *Kweichow is not "a land of milk and honey" — speaking either figuratively or literally — but, even so, a man with a bit of grit and with good health can always find something to keep him busy and arouse interest in his work — his one and only work — the winning of souls to Christ. And then, when the boys from Almonte begin to pour in here, we'll soon make Kweichow "the hub of the universe."*

And from a letter to Almonte staff and students in 1922:

> *... (I received) a petition addressed to me from the catechist of Yuen-Ho-Su, a small town .... begging me to come as soon as possible in order to give final instructions, and administer Baptism to 100 families who had been under instruction and who were now almost ready for Baptism. One hundred families! Just think of it, boys! Between 500 and 600 persons, all well disposed and prepared to enter the Church ...*
>
> *Surely our Canadian Apostles are destined to outrival St. Francis Xavier himself! Surely, the record of Canada's future missionaries to China will be the brightest in Canadian Church History!*

By January 1924 Father Carey had been "recalled from China for campaign work in Canada".

* * *

Twice in the first half of the Twenties J. M. Fraser travelled to Rome: early in 1922 to confer once more with Cardinal Van Rossum, Prefect of Propaganda, and again for an extended period in 1925. That year, after some hard bargaining with Vatican authorities, Fraser agreed to accept the mission territory which was not his first or even second choice in China: the mountainous region of Chuchow/Lishui.

Bearing this mandate from the Holy See, Father Fraser returned to Scarboro. Now approaching 50, he intended to head the first mission band scheduled to leave for China late in 1925. However, the episcopal members of the Board of Control and senior seminary staff were reluctant to see the college founder lead much younger men abroad. Perhaps board members anticipated that Fraser, who excelled as an individual missionary, would not prove an acceptable team leader in the field. But he was to have his way. Monsignor Fraser's version of what transpired, as described in his autobiography:

> *At the next meeting of the Board of Control I proposed to go to the new mission with Fathers Morrison and Serra. The Bishops were taken aback, and stated it was the most momentous decision they had ever been called upon to make, afraid the work would collapse if I left, but I was afraid that young missionaries would get discouraged if I did not go with them.*

> *"What if I got sick?" I said, "or died? Would the work (in Canada) collapse?" I had already sent two priests to China and they came back. This time I wanted to make sure they would stay, and so forth. My arguments prevailed and they gave reluctant consent.*

The first mission team of J. M. Fraser, Vincent Morrison and Ramon Serra was the centre of prayerful attention at a departure ceremony in St. Michael's Cathedral, Toronto, on December 13, 1925. This ceremonial occasion marked "the end of the beginning" phase of the missionary movement Fraser had founded in November 1918.

When the three Canadians arrived in China early in 1926 they travelled to their destination in the style Westerners then took for granted — without any thought, it seems, about the image left with their hosts:

> *Chuchow, Feb. 1, 1926 — On Wednesday, January 27 (Father Fraser reported to* China *readers) we left Wenchow amid the fervent good wishes of the Vicar-General and Father Aroud and assistants. We rode in rickshaws, the men who pulled them ringing bells and shouting continually to clear the way through the narrow, crowded streets to the river bank where our boats lay . . . . Father Fong and I were in one boat, Fathers Serra and Morrison in another, and our baggage in the third and fourth . . . .*
>
> *A score of Christians were at the landing place (in Chuchow) to welcome us and as they conducted us to the church the bells pealed forth joyously and thousands of firecrackers were set off. Our first act was a visit to the Blessed Sacrament to offer fervent thanks for the successful termination of a long, long journey . . . .*
>
> *We have seen the whole city in the last few days. It is not much of a place from an American standpoint, but in population it numbers about 40,000. Today we visited the electric power house, to which is attached a match factory and rice mill. We partook of refreshments at the proprietor's house. He is a pagan, but very well disposed towards the missionaries. There is no anti-foreign feeling here, thank God.*

Three more mission bands were to follow in the remaining years of the Twenties. Altogether 12 graduates of St. Francis Xavier China Mission College travelled to China that decade, plus Father Fraser, his brother William, who arrived in 1926, Fathers Sammon and Serra.

The 1920s roster of Scarboro pioneers: Daniel Carey, Joseph Lachapelle, Paul Kam, Vincent Morrison, Joseph Venini, William Amyot, Lawrence Beal, Bernard Boudreau, Michael Dunne, Aaron Gignac, Hugh F. X. Sharkey and Desmond Stringer. As well, the seminary rector, Dr. John E. McRae, made his first official visit in 1928.

When the fourth group of priests sailed from Vancouver in November 1929 the first three Grey Sisters of the Immaculate Conception from Pembroke also were aboard, en route to the Canadian mission as nurses and teachers. Sisters Mary Anthony (the religious name Catherine McHugh chose), Mary Catherine (Catherine Doyle), and St. Oswald (Christine McDonald) were the first of 15 women religious who were to serve in China.

"When we went to China," Hugh Sharkey recalled in a conversation 50 years later, "we were more or less imprisoned in a system." Roman Catholic missionaries "had to operate according to the rules of this system, like it or not," he explained. "Like most systems, it had its good and bad points."

Father Sharkey spoke of his "fascination" with all things Chinese, especially the antiquity of this Oriental society. Despite the many difficulties he encountered, "I never lost my fascination for China," he said. Most other China Hands evinced the same lasting enthusiasm when interviewed many years later.

* * *

Letters from other Scarboro pioneers, culled from the pages of **China** published in the latter years of the 1920s, show that the euphoric approach of Daniel Carey continued. Evidently these optimistic accounts were popular with readers of the magazine. By the end of the decade circulation was said to be nearing 100,000 subscribers.

"We are not free from troubles, but they are only slight," Ramon Serra wrote from Lungchuan early in 1928. "Christianity is gaining ground and the number of catechumens is increasing." His colleague at Lungchuan, Paul Kam, reported that the mission had "contracted for 70,000 bricks and 90,000 tiles for a new church".

John Mary Fraser, meanwhile, remained ever aware of the magnitude of the evangelizing task undertaken by the handful of Canadians. From the main mission compound at Chuchow, he wrote in 1928:

Ramon Serra with two Chinese carriers.

> *The last three days there was a regular orgy of idolatry, the people all seeming to vie with one another for the honor paid to the idols . . . three popular goddesses. All the temples of the city, and there are over a hundred, were decorated and illuminated at night, and candles and incense lighted before all the idols without exception. If anybody thinks that idolatry is dead or dying in China, let him come here in the first moon of the year.*

Another Fraser letter followed soon, this one describing a Christian schoolboy's account of experiences at home:

> *. . . (He) tells me that when I was at Lungchuan his father beat him unmercifully with a big stick to try to force him to commit an act of superstition, but that he persevered in the Faith. I congratulated him on having shed some of his blood for Christ — for the beating actually brought blood! and told him the story of St. Stephen and St. Lawrence. Perhaps he would have been actually martyred had he not succeeded in extracting himself from his father's grasp, and fled to the Church for protection.*

Hugh F. X. Sharkey, SFM.

The Scarboro magazine also featured reports and letters from Dr. McRae describing impressions of his 1928 tour of the Canadian missions on behalf of the Board of Control.

Paul Kam later described a raid on Lungchuan, where some of his own family resided, by several hundred armed bandits:

> *During Mass there was the noise of a great deal of shouting going on in the town. I was really very much alarmed but to all intents and purposes, for the sake of the people, I remained "Kam" (calm). The robbers were looting and pillaging all through the main business section and in the homes of rich families.*

Father Kam had heard rumors that 900 Communists were approaching Lungchuan, while over 1,000 refugees were said to be coming into the town from another direction. "With all this what can we do for the mission work?" he asked, candidly admitting that "our minds are not well fixed" in such situations.

In contrast, Vincent Morrison sent a matter-of-fact report telling of "the ordinary routine of missionary work here in Chuchow". Being surrounded by thousands of pagans constantly reminded him that "the harvest indeed is great".

Lawrence Beal was one of the first correspondents who referred to the mounting strife between Nationalists and Communists: "China is in the throes of a civil reformation, and the spirit of Russian Bolshevism is trying to make an entrance." He presumed his Canadian readers knew "the absolute futility of a Bolshevistic utopia." Father Beal urged Catholics at home to "pray that China will survive this struggle and obliterate the name of Sovietism, and that the infant Church will grow and lead her millions who are still living in darkness to the feet of Christ".

* * *

The Canadians' fear of Marxists increased after army units occupied some of their mission posts early in 1927. The Scarboro teams soon returned to their respective stations after a proclamation promising them protection in future. Whether in fact the occupying soldiers had been loyal to the Communist or Nationalist cause, these "Southern demons" invariably were described thereafter as "Reds." Letters from the priests at the time, however, were not that specific in identifying the marauders. Excerpts from reports carried in **China** during 1927 stand in some contrast, for example, to the recollections of Monsignor Fraser in his autobiography.

Joseph Venini, writing from the mission of Tsingtien early in 1927:

> *Troublesome times have descended upon us, and have scattered us to the four winds of Chuchow and further. For nearly two months the province of Chekiang has been overrun by soldiers, if such they may be called, of the northern and southern parties. Personally, however, we of the Chuchow district were in no way molested until, unfortunately, a few days ago a large horde of the southern demons in human form reached us on their way north.*

From a diary kept by Ramon Serra in Chuchow, and reproduced in the June 1927 issue of **China**:

> *Seventh day: One of the officers told me today that it is the intention of the southerners to occupy every Catholic mission in the province if they are successful and convert them into schools where Communism will be taught . . .*

Ninth to fifteenth day: There has been nothing unusual. For the most part the soldiers have been very civil . . .

"Conditions throughout the district are evidently returning to normal," the magazine added in a postscript, which was based on a cablegram received May 13 saying that J. M. Fraser was returning to Chuchow. Then this reassuring if puzzled report in the July-August issue:

LATEST NEWS FROM CHINA

As we go to press, word comes from Father Fraser that a proclamation has arrived in Chuchow signed by Chiang Kai-shek, former generalissimo of the Cantonese armies, to the effect that missionaries and mission property in the district are not to be molested.

So little is known by anybody about the real political state of affairs in China just now that is hard to say what force attaches to the proclamation. . . .

Writing many years later, Monsignor Fraser gave this account of the incident:

We were only a year in Lishui when the Reds invaded our district. The British sent a destroyer to Wenchow to take us to Shanghai . . . .

Two Red officers occupied my bedroom. They allowed a Chinese priest, the catechist and house boys to occupy one room. One day they entered with revolvers and flashlights and hunted for me under the bed.

Once back in Chuchow/Lishui, Fraser posted Chiang's edict on the rectory door. There all could read the generalissimo's order "assuring peace to the Church and forbidding anyone to molest us".

Thereafter for most of the Scarboro team Chiang was the heroic leader who personified all that was most promising in China, while Mao Tse-tung came to represent all that was most menacing. Some of the Canadians must have noted, even so, that Chiang and Mao actually had a changing, complex relationship over the years. These disciples of Dr. Sun Yat-sen first competed for power, then collaborated against the Japanese invaders, and later warred against one another until one of them emerged as the final victor on the mainland.

* * *

Even though he referred to local living conditions much less often then he did to pagan practices, Father Fraser was not indifferent to the wretched living conditions endured by the masses of people around him. "One would have to see it for himself to believe the depth of poverty and misery with which many of the Chinese are afflicted," he wrote in 1927. Whole families in Chuchow labored late into the night making match boxes for a few cents an hour. A tailor the priest had engaged asked for a payment of less than one Canadian dollar for "work and thread" after five days of cutting and sewing:

> *With pork at 12½ cents a pound Canadian money, needless to say they cannot indulge to a great extent in that commodity. Perforce they must partake themselves to rice and vegetables at three or four cents a pound, and even then curb their appetite.*

Reflecting on his first Christmas in China in 1929, Bernard Boudreau wrote:

> *All this (celebration) took place within the four walls of the mission compound. Outside life went on in the same everyday way. Our mission was a Bethlehem. Maybe in 30 years' time it will have spread over the whole city. It certainly stands in great need of it.*
>
> *Why such conditions exist after 2,000 years of Christianity is a mystery. Some day it might be said of our Western civilization that if in China had been done the things that were done for us they wouldn't have neglected to pass on the Faith.*

10 THE TROUBLED THIRTIES

"An endless fight against poverty and the Communist evils which it begets is the lot of the average peasant resident in Chekiang province," Desmond Stringer told the **Ottawa Citizen** in an interview that was reprinted by Scarboro's **China** in February 1938. Some of Father Stringer's observations about the mission field to which he was returning, as reported in the national capital daily:

> *Born into poverty, millions of Chinese barely manage to eke out an existence. Rice is the main item of diet and it is rarely that a person has meat to eat more than three or four times a year . . .*
>
> *An inherent devotion to their families and a deep and abiding love for the land which provides them with daily sustenance appear to provide the incentive for these peasants to live on and endure the hardships of their lot. . . . to be allowed to live quietly and peaceably, to be able to till their little plots of land, and at last, to be laid away with their ancestors, is all that the Chinese peasant asks of life . . .*
>
> *The bandits, he explained, were usually communities of peasants who, owing to the fact that they were facing starvation, took to banditry that they might live. Were economic and social conditions better, banditry would naturally cease to exist he believed . . .*

The social analysis of Desmond Stringer reported in **The Citizen** was more revealing than most accounts published in the mission magazine. **China** specialized in reports of mission journeys and religious ceremonies. Only occasionally did readers learn how the Canadian missioners felt about the host culture they were laboring to convert.

A more candid side of the China years lies in the archival records of the Society. Understandably, many of the letters exchanged between men in the field and their superiors in Canada dealt with matters of a confidential nature. Such letters should remain private, of course, except for those portions which shed light on the missionary endeavor itself — how it was seen as the years passed and how priorities and programs evolved. With this distinction in mind, selected correspondence in the SFM archives was carefully researched and interpreted by C. J. Eustace. His excerpts and findings were used extensively in preparing this chapter and several others.

* * *

Statistically speaking, the Thirties were the most promising 10 years for the Scarboro beachhead in Chekiang. During the deacde 29 priests — more than half of the total number who would go to China — crossed the Pacific. And nine Grey Sisters travelled to the Lishui-Kinhwa region in the Thirties, where they joined the three colleagues who had arrived late in 1929.

The Thirties' roster of Scarboro members and associates who followed in the footsteps of J. M. Fraser and the first mission bands of the 1920s: Joseph King, John J. MacDonald, Arthur Venadam, James MacGillivray, William C. McGrath, William McNabb, Gerald Doyle, Hugh McGettigan, Craig Strang, Leo Curtin, Leonard Hudswell, James Leonard, Lawrence McAuliffe, Lorne McFarland, William Matte, John Maurice, Patrick Moore, Harold Murphy, Ronald Reeves, Michael Carey, Edward Lyons, Alexander MacIntosh, Gerard McKernan, Daniel MacNeil, Allan McRae, Edward Moriarty, Thomas Morrisey, Charles Murphy and Harvey Steele. In December of 1939, soon after the beginning of the Second World War, five more prospective missionaries sailed for the Orient; they head the list of the 11 who would first arrive on Chinese soil in the turbulent 1940s.

* * *

Record number of clergy notwithstanding, the Scarboro enterprise itself was a far from happy one during much of the 1930s.

The "times were out of joint" during this troubled decade. Economic depression and destructive droughts afflicted the richer Western nations, Canada very much included. Falling incomes in turn meant reduced donations to the SFM coffers and hence less funds for the growing mission teams abroad. China itself was torn first by the continuing civil strife and then by massive Japanese invasion. And the Second World War was about to come to the Far East as the Thirties ended.

Chiang Kai-shek's strength in the prolonged Nationalist-Marxist struggle was anchored in the southern provinces and urban centres. In contrast, the Communists under Mao Tse-tung gradually became identified with the rural masses — a notable departure from the

Marxist-Leninist theory that envisaged revolutionary change arising first among the proletariat in the cities.

One of the most dramatic events in the 25-year history of the civil war took place between 1934 and 1935. In what became known as The Long March, Mao led a starting army of 300,000 on a circuitous 6,000 mile trek from the southern provinces to Yenan in northwestern China. En route the marchers fought off better equipped and larger units of the Nationalists. Less than 30,000 arrived at the final stopping point, where Mao regrouped and strengthened his depleted army. The Nationalists also sustained substantial losses in men and supplies.

By this time invading troops from Japan had occupied Manchuria and were about to push southward into the Chinese heartland. In order to resist the invaders, a truce was reached by Mao and Chiang in 1936. This uneasy Nationalist-Communist coalition would last through the Second World War. The Canadians in Chekiang watched with apprehension as this three-way struggle approached, then raged around them.

Chiang, whose 1927 proclamation had afforded protection to foreign missions, was the Chinese leader whom the Scarboro men and Pembroke sisters highly favored. **China** sometimes published approving articles about the generalissimo's "New Life Movement."

Early in the 1930s the Nationalist commander issued 79 commandments for a "rigorous regulation" of Chinese life styles (as if most were not already living frugally!). His commandments ranged from "good manners and table etiquette" to the maxim, "Don't borrow unless in dire need."

Once Chiang summoned Protestant and Catholic missionaries to enlist their support for his "New Life" program. Father McGrath was one of those much impressed by this initiative. In 1937 he confidently predicted that the "nefarious cause" of the Maoist Communists would "make no headway against the inherent common sense and social sanity of the Chinese people." Another early enthusiast was Dr. James G. Endicott, who became one of the most influential Canadian Protestant missionaries in China. Eventually Endicott condemned Chiang's regime and switched his allegiance to Mao Tse-tung. In 1947 Dr. Endicott declared that Mao deserved to win the civil war and predicted that he would. This public stand made the missionary one of Canada's most controversial figures at the height of the East-West Cold War.

Christmas in Chuchow, 1931. Upper row, left to right: Fathers J. J. Macdonald, J. P. King, L. A. Venadam, A. Gignac, B. Boudreau. Lower row, left to right: Fathers W. K. Amyot, V. Morrison, Wm. C. McGrath, R. Serra, P. Kam.

This is a further indication of the politically unstable and sometimes dangerous milieu in which Canadian Protestants and Catholics were trying to proselytize. And among the Scarboro priests in the 1930s there also were "personality conflicts" centred on a succession of regional superiors. Concurrently, each band of new SFM arrivals experienced cultural shock when they encountered the rigorous living conditions, compared to Canadian standards, and alien social circumstances for which they were not well prepared. Disease, other illness and depressed states of mind took an annual toll among the missionaries.

During the Thirties under the administration of Dr. McRae and his colleagues in Scarboro, the missioning pattern initiated in the 1920s was further developed. Small groups of newly ordained priests arrived in Chekiang almost yearly. Immediately they began language studies, although few are said to have become skilled in local dialects. Newcomers were assigned their first duties under more experienced men, and later became local pastors in their turn. Periodically, each priest returned to Canada — on vacation furlough, to campaign for mission funds, for other assignments more suited to personal aptitudes, because of illness or for other compassionate reasons.

* * *

In 1930 John Mary Fraser returned to Canada. Scarboro's founder was assigned to promote vocations and raise funds for the mission college, now starting to experience the effects of Canada's economic stagnation. As he would recall:

> *During the two years of mission work I preached 120 sermons in churches, and gave 102 lectures in seminaries, colleges and schools. But the results were not so good financially. The depression was on and priest and people had little to spare. One pastor told me he had to support 60 families, who formerly were supporting him.*

Father Fraser wanted to head back to China. Archbishop Neil MacNeil of Toronto instead suggested that the veteran missionary take charge of a new mission in Vancouver where he could be pastor to 20,000 Chinese Canadians. "I countered that it would not be reasonable to leave 2,000,000 for 20,000," Fraser wrote later. Again he had his way.

In 1932 Bishop Favreau of Hangchow named J. M. Fraser pastor of the Kinhwa area which adjoined the Lishui region. There he would remain until 1941, pursuing what he did best — individual evangelizing, unencumbered by any regional superior named by the controllers in Canada. In Lishui, meanwhile, the personality conflicts did not end with Father Fraser's leaving. Sister St. Angela was to write sympathetically about the men and their leader at that time:

> *Scarboro priests in China . . . were young, vivacious, daring, caring and totally dedicated. They had spirit . . . Without Father Serra and his great friend Father Amyot, I wonder whether Scarboro could have survived in China. He (Ramon Serra) was without doubt the man who anchored Scarboro's frail ship when it was being sorely loaded during the founding years in China.*

However, when the Vatican upgraded the mission region of Lishui to that of a "prefecture apostolic", the last step before autonomous diocesan status, it was not Ramon Serra who was named regional superior. Headquarter's choice was William C. McGrath, the seminary's vice rector.

This decision would be widely criticized as fair neither to the men already in the field nor to McGrath himself. The gifted writer and preacher took over without any personal experience in the Orient and without any knowledge of the Chinese language. From the beginning this handicapped his efforts to supervise, while some at least of the experienced men in Chekiang might well have felt "passed over" by headquarters in Canada. And once on the job, Father McGrath would find that he and Dr. McRae did not always see eye to eye.

William McGrath's China tenure was further complicated by bouts of illness — physical afflictions, sometimes linked to depressed states of mind. He spent time back in Canada on sick leave, while the ever faithful Father Serra filled in as temporary mission leader. In a frank letter written in September 1935, Father McGrath in effect answered his critics:

> *. . . bear in mind that there has always been a spirit of discontent in Chuchow, during Monsignor Fraser's regime, during my own tenure of office, at least on the part of a minority . . . . It makes me wonder if a sufficient sense of discipline and real missionary spirit have animated our men to date, even allowing for the very real difficulties of missionary life and the Fraser "situation." Bishop Walsh (of the American Maryknoll Missionaries) speaks of those who "go to China to convert the pagans and remain to confound one another".*

William McNabb, SFM (left) and James McGillivray, SFM., who died in China.

Like most of us, McGrath did best what he best liked doing. He made his personal preferences very clear in the same 1935 letter to his superiors. Stating that he did not want to return to China for any long period, he continued: "By lecturing and writing, I could do something definitely helpful and something which I find easy and congenial."

He was back in Lishui by December of that year, but not for long. In 1937 Father McGrath helped inaugurate a religious program at a Shanghai radio station. In May of 1939 he sailed to Canada.

(For his part, Father Serra returned to his native Spain. A few years before his death in 1972 he wrote to Scarboro's superior general, then Paul Ouellette, "I can recall very vividly my years in China," the aged priest reported. Sadly, his Spanish colleagues "think I am talking deliriously".)

With a journalist's eye for detail and a preacher's penchant for sweeping declaration, McGrath in the 1930s had penned some of the most vivid accounts of the Canadians' evangelizing labor in China. **The Dragon at Close Range**, published by the Scarboro seminary, contained a number of his compositions which make compelling reading today. "Bringing Tidings of Great Joy" is a rather poignant example. An excerpt:

> *We wish you could have been with us last evening . . . in the house of a pagan. After supper most of the men of the town (of Siao Van) came to see who these foreign visitors were and what they had to say for themselves. After the usual courtesies had been exchanged and we had offered them some foreign tobacco . . . they wanted to know if we would be good enough to explain what was our honorable business.*
>
> *The catechist did explain and well . . . He also told them why these foreign Priests had left their fathers and mothers, sisters and brothers so many thousands of miles away and had come to China to teach them how to escape from the power of the devil . . .*
>
> *They were a bit sceptical about escaping the power of the devil . . . Besides, they said, it was the first they had ever heard that the souls of men didn't return after death to enter into cows or oxen.*
>
> *But the doctrine did sound reasonable. And beautiful! Imagine a place where they could have peace forever and where the devil had no power! They certainly wouldn't mind working hard all their lives if they could look forward to that after death. This life, they said, was a pretty tough grind . . .*
>
> *It was with a feeling of sadness that we left Siao Van and began the trek along the cobblestone road that leads to "home." There is still no Priest available for these poor people, nor for the thousands of other little villages lost among our mountains of Chekiang. If there were —*

Elsewhere in this attractively illustrated collection Father McGrath remarked that "we would a thousand times prefer to deal with an unspoiled and unsophisticated and thoroughly superstitious pagan than with the product of the modern 'Oh Yeah' school of what passes for thought".

* * *

Leo Curtin, a diocesan priest formerly attached to the Archdiocese of Ottawa, was appointed to replace McGrath as regional superior in the Lishui prefecture. An older man, Father Curtin found the burdens of field leadership as heavy as his predecessors had. Deafness sometimes complicated relations with fellow priests, and was said also to have prevented him from acquiring any facility in the local Chinese dialect. Still, prospects appeared better than usual.

"Throughout the prefecture of Lishui things are going remarkably well," **China** reported in 1938. And so it seemed at the time. Five men were then working in and around Lishui, while 13 more were stationed at five principal mission stations: Tsingtien, Dolu, Pi-Wu-Ka, Sungyang and Lungchuan. Two were temporarily in Shanghai and four missioners were back in Canada on regular furlough or sick leave. The progress report in the Scarboro house organ foresaw still brighter days ahead:

> *People are turning towards the Church as never before, and if we had but the funds, mission activities throughout the district would be at the peak. In all parishes the schools are well attended, and the crowds of catechumens are increasing. They seem to appreciate deeply the fact that we are standing by them; the Sisters, as ever, are doing wonderful work in their administrations to the sick.. In spite of rumors of danger, we are going ahead as never before.*

Moreover, 11 priests, a record number, were preparing to join the next mission band, scheduled to leave for the Orient later that year. It seemed that more young Catholic men in Canada were welcoming the challenge posed by "the big task of converting more than a million and a half pagans in the Prefecture of Chuchow". Perhaps some of them had been inspired by the frequent exhortations of Monsignor McGrath. In one of his published letters to Scarboro seminarians he had sketched an uncompromising "picture of life for all of us":

> *A few short years at the seminary and then China 'till the end. My dear boys, do you think creation ever held up a nobler picture for the scrutiny of God on High? Everything that life holds given up cheerfully for Him!*

The mission team about 1939:
Top row, left to right: Dan MacNeil, Gerard McKernan, Harold Murphy, Lorne McFarland, Alex MacIntosh.

Third row, left to right: Ed Lyons, Charles Murphy, Joseph Venini, Vincent Morrison, Leo Curtin, Edward Moriarty, Harvey Steele.

Second row, left to right: Mary Genevieve, St. Angela, St. Kenneth, Mary Angela, Mary Vianney.

Front row, left to right: Mary Catherine, St. Julitta (Mother Superior), William McGrath (SFM Regional Superior), Mary Daniel, St. Martin.

Paralleling these promising developments for the small Canadian enterprise, the indigenous Catholic leadership in China had been expanding since Pope Pius XI had named the first six native-born bishops in 1926. By the late 1930s nearly 40 per cent of the 3,000 foreign and native Catholic clergy on the mainland were said to be Chinese. An estimated 5,000 seminarians were studying abroad. Chinese Catholics numbered an estimated 2.5 million in a national population then approaching a half billion.

"Although converts were few, respect for the Church was enormous, literally hundreds of times greater than its numbers warranted," one missioner would say subsequently. This was so, he explained, "because of the good works done in medical and educational fields." Free treatment clinics, for example, ministered to "tens of millions," and hundreds of Catholic orphanages were "refuges for girl babies abandoned by their mothers so they would not be drowned".

* * *

"If survival was the name of the game among the majority of poor people in China," C. J. Eustace concluded after his research studies of some SFM archival records, "it was also the motivating reality that governed the lives of many of the missionaries." Some excerpts from Mr. Eustace's draft account of his findings — an account that clearly strives to be both fair and forthright:

> *. . . survival was on two levels — one level for the priests, the other for the Chinese.*
>
> *Many of the missionaries never really mastered the Chinese language but most of them could make themselves understood . . . There was a cultural barrier also. The missionary priests lived as closely as possible together in a Canadian way . . . So they lived their own life style inside their own houses and there was little close relationship with individual Chinese.*
>
> *There was also, it seems fair to say, a continuing disillusionment in the type of mission work they were doing . . . (It) often seemed far from clear to them that their approach to the job was the right one. It was a matter of constant improvising, of continual hardship and of primitive living conditions beyond anything they had experienced at home. Most of them did not question their vocation. They were content just to bring the Sacraments to their Chinese converts — to baptize, to give Holy Communion, to hear confessions, and to give Christian burial . . .*

There was a certain number of Chinese converts who were referred to as "rice Christians" for whom a pound or two of rice and provisions made all the difference between survival and extinction . . . It was in many cases difficult for the missionaries to distinguish between those who were genuine in their religious profession, and those who were mercenary. But despite these problems the Canadians made a number of real friends among the Chinese, including some fervent Christian families.

* * *

The magazine **China** reported other major developments, most of a positive nature, during these troubled 10 years.

In 1933 the first Chinese mission in Canada was established in Vancouver under Scarboro auspices. Hugh F. X. Sharkey was placed in charge. St. Francis Xavier Seminary had reached its 15th year of operation. In extolling "the remarkable progress achieved by the institution," Alphonsus Chafe reported that total enrolment that autumn would be nearing 50 men in several stages of missionary preparation.

Dr. McRae in 1934 made his second official visit to the Chekiang region assigned to Scarboro under the episcopal watch of the bishop in Ningpo.

In 1934 James MacGillivray was the first of two Scarboro men to die on Chinese soil. That summer he was stricken with malaria and after four days died on August 6 at the age of 38. His body was buried on a Chekiang hillside. Soon after his arrival as one of the 1932 mission band, Father MacGillivray had shared some of his first impressions with readers of **China**:

. . . the poverty of the ordinary people is something to wonder at . . . When our Lord said, "Whatever you do to one of these, my least brethren, you do unto me," he must have had the Chinese in mind.

William McGrath would dedicate his collection of missioning articles, **The Dragon at Close Range**, to the memory of Father MacGillivray.

Beginning in 1937, when Japanese forces made a massive thrust southward from Manchuria, there were repeated air attacks on Kinhwa and Lishui. Shanghai, meanwhile, was under sustained assault. In his autobiography J. M. Fraser shared memories of

Japanese bombing raids on Kinhwa. From his terse and graphic accounts:

> *For four years Kinhwa was intermittently bombed. Many were killed and many houses destroyed . . . My washerwoman and her son were killed. She was found dead with her rosary in her hand. I buried them in our Catholic cemetery. My night watchman's son was found minus his head. His father recognized the body only from the clothes.*

Despite the growing hazards in Chekiang, Scarboro despatched the largest mission band ever in 1938. The new arrivals were welcomed with extra warmth by their fellow Canadians; not since 1936 had reinforcements arrived.

The year 1939 saw the outbreak of the Second World War in Europe. In Lishui the Grey Sisters were placed in charge of a new hospital unit that was to see capacity use. In December several new Scarboro priests set sail for China.

* * *

China occasionally provided informative glimpses into the priests' and sisters' reactions to daily experiences.

The Chekiang Chinese, one missioner complained anonymously, "believe that the average missionary is a millionaire":

> *They wouldn't think so if they knew of his worries to make ends meet, and pay the cook and catechist and teacher, and find the money to build chapels and support the schools in the various missions where pupils pay nothing, or perhaps only a few Chinese dollars a year . . .*

Bernard Boudreau described his frustrations when he took pastoral charge of the mission at Pi-Wu-Ka: "I got all records in shape after a month of chasing around. It is really marvellous how this place has existed up to now." For example, mission records dating back about 50 years listed as dead or "about to die" some local residents who were still alive!

"It is a sad fact that many little Chinese babies are exposed to the horrible fate of being either drowned, suffocated or abandoned to die of hunger and exposure by parents," Joseph King wrote. Infant daughters suffered most; male babies were "much more favored".

"On Christmas Eve (in 1932) I had the happiness of baptizing six

Scarboro members Joe King (left), Bernard Boudreau (centre) and Paul Wong (right) with students at the mission school in Piwa, Chekiang, 1937.

boys and one woman — my first Baptisms here in China," William McNabb reported. He noted that the Grey Sisters "do not believe in Christmas vacation, for the day following the feast they were very busy attending to the dozens of sick people who sought foreign medicine."

"Depression!" Joseph Venini told his Canadian readers they should count themselves as comparatively fortunate. Economic hardship "has been the chronic state of the Chinese people for millenia. It has been said that the Chinese could live on the land left uncultivated in the fence corners of American farms."

Another point of view appeared in the next issue of the Scarboro house organ. A May 1933 editorial, appealing for more donations from readers, quoted an unnamed missioner's plea, "We are up against it good and hard."

Reporting from the mission post of Wong Da in June that year, Fathers Amyot and King said they finally had "glass in the windows now, and a room apiece, and the rain doesn't come through the chapel roof as much as heretofore".

Aaron Gignac described his horror on witnessing the execution of two men who had been condemned, according to placards around their necks, because they had "enlisted with the Reds". They were "forced to their knees and shot by soldiers. Shot in the back of their heads . . . It was a sickening sight. Not the least disgusting part of it was the morbid curiosity exhibited by the crowd."

James Leonard wrote from Shanghai late in 1937:

> *Strange city this Shanghai. Part of the town lay in ruins from Japanese shelling and bombing, while day by day in December I noticed the shop windows filled with Christmas toys, specializing this year in toy tanks, aeroplanes, armored cars and battleships.*

Craig Strang described a Corpus Christi procession in Lishui as "triumphant". It was "the first great public demonstration of Catholic faith in Chuchow," he wrote. "It was that of a fresh conquest."

Yet Arthur Venadam was moved to wonder about the unfathomable ways of Providence — as many of his Scarboro brothers and the Pembroke sisters must often have wondered too:

> *Why it is that the Holy Ghost picks such scattered spots to work His designs is not ours to ask, but the fact remains that right here near Lishui there are lots of little towns that surely must know about us but have so far discouraged all our advances, and yet, away up in the country there are communities that send regularly for the priest and regard his visits as the outstanding event of the year.*

11 THE FORTIES – – RETREAT AND RETURN

China, which had not enjoyed peaceful times for generations, was more ravaged than ever during the 1940s by external invaders and internal strife. And for the Canadian priests and sisters in Chekiang, one emergency situation after another made sustained mission work almost impossible.

There were a few periods of comparative calm — some months in 1946-47, for example, but these peaceful intervals were shortlived. Most of the time the hard-pressed Canadians had to contend with bombing attacks, disease and depression within their own ranks, an agonizing retreat into west central China and, for some, confinement in Japanese internment camps. On returning to Chekiang in mid-decade, the missioners found their small flocks diminished by casualties or flight. Finally, as the 1940s ended the Scarboro members and Grey Sisters faced imminent Communist rule throughout China.

* * *

Reports by four principal participants provide an overview of what the 1940s felt like for these Canadians in an embattled country.

"Fortunately, missionaries have learned not to judge their measure of success by statistics alone," Leo Curtin, superior of the China missions, wrote in the fall of 1940: "If we did, I fear we would get but cold comfort from eyeing the annual report which has just been compiled for the Prefecture of Lishui."

Stressing that "the value of human souls can never be measured in dollars and cents, nor in terms of human effort expended," he noted how modest the Canadian endeavor was in relation to a "pagan population" of over 850,000 in the immediate vicinity of Scarboro's mission territories. Highlights:

> *We count 2,512 Christians in good standing at the present time. (Editorial note: this number and others following do not agree with statistics cited elsewhere in our story. The data came from various sources, all of which made different*

estimates or calculations, often in reference to smaller or larger population areas) . . . .

To aid souls get to Heaven is the major objective of any missionary. Our missionaries in Lishui baptized 208 adults who were on their deathbeds, and administered the saving Sacrament to 469 dying infants (in the year under review) . . . .

Mission personnel consisted of 22 Scarboro Fathers in Lishui, plus 11 at language school in Peking or Shanghai; two Chinese priests, nine Grey Sisters, and 53 lay catechists, most of them men, who were responsible for most of the doctrinal instruction.

Near the midway point in the Forties, when the Allies were defeating the Axis powers in both the European and Asian theatres of the Second World War, John McGoey reviewed Scarboro's wartime experiences in China and looked ahead with qualified optimism to evangelization efforts in peace time. In a Catholic Youth Broadcast carried by an Edmonton station in 1944, he asked:

Would the future see us at it again? . . . . It could never be a failure. We would go back one day, and soon. But when we would come back it must be with greater numbers, greater organization, greater means at our disposal. The efficiency demanded in a material world must be applied in the spiritual world . . . . What the price of a single Superfortress (a major U.S. bomber plane) wouldn't do!

Predicting that Christianity could become "a leaven for a better China," he invited more young Canadians "to offer their lives as priests and sisters for this work". Father McGoey claimed that true faith and social advance went hand in hand:

. . . Christianity for China or any other pagan country is the key to progress, to the elevating of the people to a higher physical as well as spiritual life. It is this which will cultivate in these nations a way of thought similar to our own, and put them on a plane with the other nations.

Such aspirations must have seemed within the realm of possibility by late 1947, two years after Japan's defeat and at a time when the renewed civil war between Chiang Kai-shek's Nationalists and Mao Tse-tung's Communist armies was still distant from Chekiang.

Arthur Venedam, then regional superior, sent an encouraging letter to Scarboro headquarters. He reported that 14 mission posts were operating at Lishui, Lungchuan, Sungyang, Pihu, Tsingtien, Yungkang, Tungyang, Pukiang, Lanchi, Tangchi, Kinhwa, Dolu, Yunho and Hwangtan:

> *There are three new missions here and we hope to have priests where possible with an army of catechists to assist them. Both the Lishui and Lungchuan clinics are operating full blast with 400 to 500 treated at each clinic daily . . . .*
>
> *We have magnificent Sisters, including the new ones. If they don't get to heaven, nobody will . . . .*
>
> *Our school at Lishui is filled to capacity and so is the branch school five li (a mile and a half) down the river and the results spiritually are very encouraging . . . . Father Hudswell is doing a grand job at the Lungchuan school. He has a Catholic principal and will likely get two or three Catholic teachers next term . . . .*
>
> *Practically all the missions are now under repair. The church here in Lishui . . . is in good shape and more beautiful than ever . . . .*
>
> *We had a wonderful Christmas, over 200 Communions, 18 Baptisms and 28 Confirmations . . . .*

Portents of better days to come? It was not to be. By early 1949, as Marxist armies advanced throughout China, the new bishop of Lishui — Scarboro's Kenneth Turner — wrote urgently to his colleagues in Canada: "Ask the readers of **China** magazine to begin a crusade of daily Rosaries that all will go well with us here. I am asking for prayers and penance. I was never more earnest in my life."

* * *

The first four of 11 more men whom Scarboro would sent to China that decade arrived in Chekiang early in 1940 — John McGoey, Gordon Stringer, Kenneth Turner and Russell White. The other seven arrived later that same year: Armand Clement, Francis Diemert, John Kelly, Thomas McQuaid, Joseph Murphy, Michael MacSween and Andrew Pinfold. They were the last mission band Scarboro would send to China. Further sailings from Canada became impossible when the Second World War spread to the Pacific in 1941.

The first year in the warring decade also saw the death of the second Scarboro missioner — Aaron Gignac. He died in China October 31 following an operation. Like James McGillivray, who had died five years earlier, Father Gignac was 38. His body was buried beside that of his fellow Canadian on a Chekiang hillside.

Ten years before Aaron Gignac had shared impressions of his first mission trip with readers of **China**:

> *We spent a week at Gui Sz Ka, visiting the Christians and exhorting them to come to Mass and the Sacraments. The catechist explained the doctrines to them and we ourselves added a word of exhortation from time to time, telling them how important a thing it was to save one's soul, that life in this world at best was short and full of trials of every kind and that the truly wise man would work for a life of happiness that had no end.*
>
> *. . . I had no idea of the appalling condition of many of our mission outposts. I childlishly thought they were buildings of fairly substantial construction and fairly comfortable. They are really only miserable hovels.*

Armand Clement, SFM, was an RCAF chaplain in World War II.

By all accounts Father Gignac became one of the most effective missionaries, well liked by the Chinese and Canadian colleagues alike. Hugh Sharkey would pay him this tribute:

> *Were I to single out some special characteristics that Father Aaron had, I think they would be his simplicity and humility. He was always just himself — and we all loved him for his unaffected, natural ways.*

"I learned more from Father Gignac in the 18 months before he died than in all my formal studies," Harvey Steele remembered. "He had an outstanding command of the language and he respected the people and their customs." Steele said that the example of his mentor encouraged him "to question the wisdom of identifying Christianity with Western Culture" and to acknowledge that "the Chinese had much to teach us."

John McGoey, more recently on the mission scene, was also deeply affected by the witness of Aaron Gignac. The young priest was with the veteran when he spoke his last words, "Jesus, Mary . . . .":

> *It was the calmest, most peaceful death I have ever seen — not the least resentment, regret, or hesitation. Just an event for which he had prepared all his life . . . .*
>
> *One thought stayed with me. If only I could die like that . . . . It is still my wish today.*

* * *

Significant developments were taking place on the Canadian side of the Pacific in 1940. In June word was received that the Vatican Congregation for the Propagation of the Faith had formally approved constitutions for the Canadian mission enterprise, which henceforth was given a higher ecclesial status as the Scarboro Foreign Mission Society. Dr. J. E. McRae was authorized to preside as temporary head until the first General Chapter met the following year to elect a superior general and General Council.

Paralleling this institutional change, the mission territory of Kinhwa, formerly under jurisdiction of the bishop of Hangchow, was added to the Lishui prefecture. Monsignor McGrath presided over this enlarged mission territory as prefect apostolic. His mission team soon would reach a peak strength of 36 men, with another seven then scheduled for early service in the Orient.

* * *

All Scarboro programs and plans were interrupted in 1941 and 1942. Following its surprise attack on American naval forces at Pearl Harbour in December of 1941, Japan entered the Second World War on the side of Nazi Germany and Fascist Italy. Henceforth Canadians in the Far East were regarded by Tokyo as enemy aliens. Japanese forces soon swept across much of China and the Malaysian Peninsula, and occupied the Philippines, where Monsignor Fraser was to spend several years in safe confinement.

In Peking, the Japanese interned Scarboro priests then studying at a Jesuit language school. Included among the hundreds of internees were Fathers Beal, Carey (until then superior of the SFM house of studies there), Clement, Diemert, McSween, McQuaid and Joseph Murphy.

Charles Murphy was confined to the warden's quarters of Stanley Prison in Hong Kong where an ill-equipped Canadian expeditionary force had been overpowered by the Japanese. Desmond Stringer would report in 1942 that Father Murphy "had the opportunity of leaving there and returning to Canada". Instead Murphy "chose to remain and care for the spiritual welfare of his charges in the concentration camp".

In January 1942, Hugh Sharkey, editor of **China**, took a stiff-upper-lip stance in response to these developments:

> *We ask our friends to continue their interest in our work and the financial assistance they have so generously given in the past. We must keep up the training of young men in our seminary; we must carry on the conversion of the Chinese people of our own country; we must prepare for the days. . . . of renewed missionary activity in the Orient.*

* * *

In Chekiang, meanwhile, the Canadian men and women spent much of their time and energy contending with bombing raids. A Grey Sister's report from Lishui described what had become almost a daily experience:

> *Imagine the sound of those heavy bombs and the screaming of incendiaries, the large columns of smoke, the explosion of gasoline and oil and other fireworks . . . .*
>
> *When the heavy bombs demolished the dispensary we thought we were all gone. Father Kelly gave us all absolution*

Charles Murphy, SFM, became a navy chaplain.

> *in the dugout . . . . About 20 were killed (in an office building within a few houses of the mission enclosure) and 10 burned to death after receiving shrapnel wounds. The screams from the burning victims were terrible. A young married couple and five girls were brought in from that section . . . .*
>
> *I worked on those five injured people all afternoon, removing pieces of shrapnel, treating large, open wounds and checking hemorrhages. All the time the thought of that poor burning soul and her shrieking cries for help were ringing in my ears . . . .*

By late May 1942 Japanese units were fast approaching Lishui. The Canadian missioners evacuated their main post on May 23. Some among them would be "on the road", except for several weeks' stay in Lungchuan, for the next six months. In this harrowing period, they would travel more than 1,500 miles on foot, by bicycle, and river boat, by bus, truck and train, until they reached Yuanling in the west central province of Hunan. Their journey — always strenuous, often frustrating and sometimes perilous — followed a southwestern, then northwestern course, which even on the map looks daunting. *(See maps)*

The main group of refugees made their way in the first week to Lungchuan, which was the southernmost mission station manned by the Scarboro team. Twenty-three priests and sisters, including some neighboring American and Irish missionaries, were received by Arthur Venadam, mission rector. He was to remain in the district throughout the Japanese occupation that soon followed.

After resting there for some time, comparing notes and making individual and group decisions, the missionaries moved on in smaller groupings and sometimes in different directions. Harvey Steele, for one, would make his way to Chungking where he would serve alongside his Maryknoll hosts as a chaplain to American servicemen. Chungking, then the Nationalist capital of China, was at least 2,000 miles to the northwest.

Most of the others travelled southward towards Nanping in Fukien province, which point they reached in late July. Then August travel on a balky old bus to Kanchow in Kiangsi province; thence to Hengyang, partly by train, which they reached in early September. And on to Yuanling via Changsha by train and river boat. There the exhausted Canadians were received November 22, 1942 by American Sisters and Bishop Cuthbert O'Gara, vicar apostolic of the Passionist missions in China. Later he would praise the collaborative labors of his Canadian guests, saying: "It was our privilege to welcome them — six Fathers and seven Sisters."

* * *

Even in the most remote areas of Chekiang province, meanwhile, the Chinese were suffering hardships and tragic losses at the hands of their Asiatic neighbors. In March 1943 Kenneth Turner described in detail what had happened to the people in Dolu, in the Kinhwa region:

> *Whoever would have thought that the full force of the war would strike this tiny out-of-the-way village of Dolu, nestling in a narrow valley between the high, bare hills? It is miles away from any place of importance . . . .*
>
> *For years and years on end Dolu village has enjoyed its placid existence, barely touched by the changes that have*

affected the outside world. Its mud walls and tiled roofs have sheltered generations of villagers in peace and isolation. Daughters have been given in marriage and left, but never go far from home. Sons have married and brought wives from neighbouring villages. Dolu's unlovely homes, walling in the narrow crooked lanes, have seen children born, and they have echoed to the wailings of the mourners as each one's time came. On the slopes of the hills are the grass-covered mounds covering the graves of ancestors. The "good earth" was their sole employment and care, and in it they rest awaiting the Resurrection . . . .

Gradually I got the story of the catastrophe . . . When a (Japanese) foraging party entered the valley attempting to take grain and cattle, there were some who resisted. Rifles blazed from the hills. In retaliation every house in Dolu and in six neighboring villages were one by one set ablaze. None were spared, not even a Buddhist shrine just outside the village . . . .

I went into the church. It was as we had left it. There was no evidence of any attempt to set the church on fire . . . .

Half a year has gone by and Dolu is emerging from its ashes. Around the church, emblematic of what gives meaning to life and suffering, the villagers have begun to raise their little cottages. The past winter has been a severe one. Sickness and want have taken their toll of life, especially of the little ones. Even in this rectory, huddled close to the kitchen fire in his mother's arms, one little boy died with the chrism of Confirmation still wet on his forehead.

* * *

Shortly before Christmas in 1943, Joseph Murphy wrote a letter home to "Dear Mother and Dad" from Peking where formerly he had been a language student and now was held as an enemy alien along with several other Scarboro men —

After the first few weeks internment was not so bad . . . . At first there was much bigotry shown towards Catholic Fathers and Sisters. Slowly, when the rest of the camp (numbering over 1,700 at one point) saw the Fathers take the heaviest of the work and the Sisters usually the dirtiest, ignorance gave way to admiration.

On January 1, 1944 Murphy wrote again. He foresaw long delays before his letter would reach his parents. "Happy New Year's wishes are in order today, but by the time you receive this it will be 'Happy Easter' — possibly even 'Merry Christmas' again." He, together with several other Canadians, would remain interned for several months more. Some other Scarboro priests were permitted to return to Canada earlier under repatriation arrangements between governments.

* * *

The last issue of **China** for 1943 recorded an historic juncture in the story of the Canadian missionary Society — one that marked the approaching end of the China chapter and the beginning of a new Latin American chapter. The first mission team bound for Santo Domingo in the Dominican Republic was hailed in print and photographs. And on a nearby page the magazine offered a "Hearty welcome to our repatriated missioners" — eight men, headed by veteran Lawrence Beal, who were returning from the Far East. Their return presaged by less than a decade what was to become the pattern in the early 1950s. How many could foresee in 1943 that following Japan's impending defeat, the civil war would resume in China, and most foreign missionaries soon would be considered "enemies of the people"?

By 1944, however, immediate missionary prospects in China seemed rather promising to some of the men still in that beleaguered land. The Lishui mission was reopened by returning priests who were "welcomed home" to the region by Arthur Venadam. Fathers Curtin, Morrisey, Kelly, McAuliffe and McKernan had returned to the area "in excellent health," **China** reported.

"Better days are ahead, I am sure," Father Venadam, by then pro-prefect of Lishui, reported in December of 1944. On a "prolonged visit to the missions" in the region he had found some of the church buildings still standing, although all had been looted. "What a difference from former years. Still, we have a lot for which to be thankful and God is certainly with us."

* * *

Back in Canada Monsignor McGrath had embraced another cause — the visions of the Blessed Virgin Mary reported by three shepherd children in Fatima, Portugal in 1917. They claimed that the Mother of Jesus had urged them and the Catholic world to pray for the early conversion of Russia so as to avoid world catastrophe. "Not since the autobiography of the Little Flower (St. Theresa of

Lisieux, France) have I found anything so profoundly touching in its spiritual simplicity as the story of the child witnesses of Fatima," McGrath wrote. "Would we save America, as devotions to Fatima have saved Portugal? When will we learn from those child friends of God's own Blessed Mother?"

At the time William McGrath was first assistant to the SFM superior general, but he was soon to resign this office and concentrate his energies in addressing mass rallies to honor Our Lady of Fatima. No doubt he was encouraged in this by reports of Pius XII's personal interest in the Fatima devotion.

* * *

Japan surrendered to the Allied Powers in August of 1945. "The war is over but the wounds are deep and angry looking," Desmond Stringer wrote in reference to China:

> *The scenic beauty of Chekiang is pockmarked, its people dazed and dejected. Centuries of belief have been shattered and lie in the dusty ruins that once were idols. If ever the strong, heart-healing qualities of mercy were needed, now is the time; now, when the old men can't dream dreams, nor the young see visions.*

By June of 1946 **China** proudly featured a two-page spread picturing the 14 missionaries who were back in the Chinese missions. Readers also learned that Monsignor Fraser had returned to Kinhwa where he was evangelizing "with undiminished zeal and courage." By December several of the Grey Sisters had also returned to Lishui territory. As a result, one of them wrote, "the whole town is ringing with excitement".

This euphoric mood prevailed through much of 1947. By the next year, however, there was growing apprehension as the Canadians learned of Communist advances southward in the continuing civil war. By then the Lishui prefecture had a new regional superior — Kenneth Turner. His "Religious Report on our Mission in China," published in the May 1948 issue of the Scarboro house organ, made sober reading on both sides of the Pacific. Here, for a change, was a leader not given to wishful optimism, even as his Christian hope prevailed:

> *. . . we have 6,364 Christians. So the percentage of Christianity to population is extremely low, viz. 0.22 (of one) per cent. It is evident that we are really only beginning to convert this area. This is a labor that will require many, many more*

priests than we have at present . . . .

The Communist menace is probably the reason for many towns imposing a curfew. In Lishui last month I had to wait until dawn (not having a pass) before leaving the mission to make my way to my sampan on the beach . . . .

We naturally want to be optimistic in predictions for the coming year but at the same time we must remember that the Church in the North is being suppressed and persecuted . . . .

Writing in July of the same year Ronald Reeves described the ruinous inflation that was sweeping through areas of China still held — but not for long — by Chiang Kai-shek's Nationalists:

The exchange hit the all-time high last week: six million of the local currency for one American dollar. An egg now cost $60,000! Rice is $20,000,000 for one hundred pounds. . . . There is a great insecurity over here, everybody disturbed; this is a new attitude for the Chinese people. They know the war is not over yet.

"We are using this (sense of insecurity) to convince them that religion is their only hope," Father Reeves continued. "Much good may yet come out of these trying times."

Later in 1948 Kenneth Turner was named Bishop of Lishui. Nearly 3,000,000 people were said to reside within the diocesan boundaries of 18 counties. Of these, as already noted, less than 6,500 were listed as Catholics on the diocesan rolls.

From its beginning Bishop Turner's episcopal tenure was threatened by the approaching armies of Mao Tse-tung. Craig Strang tried to sound optimistic in a letter written in November of 1948: "As for the Reds coming this way — many whose judgment I respect seem to think that unlikely for a long time," he reported. "They argue: the Reds are divided among themselves and that will show to our advantage when they have a bigger territory to govern . . . . In a nutshell, our territory *may* not be occupied; if so, there is little concern for personal safety."

Within a few months, however, Bishop Turner would say that he was "never more earnest in my life" in asking Canadian supporters for their prayers.

* * *

While the Second General Chapter of the Society was meeting in Scarborough during the late summer of 1949, approximately 20 priests and sisters still were in mainland China, most of them ministering as before in the Diocese of Lishui. Hugh McGettigan, Scarboro's procurator in China, was in Shanghai, which had been under Marxist control since May of that year. Also there: John McGoey and Gerard McKernan. They were leading figures in interchurch and international programs of postwar relief and rehabilitation.

Father McGoey later described his experiences as a welfare co-ordinator in fascinating detail and with provocative comment in **Nor Scrip Nor Shoes**. He and an American Vincentian priest started the Catholic Welfare Committee, which on behalf of China's 140 Catholic bishops worked with various donor agencies in the rehabilitative field. These included the American Advisory Committee, whose members oversaw contributions by 23 Protestant groups in China. McGoey's efforts brought him into personal contact with high officials of the United Nations, the U.S., the Nationalists in China and later with Communist authorities.

As he saw it, the Americans were duped into believing that Mao's forces were mostly "agrarian reformers" rather than ideological militants. After Communist troops occupied Shanghai in the late spring of 1949, Father McGoey said orderly rehabilitation work became impossible:

> *All the groups which had been so delighted to see the Communists were now taking a sober second look. They found out that working for the "bloodsucking capitalists" was admittedly tough, but not half as tough as working for "the People." You could complain about the capitalists, at least; you could not complain about the People. And daily it was becoming more confusing who the People were. There was the People's Currency, the People's Bank, the People's Army, the People's Will — but just who were the People? The answer to this became all too grimly plain as time went by.*

* * *

At this point in our decade-by-decade review, we will double back to trace in some detail the parallel story of the Grey Sisters in Chekiang.

12 PARTNERS IN MISSION: THE GREY SISTERS

An historic picture with caption that is more revealing than any thousand words is prominently displayed in one of the busy offices of the SFM headquarters. Shown in the 1938 photograph is the Canadian mission team in the Lishui-Kinhwa regions. The central figure is that of Monsignor John Mary Fraser, Scarboro's founder, whose photographic image has been retouched in bright tints. The 21 assembled priests standing on either side of him appear in the black and white of the original print, with their names listed under the group portrait — left to right, row by row. And there is one row of nine Grey Sisters of the Immaculate Conception from Pembroke. As known by their religious names then, they are not identified by name in the listing under the framed picture. They were left to right: Sisters St. Kenneth, Mary Genevieve, St. Angela, Mary Daniel, St. Julitta, superior; Mary Angela, Mary Catherine, Mary Vianney and St. Martin. *(See Roster of Sisters in Appendices.)*

The group photograph is another reminder that hierarchical order and masculine supremacy prevailed without open questioning in Catholic circles in the decades before civil trends and Vatican II fostered alternative perceptions.

However, it would be a mistake to read too much into this 1938 portrait as viewed from the early 1980s. True, the notable contribution to mission made by 15 Grey Sisters from 1929 to 1952 has to date been a comparatively neglected aspect in most accounts of the Canadian years in Chekiang. Yet several of the surviving sisters and priests who were there insist, and strongly, that no slight was ever intended by the men who worked overseas alongside these religious women.

Perhaps editors of **China** in Scarboro sometimes overlooked "the sisters' angle" in deciding the contents of the monthly magazine. If so, this would have reflected the mentality of the times. Then even more than now, it was pointed out, religious journalism gave priority attention to the hierarchical Church, to the pope and bishops first of all, to priests before sisters, to clergy and religious women ahead of the laity, almost always to men before women.

In Chekiang the Grey Sisters' life-sustaining labors as nurses and

The much discussed group portrait taken outside the church at Lishui in 1938.

Back row, left to right: Harvey Steele, Harold Murphy, Ken Turner, Jack McGoey, Gordon Stringer, Russ White, Charles Murphy, Len Hudswell, Ed Moriarty, Dan MacNeil, John Kelly.

Middle row, left to right: Sisters St. Kenneth, Mary Genevieve, St. Angela, Mary Daniel, St. Julitta (Superior), Mary Angela, Mary Catherine, Mary Vianney, St. Martin and Fr. Paul Kam.

Bottom row, left to right: Arthur Venadam, Aaron Gignac, Larry Beal, Leo Curtin, John Mary Fraser, Vincent Morrison, Desmond Stringer, Larry McAuliffe, John Maurice.

teachers were never overlooked, Scarboro veterans emphasize. In fact, John McGoey claimed they were "reverenced as the greatest asset of the mission".

"It would be impossible to express the appreciation we priests had for the Grey Sisters," Bishop Ken Turner declared. He did recall, though, that they were "shy about publicizing themselves."

Probably oversight — more understandable as the years passed — explains the fact that a succession of special anniversary issues of the SFM magazine ignored these partners in mission. For example, the June 1951 issue of **Scarboro Missions** which feted Monsignor Fraser's golden jubilee, did not make any reference to the women who had been willing helpers in China for many years. Nor did the 1968 edition marking the 50th anniversary of the priests' Society. And three special issues of the magazine during the SFM's 60th year in 1978 did not once refer to the missionaries' collaborators during most of their China years — although the same 1938 group portrait was reproduced, again without naming the Grey Sisters.

* * *

One week before the 1929 stock market crash precipitated the Great Depression, a happier event for those present took place in St. Columban's Cathedral, Pembroke, Ontario. It was the departure ceremony to convey blessings and best wishes to the three Grey Sisters who were about to travel to the Scarboro foothold in faraway China. Thirty-four members had responded to Mother St. Paul's call for volunteers. From this large number three were selected to practise their nursing and teaching skills in the Orient: Catherine Doyle (Sr. Mary Catherine), Christine McDonald (Sr. St. Oswald) and Catherine McHugh (Sr. Mary Anthony).

Their religious community, like some others in Canada and the United States, traced its origin to the nursing order founded by Blessed Marguerite d'Youville of Montreal in the 18th century. The Grey Sisters of the Immaculate Conception were invited to send members to China as a result of prolonged discussions that began in May 1928. These involved Father Fraser, his episcopal superior — the bishop of Ningpo, China; Dr. J. E. McRae, rector of the Scarboro mission seminary, the Congregation for the Propagation of the Faith at the Vatican, Bishop P. T. Ryan of Pembroke and Mother St. Paul, the Sister Superior.

The three chosen volunteers arrived in Shanghai in December 1929. There they had a foretaste of the often disappointing and always demanding apostolate they were undertaking. As described by Sister Mary Lawrence, author of "a sketch" on the missionary experiences of Mary Catherine:

> *.... at the dock Rev. John Fraser, superior of the Chuchow mission and Sr. Mary Louise, a Sister of Charity, met them. Father Fraser gave them a very cool reception. The reason for his unfriendly attitude became apparent later. He had been greatly disappointed when the Grey Sisters were chosen as he preferred religious of another congregation. (vi) .... Unknown to the Sisters, Father Fraser had been recalled to Canada and Rev. Ramon Serra had been appointed in his place. Father Serra had sent Rev. William Amyot to meet the Sisters at Shanghai but he had been delayed by the threat of an attack by bandits.*

The new arrivals learned they would have to wait for what turned out to be one year before they could begin their intended good works in Chuchow/Lishui. Instead, they were escorted to Wenchow, some 80 miles distance, where they were to reside as house guests of the Sisters of Charity. Here the Canadian trio were initiated in the missioning practices, while in Chuchow Father Fraser and his priest brother, William Fraser, oversaw construction of their convent residence.

Fathers Serra, Amyot and Lawrence Beal in Chuchow were said to have done all they could to make the newcomers feel welcome in China, and to assuage their disappointment.

In June 1930 the Scarboro magazine carried the first published letter from one of the Grey Sisters, writing anonymously. Her initial impressions in Wenchow were vivid ones:

> *Conditions are terrible here owing to the severe famine. The poor gather in hundreds at the Sisters' gate awaiting a few pennies or a bowl of rice. All receive something. No one is ever turned away empty-handed. It is pitiful to see the little children crying for food and their parents unable to provide for them.*
>
> *Those poor children are received in the dispensary every morning and it is our privilege to serve hot tea and rice cakes*

(vi) "Another congregation" — This probably refers to the Sisters of St. Joseph, the order to which one of his own sisters belonged.

to the little waifs. If you could only see the happy faces as they receive their portion, you would soon realize how privileged we have been to receive so great a calling to labor among Our Lord's suffering.

After J. M. Fraser's departure for Canada in 1930 Fathers Serra and Amyot hurried along the final stages of convent construction in Chuchow so the Grey Sisters could take up residence no later than December 8, the principal feast day of their community. William Amyot wrote an enthusiastic account of their reception in Chuchow when they arrived by river boat from Wenchow:

The rain, which perhaps had been one of the factors that had kept the bandits away, still pattered down a little, but it could not dampen the ardor of the huge crowd of welcomers assembled far ahead of the landing stage. Just as the boats drew up, however, the last drop fell, umbrellas were put away and flags began to wave. There was Father Serra. Yes, and all the other priests too, the catechists, school children and Christians all were there, with many pagans thrown in for luck to swell that happy throng . . . .

Sisters Mary Daniel (left) and Mary Genevieve (right) on their way to Chuchow by "floating hotel" in the early 1930s.

Out stepped the Sisters. A few words of greeting alone could be heard, so great was the noise of the festive firecrackers and the babble of enthusiastic voices on every side . . . .

It was still the Feast. Our prayers had been heard and our wishes granted . . . .

The same issue of **China** also published part of a letter from one of the women. She reported her first experiences in Chuchow, henceforth also the main mission for the Grey Sisters:

. . . we visited an old lady who was dying. Oh! such a hovel for any sick person to live in . . . . That same evening a man was brought in on a stretcher, dying. We gave him conditional Baptism and I hope he is in Heaven by now. Since Saturday we have treated about 50 daily.

Our consolations are numerous, but it is heart-rending to hear those poor people appealing for help. They are so grateful for the smallest service or least act of kindness.

Years later Sister Mary Catherine would recall the pattern of nursing care that developed from this very first day "on the job":

In the afternoon we made our first sick call. Sister Oswald kept house while Sister Mary Anthony and I accompanied by Father Serra as interpreter went by rickshaw to the home of a well-to-do merchant whose daughter was considered in a dying condition. When we reached the house the crowd which followed us amounted to over a hundred. We discovered the child was suffering from typhoid fever. We did what we could for her and left the rest in the hands of God. The following morning the parents happily reported a slight improvement — the child had her first night's rest in three weeks.

The good news spread throughout the city. After our second visit to the typhoid patient we found a large crowd waiting for us outside. We held an open-air clinic while our medicine lasted. Father Serra told the remaining patients to call at the Convent where the Sisters would care for them. By three o'clock fully 100 had gathered at the mission gate and in the guard's room we held the first clinic.

And so it was every day afterwards. Hundreds of thousands of sick would, through the years, seek relief at our clinic. When the patients were too ill to come we went to them on foot, by rickshaw, sampan or sedan chair to heed the call of those who needed us.

Mary Catherine Doyle, an experienced pharmacist, knew the secret of making pills and mixing ointments. Medicines were expensive, with Shanghai the only reliable source of supply. In her words, "One has to be ingenious. As bandages and dressings were acutely needed, they could be washed, sterilized, re-rolled and re-used, extra work for the Sisters but there was no alternative."

The Canadian women also concentrated on schooling for local children. Homemaking skills ranked high in the classroom program, one of the Grey Sisters reported in 1932. Each day there was a sewing class — "as every Chinese girl must learn to make her own clothes and shoes". Washing rice bowls thoroughly, and cleaning rooms were other class pursuits, as the sisters stressed hygienic habits. Children enjoyed school, the writer said, if only because their brothers and sisters at home usually had to work long hours "accomplishing arduous tasks which are often more than they are fit for".

* * *

Happier times! School recess scene in the mission compound.

In their more than 20 years overseas the sisters from Pembroke usually worked in unsettled social conditions and sometimes dangerous circumstances. When the principal hazard did not arise from the intermittent civil strife between Chinese Communists and Nationalists, major perils in the early Thirties included feuding warlords, roving bandits, sudden floods, famines, epidemics and other emergency situations. Still to come were bombings and subsequent invasion by Japanese forces and, later on, Maoist control of the mainland.

The dozen more Grey Sisters who later joined or replaced some of the original threesome, in the order of their arrival: Sisters Mary Daniel (Annie O'Connor) and Mary Genevieve (Jean Jedrzejezyk) in 1931; St. Julitta (Mary Jane Fleming) and St. Angela (Mary Helen Lynch) in 1932; St. Martin (Catherine Gervais) and Mary Angela (Mary McCarthy) in 1934; St. Kenneth (Kathleen Radey) and Mary Vianney (Iona Bertrand) in 1938; and Sisters Mary Esther (Margaret Deverish), St. Joan (Susan Daly) St. Matthew (Florence Pinfold) and St. Nicholas (Genevieve Grace) in 1947.

Nine still were living, most of them in retirement, as of June 1981. Mary Catherine Doyle, first to volunteer, one of the first three to arrive and one of the last three to leave China, lived until March 1981.

* * *

As the 1930s were ending, Leo Curtin, acting mission superior in China, wondered in print:

> *One of the characteristics of the missionary Sisters is their habitual good humor, enigmatic as it may seem. The reason seems to be wholly supernatural. Humanly speaking, they should not be happy. They have given up everything, home and friends, and the almost certain chance of a very lucrative nursing career, to devote their lives to the alleviation of suffering here in pagan China; but in spite of it all, they seem to be the happiest people on the face of the earth.*

From 1937 onwards the Japanese invasion of the Chinese mainland moved southward on an increasing scale. The bombing raids on Lishui and Kinhwa soon became frequent and intense. When Japanese troops penetrated deeply into Chekiang province in 1942, the Canadians were advised as enemy aliens to leave the Lishui region.

Sister Mary Catherine later would recall some highlights of the exodus by priests and sisters from Lishui near the eastern coast deep into west central China:

> *We stayed with our stricken people until one day in May, 1942 a breathless messenger arrived to tell us "Vacate the city immediately; Japanese are only 20 miles away!" Within five minutes we were ready, leaving dinner still on the table and all our possessions behind us . . . .*
>
> *The Sisters from our other mission, Lungchuan, further inland, joined us when we reached them. Then we continued our flight under strafing and bombing, by foot, sampan, bicycle and ammunition trucks over the treacherous roads of interior China, always a step ahead of capture.*
>
> *At night we stopped to rest, sometimes at a Catholic mission, sometimes a Protestant one. If these were not available, we slept on a sampan or along the roadside. The most unusual one was in a large haymow in a shelter for donkeys. We obtained our food, which consisted of rice, at times supplemented by pieces of chicken, from farmers and stores in small villages.*

* * *

A detailed account of the journey, almost day by day in regularity, was kept by Sister St. Angela during the Canadians' long march. "Refugees' Diary" subsequently was published by instalments in the Scarboro magazine. Excerpts indicate the lively content and convivial flavor of her compelling story:

> *May 23rd . . . . Just about noon we were ready to start, and amid tears and prayers, we bade goodbye to Lishui.*
>
> *May 29th . . . . While at Lungchuan we had many alarms but no serious air raids. Rumors, some of them half truths and others mere figments of the imagination, beset us at every turn; what to believe?*
>
> *July 28th . . . . We were to leave this morning, but after spending the day waiting we returned to the convent with the idea that the trip was cancelled, as military officials had claimed our truck . . . .*
>
> *Sunday, August 2nd . . . . They stood on the river bank — four of them — farmers all. They wanted to cross the river*

to the village, but how could they with us sleeping in the ferry? The sun was not up yet, and we were not anxious to rise before it did come up. What to do? One of the men politely told us to remain under our nets. He and his friends would ferry us across the river and when their business on that side of the river was done, they would row us back. Nice of them, but we could not fancy five sleeping Sisters afloat, so we voted on disembarking, which we did. A wash up in the river, then breakfast of fried pork and rice. The day is hot and we find a cool spot in a house. After dinner the truck driver tells us that a new engine is being brought from Lungchuan and that we leave that night. Tonight comes but no engine with it. We prepare supper — more rice and pork. It is dark when all is prepared and we sit around the truck and take our rice by candlelight. The old boatman comes along to see about renting his craft again. Another night under the stars, cradled in the little boat and rocked to and fro in the waves. Sleep we all did, and the truck driver's announcement that the new engine had arrived was our call to get up . . .

Tuesday, August 4th . . . The roosters crowed us out . . . and if they understood human language they knew just how we appreciated their vocal efforts. We had breakfast in the station, candied rice and canned milk . . .

Friday, August 14 . . . We are certainly seeing China inch by inch. Now we are on again, now we are off the truck again, no trees in sight and plenty of sun. Not a drop of water to drink, and we are so thirsty that the muddy water in the rice paddies looks tempting . . .

Saturday, August 15 . . . The inevitable has happened — we are not on but off the roadside this time. Fr. White is being treated by a Chinese quack, and Fr. Steele is working on Sister Superior's arm. Our truck turned over into a ditch just two hours ago. Thank God, none killed, though for awhile we thought ourselves dead . . .

Saturday night . . . We all feel safer on two feet than on four wheels now. No need to coax us to walk the hills now, Mr. Driver, we'll walk anytime you think there is anything resembling a grade from now on . . .

Monday, August 17th . . . We are stranded again, and I cannot say we are sorry. If the lights and livers are not shaken out of us, it is not the truck's fault.

Friday, August 21st . . . Our boatmen are working well, though we are held up by a heavy wind. At about five in the afternoon we change to a smaller boat, and in an hour's time we shall be in Kanchow. We arrived a little later than expected, and Sister Vincent Louise of the Sisters of Charity welcomed us to her lovely convent. She had our dinner all prepared and our beds too. She turned the Sisters' community room into a dormitory for the refugee Sisters. To sleep in a bed again, the second time since we left Lungchuan nearly a month ago — what a treat.

Sunday, August 30th . . . Frs. McGoey and Curtin have joined us . . . We move on two li, and are now resting in a cemetery, the only place around which affords any kind of shade.

Wednesday, September 2nd . . . Mass at 4 a.m. After breakfast we again covered the long distance to the truck. Strange, the driver is all set to go, and in no time we are off. Waiting for you, he had the nerve to say . . .

Thursday, November 19th . . . Slept little last night (in an inn at Chen Chia) — bedbugs and fleas too much at large. People call us out to visit their sick, and this helps to fill in the time. There's always an audience around to watch us eat . . .

Sunday, November 22nd . . . At 4.30 we reached Yuanling and what a welcome we received from the . . . Sisters of Charity from New Jersey . . .

Monday, November 23rd . . . We are getting acquainted with our new surroundings. It seems so strange to be settled after being so long on the road with no set abode. To be putting our clothes away in a cupboard again — to have a fixed address — it all seems queer after suitcasing for so many months and expecting to move on any day . . .

* * *

Less than six months after most of the Canadians took refuge in Yuanling, Sister Mary Daniel (Annie C. O'Connor) died May 9, 1943 of typhus, which she had contracted during visits to the sick. Sister Julitta, the superior, wrote a poignant letter to Mary Daniel's relatives in Canada. The letter was addressed to Mother St. Patrick in Toronto, a Loretto nun and blood sister of the deceased:

God surely asked the supreme sacrifice of everything. She died away from her Canadian and away from her Chinese home, and she loved them both. During the past five years she had much to suffer as she was so frightened of air raids and she has the merit of having gone through nearly 200 of them. Having to evacuate was a heavy cross and the long trip was not easy but she saw in all the will of God. All these little things Sister had the merit of offering to God before He asked for her all.

Two other members, Mary Vianney and St. Kenneth, made their way to India where they nursed "in a rest home for 3,500 servicemen of all creeds and races, many of them fliers of the RCAF". Other sisters of the Pembroke community went back to Canada during the remaining war years, ready to return to Chekiang at the first opportunity.

* * *

That "homecoming" occurred in December 1946 for six of them. St. Angela, always the diary keeper, wrote a few days before the Christmas feast:

We have been very busy meeting our old friends. Yesterday morning (December 22nd) Sister M. Catherine and I went on a sick call, and as we went along the streets old familiar faces came out to greet us — they followed us and by the time we reached the sick house we had quite a procession. Poor people, they were never so wretched.

It would be the same story in Kinhwa a few months later. Monsignor Fraser, recently returned to familiar mission territory, reported in July 1947:

Last week two sisters came from Lishui to treat the sick and distribute medicine. We announced their coming in the local newspaper. They stayed for three days and in that time they treated over a thousand cases! People came from far and near with every disease under the sun. Most of them were walking cases but some came in chairs or litters. I counted at one time more than 200 on the grounds.

We took out all the benches in the church and they sat patiently in the shade of the trees until their turn came. The sisters worked very hard — 12 hours each day without rest. When one was taking lunch the other was treating the patients. They gave injections, pulled teeth, applied remedies and treated every ailment without exception and all absolutely gratis.

Their visit greatly enhanced the reputation of the Church. Nor was their work without spiritual benefit; 25 persons, principally infants in danger of death, were baptized.

Generous, if delayed, praise from Scarboro Missions founder!

Len Hudswell wrote in similar vein from Lungchuan in the October issue of **China** that year. He too sketched a memorable picture and offered some reflections on the close links between medicines for body and spirit:

. . . before Mass has ended, the sick begin to arrive at the dispensary. All manner of men arrive: rich and poor, well dressed and ragged, women with children and the old men. These latter are often due to leave the world and take the journey to the other side of the mountain to see the old king who will judge them (the local version of the judgment day).

With their pagan mentality and absolute fear of death, these old folk will do anything to postpone such a hopeless experience. They know nothing of a God of love. Hence the utility of a catechist who can explain the true doctrine when they are in such a receptive mood. The catechist here is a well-instructed Christian who is trained to explain the Faith. He gets to know the patients at the dispensary, especially those who must make many visits, and gradually he suggests the advisability of medicine for the soul as well as for the body.

* * *

Communist forces occupied the Lishui-Kinhwa regions in the summer of 1949. "A Letter from a Sister in China" described first experiences under the new regime:

Mail is coming through again and so our bamboo curtain is raised a little to the outside world . . . God has been careful of us and so far we have had nothing to suffer. Everything in fact is as usual and we go about work as in "pre-lib" days. The officials are most courteous and seem to appreciate our work for the poor . . .

Lately we have been having a considerable number of lepers. It is impossible to cure them and hard to make them understand that there is no magic in our medicine. We dress their wounds but beyond that we are powerless to help them.

At the moment we are in the throes of a treacherous measles epidemic. Children are dying like flies and we find it well nigh impossible to keep pace with the number of afflicted. With constant care and the powerful aid of pencillin we succeeded in saving several of the children. This news spread through the town and into the mountain villages. The result is that the babies are being brought to the convent at all hours and from all directions, and the poor distracted parents expect us to restore health to their little ones who are often beyond hope. We have baptized many babies these last days and that is some consolation anyway.

We are still caring for the refugees. Most of them were once wealthy people who are now reduced to the extremist poverty. They are not allowed to live inside the city gates and so have little settlements of straw huts outside the city . . . We do our best to keep them from starvation.

"They have loosened up a great deal lately and are quite friendly now," another Sister wrote in referring to local Maoist officials. "They just sort of kept their distance until recently when they have come to the point of being friendly. We have them daily in the clinic and I think they see that we have no evil designs on the Good Earth." The correspondent added, "Actually, we have more freedom than the Fathers as the officials seem to think the Sisters are more useful to the people. We are often amused at their comments."

Before the next spring, however, "things began to change," Mary Catherine would recall. An order was given that local Christians were not to assemble for any religious services, although the Scarboro priests were allowed to celebrate Mass with the Sisters present behind locked doors. Mary Catherine was taken into custody in April 1950, interrogated by relays of "judges," and released with the warning that her punishment for baptizing a dying woman was still pending:

A few days afterwards they took our convent and practically everything we owned. We with the clergy were confined to an old wing of the hospital. The clergy and several "Comrades" occupied the lower part while two rooms in the loft served as our quarters. We were able to fit up one room as a chapel with the Blessed Sacrament reserved . . .

The Korean War, which saw Chinese and Canadian forces on

opposing sides in that still unsettled conflict, added to the precarious isolation of the missioners in Chekiang.

In February 1952 Bishop Ken Turner, several priests and other religious women joined Sister Mary Catherine in a restrained celebration of the 20th anniversary of her final vows, which she had made in Lishui in 1932. Later Craig Strang would compose "A Canticle of Sacrifice" inspired by this event:

> *This year also the scene was happy but lonely; happy because it marked another year of consecrated life still in the same land of her calling; lonely because of the isolation brought on by adverse circumstances. No friends, not to mention relatives, could come and visit her and rejoice with her, and a greater calamity, she could not go to heal, help or encourage any . . .*
>
> *Are then these 20 years in vain? . . . To all lovers of Christ the answer is NO, for the glasses of cold water — the phials of medicine, the long journeys, the loving care, the understanding patience, and the multitude of prayers which Sister and others like her have offered in His name shall never ever lose their reward . . .*

Several months later the last three Grey Sisiters in Lishui — Mary Angela, St. Matthew and Mary Catherine, were granted exit visas from the People's Republic. They crossed the border into Hong Kong in mid-October 1952. So ended a notable feminine presence of more than two decades by 15 Canadian women in the Old China.

* * *

Undoubtedly, being as human as their male partners in mission, the Grey Sisters in Chekiang had "family problems" within their ranks as they worked to relieve others' needs. As one of the sisters noted in a letter:

> *Given the isolation, a concern for the people dear to us who were suffering, the tension brought on by ill health and an uncertain future, there certainly were times when nerves were frayed, but this was far from being the prevailing spirit. My experience was that we grew closer together as difficulties increased. Bonds were formed during those years which unite us today, in spite of the years of separation and work in other fields.*

Frayed nerves or no, the Scarboro men who observed them at

work in China under trying, sometimes perilous conditions were for once unanimous in agreeing that the Grey Sisters always gave a generous and courageous witness to their Christian commitment.

Nearly 30 years later, St. Angela, the diary-keeper in China, was teaching at the Chinese Catholic Centre in Vancouver. To celebrate her 50th jubilee as a religious, she had, with typical daring, returned to China for a two-week visit in July of 1980.

In a long distance telephone interview in May 1981 St. Angela shared some of her impressions of the land and people she had not seen since 1952. "For me, it was going home," she said, speaking with a vitality that belied her years. She was the only Catholic member of a Christian tour group of 13 Canadians and Americans; the remainder were "evangelicals of some kind" whom she found friendly and supportive on the journey.

The North Americans entered the People's Republic from Hong Kong. Principal stopping points included Shanghai, Sian, Peking and Hangchow, the last not far northeast of the Lishui-Kinhwa area. St. Angela's facility in Mandarin quickly came back to her, she said, so that she had "no difficulty" in communicating with her hosts.

Some highlights of the veteran Grey Sister's experiences, paraphrased from notes:

> *I went back to China with the closed mind I had come out with in 1952. It's still under Communist rule but I got a pleasant surprise . . . Everyone was marvellous to me, especially the Christians who hadn't seen a Sister in nearly 30 years . . .*
>
> *Yes, I had decided to go in wearing a full religious habit. In Hong Kong an American reporter wished me God's blessing, saying to me that Chinese Christians were lonely and hungry for outside contacts. It was true. Everywhere I went people nearly mobbed me. Their courtesy was just wonderful. I also found the authorities most gracious . . .*
>
> *In Hangchow I met one of our own Christians from before. When this man saw me, he started yelling, "The Sisters are back! The Sisters are back!" We talked quite freely . . .*
>
> *My guide would have taken me to Lishui and Kinhwa from Hangchow. But I was in Hangchow early during our trip and I was still afraid at that point that visiting with our Christians might make difficulties for them. If the opportunity had*

come up later in the tour, I would have gone to speak with them . . .

The people seem to have quite a bit more freedom than when we were expelled in 1952. They do not seem fearful. I was amazed at the questions some of them asked. What did we in North America think of Communism, and so on.

Many are sad about the restrictions on the size of their families. Couples are supposed to have only one child. This is very hard for people with such a strong family tradition . . .

"I just wanted to stay," Sister St. Angela mused. Then with wistful humor: "I was hoping they'd put me in jail so at least I'd be close to the Chinese people."

13 MAO'S TRIUMPH, SCARBORO'S EXPULSION

"A new China is being born; a new apostolate is about to begin; and we must furnish a new missionary," the Oriental visitor told his Toronto hosts at the first Canadian National Missionary Exhibition. It was October 1943 and the speaker was Bishop Paul Yu-pin, then vicar-apostolic of Nanking and bishop of Sozusa.

In calling for 100,000 missionaries for China after the Second World War, the native churchman spelled out some essential qualifications:

> *It is obvious that the missionary should not bring with him any superiority complex, for the day of special privilege is finished . . . The man who would live in the past with the privileges of the past is doomed to failure. We must expect only . . . common rights, not privileges.*

He commended Chiang Kai-shek for the Nationalist leader's support of missionary efforts undertaken with "an open mind". The Nanking prelate declared: "China is on the march; China is changing, and the new missionary, under penalty of stagnation, must change with her."

Good advice, but already too late. In the same month only six years later Mao Tse-tung would stand before 200,000 cheering followers in Peking to declare that his government was the sole legal authority in all of mainland China. And for the next quarter century this new People's Republic would restrict, harass, deport, imprison or exterminate numerous foreign missionaries as "enemies of the people" — a process that accelerated when the Korean War pitted Chinese and North Korean forces against American, Canadian and other United Nations units from the missionaries' home countries.

* * *

By all accounts priests of the Scarboro Mission Society and Grey Sisters of the Immaculate Conception fared better than most foreign clergy and religious in the People's Republic. In time all the Canadians returned home and most of them were assigned to other missions or apostolates. Only one SFM member did not leave the mainland — Paul Kam, the native Chinese priest.

The "Red takeover" began quietly enough, according to the first reports from the mission field. "The occupation of Lishui diocese by the Communists was more or less peacefully accomplished," Hugh McGettigan reported in a letter written in July 1949. "To date there have been no untoward incidents." The rest of his published letter and correspondence from Harold Murphy and Gerard McKernan that summer were uniformly calm in tone.

"Everything is peaceful," Father Murphy reported. "My health is excellent. The Christians are in fine fettle: more fervent than ever before."

"Well, we came through the war all right," Father McKernan wrote from Shanghai in similar vein. "There were a few sleepless nights but that is all over now, and all is well." He added that the Communist "soldiers have behaved very well. We have not been molested in any way."

Father McGettigan said that Bishop Ken Turner "has been making the rounds, administering Confirmation. His trips have been very fruitful, spiritually". An indication of restrictions to come also was noted:

> *The military borrowed Father Moriarity's jeep for 10 days and then returned it to him in tip-top shape, greased and with a tankful of gas. However, he has not been permitted to drive it from mission to mission.*

* * *

While the group in Chekiang was adjusting warily to their new civil governors, at Scarboro headquarters the Second General Chapter of the Society recorded apprehension about the future of the China mission and the fate of the Canadians still here — people whose spirit, the Chapter said, had been "tried and proven in recent years". It must have pained in particular the retiring superior general, Dr. John E. McRae, to see this crisis-haunted endeavor entering another and probably final testing.

* * *

"I have not been able to see Fathers Harold Murphy, Morrisey or Hudswell for months," Bishop Turner was reporting by December of 1949. "I applied for a permit to travel up to Kinhwa months ago but have had no answer . . . However, I was able to confirm some of Father Craig Strang's Christians in Pihu last week."

Three priests were residing with the SFM bishop, all of them mostly confined to their living quarters. Elsewhere in the building there were uninvited house guests — agents for the local authorities who kept an eye on the Canadians. Mindful of mail censorship, Bishop Turner described this situation cautiously:

> *I have a room upstairs and a small sleeping cubiculum. But in the room are five chairs, four trunks, a small box, two bookcases and a small shrine to Our Lady of Fatima and believe it or not, my bicycle. Father Kam occupies the room*

Ed Moriarty, SFM and the trusty jeep, plus a bicycle — just in case!

> *opposite and Fathers Venadam and MacIntosh have a room each downstairs. We still eat in the same refectory. All the other rooms are occupied by "others." We say Mass in the Cathedral usually at an early hour so as to allow them to start their meetings on time.*

* * *

In Canada Scarboro members were analyzing the defeat of the once powerful Chiang Kai-shek by Mao Tse-tung. John McGoey shared his interpretation with readers of **China**. Chiang came out of the Second World War in 1945 "complacent from arms and money thrown into China by friends abroad," while the Communist forces were mostly "bottled up" in the north. If the Nationalists enjoyed such a clear advantage, why were they defeated by their adversaries? Chiang "forgot to strengthen his people," Father McGoey believed:

> *The reforms for which he had fought as a young man, the reforms which drove him to join the Communists in the early days, did not materialize under his leadership. He did what so many politicos in our country have done. Got himself into power, and then paid off his friends and forgot the people for whom he was supposed to be working. The reforms that he made were paper reforms, not actual ones . . .*
>
> *Matching their arms with propaganda the Communists soon convinced the people of China that Chiang never had intended reform and that such was the corruption of his government that the only solution was to try communism which would truly give them heaven and earth, and heaven on earth.*

The priest who had seen much of China's struggle at first hand during the 1940s was not at all sure that Canadians would profit by the Oriental nation's experience. He felt that the Western world probably would "have to learn the hard way that freedom is a glorious thing, a gift of God to man, to be used, not abused, like any other grace He gives".

CANADA SHOULD SAY "NO." This headline introduced an emotional editorial in **Scarboro Missions** in July-August 1950. "As a Society . . . we believe it would be a disgrace and a calamity for our country to give recognition to Red China," the editor declared. "Let Canada . . . not betray Christian principles by following mere expediency and harkening to the voice of noisy and publicity-seeking minorities for kinship with Communist China." As it turned out, the

Canadian government did not establish full diplomatic relations with the People's Republic until 1970. On the same occasion Ottawa also began exchanging ambassadors with the Holy See.

* * *

"Mo was a character, an individualist, but unlike most individualists, his was a type which made him the friend and companion of his fellow priests," Roland Roberts wrote in appreciation of another SFMer, Vincent Morrison, after the China veteran died as a result of a road accident in October 1950. Born in Prince Edward Island in 1883, this pioneer member of the first mission band gave 18 years of his life to evangelizing in Chekiang.

Two other missionaries of the 1920s also were to die in the early Fifties — William Fraser, brother of Scarboro's founder; and J. J. Sammon. Although associated with the Scarboro enterprise in its early years, neither man became a member of the Society.

* * *

The Korean War meant that Canadians in China were "enemy aliens," as well as being "enemies of the people" in most Marxists' eyes. In mid-1951 exit visas to leave China were granted to Harold Murphy and Ronald Reeves for reasons of ill health. By this time four other priests and four religious sisters at Lishui were confined to the Grey Sisters' convent; those in the Lungchuan mission had been previously "expelled". Most of the Canadians applied for permission to leave the mainland, realizing that there was little prospect they could resume their missionary efforts in the foreseeable future, and expecting that they would have to wait indefinitely for replies to their requests for exit visas.

By Christmas of 1951 those at Lishui still were waiting. Craig Strang described the restrained way the seven housebound priests and sisters observed the feast that year:

> *After the Masses we all received the Bishop's blessing, wished each other Christmas greetings, and exchanged what little presents our restricted circumstances permitted. Amongst the latter we may mention the following: The Bishop gave each of the Sisters a fire-pot or small portable stove by which hands, wrists and feet can be kept warm — the universal Chinese method. To others he gave various presents of socks, cigarettes and prayer books. He received in return handkerchiefs, fruit, rice candy, an ecclesiastical calendar for 1952 done in water color, and five cigars . . .*

Harvey Steele, SFM.

> *The Sisters and Father MacIntosh, the bursar, exerted their utmost to make the Christmas dinner as nice as possible, and they succeeded so well that we lacked but a few of the luxuries of home. We had a lovely soup and roast chicken; even potatoes, which are indeed a rarity, and turnips and cabbage. For dessert Sister Catherine had a molasses pie and a dark cake with "Happy Christmas" marked with red paper on the top. It was indeed worth looking forward to . . .*

"The picture of this diocese — in fact of the church in China — is epitomized by the day-long view from my window," Bishop Ken Turner wrote at Easter 1952:

> *A bare 30 feet across the cobblestone lane are the gates of my Cathedral of the Sacred Heart, padlocked these long 18 months. Elsewhere in the diocese the ban on public worship has been in effect for varying slightly shorter periods. No*

John McGoey, SFM.

instructions or exhortations can be given to the faithful for we never see them. The fact of our being foreigners further aggravates the cleavage between pastor and flock, making the least intercourse suspect. Our Faith has been classified as one with the superstitions . . .

He had heard word-of-mouth reports that bishops, priests and religious women in some other areas of China were "in chains or deported," while a "State-sponsored church seems to be planned." This would become known as the Patriotic Catholic Association, which rejected any official ties with the Vatican.

* * *

"We should remember, fellow Canadians, that red is for danger and that pink is a tone of red," warned **Scarboro Missions** in a June 1952 editorial:

The lessons of Russia, Europe and Asia go unheeded or, if recognised, are cast aside with the trite expression: "It can't happen here." But it can happen here and it is happening here. The almost totally red Miners' and Smelters' Union of Northern Ontario and the Communist-led Lumbermen's Union of British Columbia are two danger spots which the majority of Canadians fail to heed. The so-called "pink" political parties — especially pink in British Columbia — are not recognized by most Canadians as a menace to their Canadian way of life and to the democratic liberties of which Canadians are so justly proud.

Concurrently, in the United States Senator Joseph McCarthy and his critics were battling in the mass media over the Wisconsin politician's accusations of massive Red infiltration in the American government. The Republican senator, in turn, was accused of smearing innocent people through "guilt by association." Internationally, the Cold War between the Soviet Union and the United States government was intensifying.

* * *

On July 8, 1952 Arthur Venadam and Paul Kam were arrested in Lishui. Military police raided the missioners' crowded premises, Craig Strang reported, arrested and handcuffed two of the priests and took them to the local jail where they could receive food from outside once each week but not visitors. Strang continued:

The formal reason for the arrest of Father Venadam was read out to us. "Instituting the Legion of Mary, being an agent of President Truman, of Chiang Kai-shek and of the bandits; anti-revolutionary activities." Bishop Turner told the officers in charge that he himself was the responsible person and that Father Venadam was acting under orders. The officer ignored this confession of "guilt."

Months passed without any direct news from the two imprisoned Scarboro men. Unexpectedly Alex MacIntosh and three remaining Grey Sisters were given permission to leave in 1952. They crossed the border bridge into Hong Kong in October. "It is rather hard to get used to the idea that we are free again and at times one falls back into the manner of speaking in guarded language," Father MacIntosh observed in his first letter from Hong Kong.

Only Bishop Turner and Father Strang remained in confinement at the mission property in Lishui, while in Shanghai Gerard McKernan was being held by the local Marxists. In November 1952

Craig Strang received word that he could obtain his exit documents in Hangchow. After three days of interrogation and long waits, plus periodic searches of his person and baggage, Father Strang was allowed to travel by train to Hong Kong and hence to Canada.

In his Christmas message that year, SFM Superior General Thomas McQuaid asked Society members to pray for their imprisoned or detained brothers in China, where they were "surrounded by avowed disbelievers in what Christmas means".

For another year Bishop Turner was by himself in the restricted portion of the Lishui mission compound open to him. "It was a lonely year," he recalled during a 1980 interview. "Prayer, reading and study" were his main daily pursuits. He thought it providential that the local authorities had not removed "some really good books," including works of Thomas Merton. Some of these he read several times.

Occasionally, sitting by the window that overlooked the lane past the cathedral, Bishop Turner said he could exchange meaningful signs with Chinese Christians who were passing by. A hand on the breast was the agreed sign of sorrow for sins. Seeing this, the Bishop would silently repeat the sacramental words used to absolve the penitent. Local Christians could not do more than exchange such furtive signs without risking arrest, he said.

"There was nothing I could do in a political way," Ken Turner explained. "They were so well organized that it would have been absolutely crazy to fight them or outwit them."

Bishop Turner's lonely house arrest came to an end in November 1953 when he crossed the corridor into Hong Kong. Arthur Venadam was released from prison the following May and later in 1954 Gerard McKernan was allowed to leave the People's Republic. Only Paul Kam was not definitely accounted for — then or later, although it was rumored that the native priest eventually was freed from imprisonment.

* * *

In welcoming home Bishop Turner and Fathers Venadam and McKernan, **Scarboro Missions'** editor angrily rejected any suggestion of future accommodation with the Communist government in China:

> *These members of our Society have suffered for the Catholic Faith and that suffering was inflicted by Militant Atheism so treacherously masquerading under the innocuous name of*

Communism — the wolf in sheep's clothing.

The deluded dupes who clamored for Christ's death, "lest our nation perish," are found today among the advocates of "peaceful co-existence." In that early day they closed their ears to the Master's warning.

A like fate awaits us unless we heed the warnings of these "other Christs" who by Word and example are trying so heroically to awaken us to our danger.

An earlier editorial in 1954 had taken a different approach by stressing the Church's social teachings on justice and peace. Responsible Christian citizens could apply these principles to current problems, the writer said, and in this provide an antidote to Marxist prescriptions:

1. *Know well the problems facing your community . . .*
2. *Know the principles . . . expressed in the social encyclicals of Leo XIII and Pius XI.*
3. *Finally, be articulate. Make the influence of sound social and moral doctrine felt in your community by speaking out fearlessly . . .*

* * *

Arthur Venadam prepared a detailed account of his 22-month imprisonment, which **Scarboro Missions** featured in its first 1955 issue. For the first half year, Venadam recalled, he had been held in the Lishui jail; then in provincial prison in Hangchow until his deportation. Some highlights from the graphic account of his experiences:

Practically every night, for almost six months, I was summoned from sleep, handcuffed and marched under military escort before a full-dress court. These sessions of accusations and interrogations would last three, four and five hours — during which I was made to sit on a chair, stand, or sit on the floor . . .

The same admonition was repeated over and over again. "Admit your crimes and you will be set free." Some of the weirdest charges were hurled at me . . . (One) accusation was that I had sent out all sorts of secret information to the British and American governments, and elsewhere, arranging to have these letters carried by special messengers among whom were supposed to be Father McKernan and Father McGoey . . .

Since I denied all these accusations, people were forced to come into court to denounce me. These poor peasants, knowing these accusations to be false and not wanting to bear false witness, stood there crying. One man in particular was forced to travel by sampan about 40 miles up river to denounce me as an anti-revolutionist. But when his turn came to speak he upbraided the court, telling everyone that I was not an anti-revolutionist, and that the whole farce was false. He was ordered to sit down and shut up! . . .

They accused me of preaching in the Cathedral and elsewhere, before the "Liberation," for the purpose of arousing the people against them. (What I had done was to warn the people against Communism and urge them to remain firm in their Faith.) They said, too, that I had forbidden Catholics to attend Communist meetings, etc., and also warned them against marrying Communists. (This, of course, I had done.) Another indictment was that I had threatened to refuse the Sacraments to Christians if they participated in Communistic activities . . .

They began to accuse me of having said, at the time of dividing up the land, that all these people who owned lands or fields had certainly not acquired them dishonestly — at least the majority of them had not, so the Government should remunerate them for the land it was taking from them. Had I not called the land-division scheme a "bandit" way of doing things and therefore implied the Government was a "bandit government"? This criticism was considered a very serious crime. I admitted I had made this observation and was in no way sorry for having done so . . .

(In Hangchow) I was taken to a bare room. There was some straw for me to sleep on . . . . They told me that they would leave me here for a month to meditate on my crimes and on everything I had done against them during my 24 years in China . . . . I lay down on the straw, exhausted and feverish, and fell into restless slumber . . . .

After another month they moved me to a damp and dark room. Because of the chill, I became ill with a cold. I told the guard I did not feel well, so he summoned a nurse. She told me not to be afraid, that they would look after me. . . . She was very kind to me. It was through her intercession that I was moved to another room . . . . I had to sit on boards all day, not being permitted to rest against anything.

I was not allowed to move even a finger without first asking permission from the guard stationed at the door. They kept me in that room until my expulsion on May 15, 1954.

Among Venadam's interrogators was a Lishui school teacher whom the priest had baptized some time before:

He denied (at this earlier time) being a Communist and insisted he still wanted to be a Catholic. As I had no certain proof he wasn't telling the truth, I continued to instruct him further and finally baptized him. When the Communists came to Lishui in the spring of 1949, this Judas came out in the open; he was appointed to the Public Security Bureau and appeared as one of my cruellest accusers . . . . .

At the (Hong Kong) border, when the British authorities asked for any identification before letting me through, I was surprised to learn that Judas had my passport in his pocket. The last time I had seen it was in Lishui, over two years ago . . . . The British authorities then let me through and as I looked back I saw my "old teacher" watching to make sure that I had gone. Then he turned and went away, back into the nightmare of murder and intrigue that is China today.

* * *

"There had to be a revolution in China," another Canadian missionary, Protestant missiologist Katharine Hockin,would write in her **Servants of God in People's China**, published in 1962. She pointed to the breakdown of the ancient feudal society, and the systemic injustices perpetuated by a privileged alliance of landlords, government officials and Confucian scholars, as well as the exploitative dealings in China by Western powers. Decades before Joseph Venini was one of the Scarboro pioneers who had foreseen the need and likelihood of revolutionary change in China.

Many years later a religious sister born in China would claim that Communist persecution of Christians to some extent had been provoked by the more militant believers themselves. Dr. Theresa Chu, member of the Society of the Sacred Heart who later became director of the Canada-China Programme of the Canadian Council of Churches, told the **Catholic New Times** in 1981 that many Chinese Catholics, her family included, had suffered when the anti-government "Three No Movement" was at its peak in 1949-55. As reported in the Toronto weekly:

> *Catholics who showed any enthusiasm for the new government were reported to their clergy by the Legion of Mary so that they could be refused communion. Fear of excommunication was rife. The Legion of Mary was heroic but fanatical — organizing Stations of the Cross in the streets, preaching total non-cooperation. Some also preached counter-revolution, but they were arrested, said Sister Theresa.*
>
> *Sister Theresa's relatives were describing this "Three-No" period to her during her most recent visit to China. One of them said, "The Church taught us to hate in those days. It didn't teach us to love."*

Gerard McKernan, the last of the Scarboro priests to return from China in 1954, was a director of Catholic relief work in Shanghai until his arrest by local Communist officials. He was held for nine months before being allowed to go back to Canada. Later he would chastise complacent Canadians for allowing the Maoists to "steal our line" — namely the Christian ideal of personal self-sacrifice for the common good, which he said the Chinese Reds had subverted for their own atheistic goals.

"China is a nation galvanizing itself into a race of dedicated messiahs all burdened with the mission of revealing the Mao-Marxist ideal to all the oppressed nations of the world," he wrote:

> *Compare this messianic ideology in its Asian context with the sickening trash they receive from Western radio. What do they think of* our *approach? They listen to our earthy materialism which has never a thought, never an indication of anything more inspiring than backyard swimming pools, juke boxes or supermarkets . . . .*
>
> *We groan over the miseries, calamities, privations of freedom and frightening upheavals that have befallen China . . . . We neglect to consider the inspiration behind the upheaval . . . the spirit of self-sacrifice for the common good . . . .*
>
> *Is it too far-fetched to suspect that . . . . the West, softened (or hardened) by its materialism, greed, individualism, is faced with a lesson that few discern? Certainly . . . we are not definitely inspired altogether by Christian ideals. In the world of today it appears as if idealism, a mystic ideal of self-sacrifice, is arising from the atheism of the*

East and a creeping materialism threatens to smother every vestige of idealism in the Christian West.

* * *

As the China chapter of the Scarboro story came to a melancholy close, insights like those of Father McKernan were a minority viewpoint within the Foreign Mission Society. Greater heed was paid by most SFM members and Scarboro supporters across Canada to other, less self-critical positions.

"Fatima or World Suicide" was the major theme of a popular Catholic crusade in North America directed by Monsignor William McGrath, former Scarboro superior in China. Beginning in September 1949, McGrath and Desmond Stringer, later joined by Patrick Moore, toured much of the continent — first in the United States, then in Canada and in time elsewhere in the Western Hemisphere. Everywhere they carried with them and made the focus of their preaching the statue of the Pilgrim Virgin of Fatima.

China and **Scarboro Missions** published regular, glowing accounts of this two-fold crusade. First of all, it promoted petitions to Our Lady of Fatima for "the conversion of Russia," which reputedly would stave off global catastrophe. Secondly, the crusade featured denunciations of Communism and sweeping indictments of "fellow travellers" abroad and at home. In all this there was comparatively little critical analysis of North America's selfish materialism, as Father McKernan had urged.

By the middle of 1951, McGrath and Stringer reportedly had logged 95,000 miles with the Pilgrim Virgin statue, while Father Moore had toured 45,000 miles in the West Indies and South America, bearing with him a replica of the same statue.

Monsignor McGrath also found time to compose a monthly column "From the Crow's Nest." Claiming to have spoken to "approximately 15 million people" by mid-1954, he wrote for readers of **Scarboro Missions**:

The Blessed Mother has made it crystal clear that we have all played a part in the spread of diabolical Communism. We have all helped create, by our own sins, the Frankenstein monster that is terrorizing the world today. "If men do not cease offending my Divine Son (here he was quoting what the apparition of Mary was said to have told the children at Fatima) . . . Russia will spread her errors throughout the entire world, promoting war and persecution of the faithful." *There is a very definite connection between universal moral delinquency today and the ever tightening stranglehold of Communism upon the world. Aided, it is true, by the almost unbelievable stupidity of Western world leaders . . . .*

To drive home his arguments, Monsignor McGrath quoted what Our Lady of Fatima was reputed to have told the three children in 1917: "Pray, pray very much and make sacrifices for sinners, for many souls go to Hell because there is no one to make sacrifices and pray for them!"

"Ten years more, that's about all! Fifteen, maybe, at the outside! By then the Reds will have taken over America," the Pilgrim Virgin crusader was predicting by May of 1955. "No war. No hydrogen bomb. No mass slaughter — till after the victory has been won." How then?:

The coup d'etat, in course of accomplishment even while you are reading these lines, will be engineered to final success by the entrenched and untouchable traitors in high places, aided and abetted by their strategically placed cohorts in the nerve centres of the nation. The men who sold 500 million Chinese into Communist slavery will finally betray America.

McGrath did commend the efforts of "a few brave souls" for their resistance to the international conspiracy he detected. They included Walter Winchell of Broadway and broadcast fame, Senator Joe McCarthy and Bishop Fulton Sheen, then a popular television star:

Apropos of what would happen in America should the Reds take over, I have before me at the moment a document that affords fruit for meditation. It is a list of 192 priests, some of whom I knew personally, who have been murdered in China and the list is admittedly incomplete . . . . All this at the hands of the Red Chinese Murderers who still hold some 900 Americans in their filthy dungeons and who, if our nitwit liberals have the final say-so, will be permitted to shoot their bloody way into the United Nations. Truly — whom the gods wish to destroy they first make mad.

Monsignor McGrath, after recovering from physical exhaustion and depression, died peacefully at Scarboro in July 1970. He had been one of the most colorful and gifted, and latterly one of the most controversial leaders in the mission society.

* * *

The forced abandonment of the Canadians' endeavor in Chekiang after nearly three decades of dedicated effort stood in contrast to some positive developments in the continuing Scarboro story. Nine young men — the second largest number since 1924 — were ordained as SFM priests in December of 1954. As that very mixed year ended, the Society counted 108 members — more than half of them serving in missions in six countries of Asia, Latin America and the West Indies.

Meanwhile, the always individual story of John Mary Fraser, the Society's founder, was still unfolding — just as it had begun before the mission Society came to exist.

14 FRASER'S TWO LAST DECADES

Nagasaki, historic heartland of Catholicism in Japan, was the second and last Japanese city chosen by the American high command for atomic bombing in August 1945. As at Hiroshima that same fateful month, tens of thousands were killed instantly, died later or were permanently maimed, and much of the city was destroyed. In the two target areas an estimated 210,000 people, most of them civilians, lost their lives. Within weeks the Tokyo government surrendered unconditionally to the Allies, bringing to an end the bloodiest war in human history.

Among the major buildings almost levelled by the bombing of Nagasaki was Queen of Martyrs Church. Only the lower part of the side walls was left standing. Worshippers within and many parishioners nearby were among the 8,000 Japanese Catholics reportedly killed or injured in the atomic attack.

Nearly five years later, John Mary Fraser, by then in his seventies, arrived at the bomb site with $2,000 for renovations which he had collected in Canada and the U.S. In June 1950 the founder of the Scarboro Foreign Mission Society was taking up his first pastoral challenge in Japan. He had come at the "cordial invitation" of Bishop Yamaguchi, who knew the veteran Canadian missionary was a man who got things done.

"During the next year and a half I was busily engaged in supervising the reconstruction of the bombed-out church," Monsignor Fraser wrote in his memoirs, "and in sending photographs of the progress of the work to friends. The response was gratifying. Among others, Cardinal McGuigan sent $1,000." The restored house of worship was formally blessed in October of 1951.

This was the first and most dramatic of several building enterprises Fraser was to supervise in postwar Japan during the last phase of his six-decade career. As well, once he had learned some Japanese, he preached, taught, baptized, heard confessions and celebrated Mass with his accustomed thoroughness, even though at an advanced age.

* * *

Monsignor Fraser's 12 years in Japan climaxed two of the most eventful decades in his exceptionally eventful life. From December 1941 until April 1945 he had been confined to Japanese-occupied Manila, the capital of the Philippines. Although originally bound for Shanghai, the ship on which he was a passenger late in 1941 put into the Filipino port when the Second World War spread to the Pacific.

In and around Manila J. M. Fraser's experiences ranged from retreat-like peace as a restricted house guest of the local archbishop to wartime terrors. He, along with other civilian refugees, was subjected to successive bombardments by the Japanese and

The Fraser brothers — William and John Mary — lay another cornerstone.

American armed forces. From his account of the bombing and shelling in Manila after U.S. units landed to recapture the capital area:

> *A young woman begged me to give the last rites to her mother who was dying in a foxhole. She was covered with blood. I wiped away the blood from her forehead and anointed her. A shell had penetrated the building and fallen right in the midst of the refugees. Fifteen were killed and 50 wounded. The chaplain and I, fortunately, had heard their confessions and given them general absolution the night before. The Blessed Sacrament had been placed under the trees on the campus.*

Together with more than 50 other priests and sisters Monsignor Fraser was a passenger on the first ship to sail from Manila for the United States in April of 1945. The returnees were warmly welcomed in San Francisco by the Americans and also by Canadian officials attending the founding conference for the United Nations. One of them was Prime Minister Mackenzie King, for whom J. M. Fraser said he had this blunt advice: "Put the Russians back into Russia."

On to "hearty" receptions in Calgary from his nephew, Bishop Francis Carroll, and in Toronto during a ceremony presided over by James Cardinal McGuigan. A year later, in May of 1946, the veteran evangelizer, accompanied by Craig Strang, returned to China. This would be his last period in that first and most loved mission territory.

The Chinese people were struggling to recover from the devastation of the recent Japanese occupation, while the civil war was resuming between the Nationalists and Communists. In his autobiography Monsignor Fraser would summarize his last three years in China in only a few paragraphs:

> *On arrival at the Lazarist Procure in Shanghai, I was disappointed to learn that the $2,000 I had sent in 1941 to build three chapels had vanished. It had been changed into Chinese currency and deposited in a bank. During the war the value of Chinese currency had depreciated to such an extent that it was now worth only $10.*
>
> *At Kinhwa I found my church in a sad state. The steeple had been demolished, the military having feared it would be a target for bombers. The altars and pews were gone and the whole building was in need of repair. The convent was*

occupied by paupers who had turned up the flooring for firewood . . . .

Before leaving China (for the Second Chapter of the Society in 1949) I had the pleasure and honor of performing the installation ceremony for Bishop Turner in Lishui. While there, the Sisters told me of the edifying death of a boy I had sent to their hospital. The poor lad had been offered to me in Kinhwa in the last stages of consumption.

He was soon sufficiently instructed to be baptized and receive the other Sacraments. The Sisters took him to Lishui in the jeep. They offered him a sweater but he said he would have no further use for it and to give it to his little brother. His pagan family were greatly pleased at the fine funeral we gave him . . . .

* * *

While in Scarboro for the 1949 Chapter, Monsignor Fraser received word that it would be impossible to return to Chekiang because of the Communist triumph in the civil war. On receipt of this disappointing news, Fraser promptly arranged to go to Japan instead, which he did within the year.

During these last decades John Mary Fraser passed two notable milestones. He observed the 50th anniversary of his ordination in July 1951, when he received a prized cablegram sent in the name of Pope Puis XII. Then came the 60th jubilee 10 years later. Concerning these he wrote briefly and to the point as usual: "I had much to be thankful for. I have always enjoyed good health and have never been too sick to say Mass and recite the Divine Office."

The dozen years of missioning in Japan which began in Nagasaki from 1950 to 1954, continued in Fukoka from 1954 to 1956 and then in Osaka from 1959 until 1962. In the two last cities Monsignor Fraser built churches and rectories that brought his career total to nearly 20 Christian structures in the Orient. As he liked to say, "I'm always building churches." In fact he was planning yet another edifice when he wrote his last known letter in July of 1962 to SFMer Gerald Kelly. He noted that "the Immaculate Conception Sisters of Montreal" have consented to come to Minato in 1963; then added: "So it will be after New Year's that I will build their convent."

* * *

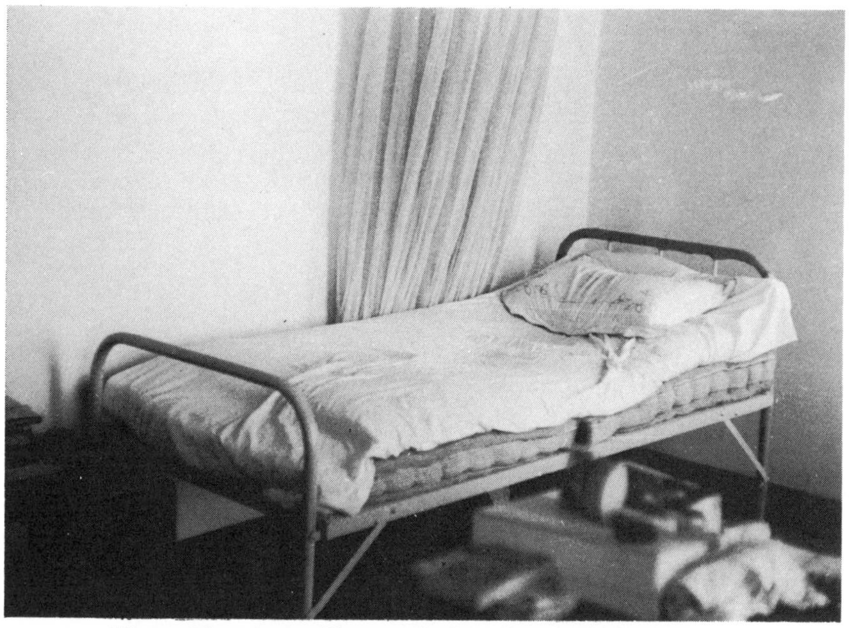

Where Monsignor Fraser died in September, 1962.

The Second Vatican Council was scheduled to begin September 12, 1962. In anticipation of this first global Catholic council of bishops in nearly a century, the news media carried innumerable reports, predictions and commentaries. In Osaka Monsignor Fraser and his assistant, Rogers Pelow, followed the Vatican's preparations mainly through the pages of the **Catholic Register**, then published in Kingston. In an interview almost 20 years later Father Pelow recalled one conversation he had with Monsignor concerning the approaching council. Paraphrased from notes:

> *I asked him how long he thought the council was going to last. "Oh well," he said in his high-pitched voice, "the Pope has it all settled. The bishops will go over to Rome just to sign the documents." I pointed out that some of the bishops didn't think so, including Bishop Alexander Carter of Saulte Ste. Marie. He had been quoted in* **The Register** *as saying the bishops weren't going to the Council just to rubber stamp what the Vatican Curia had drafted beforehand.*
>
> *I gave the Carter story to Monsignor Fraser. We never discussed the question again. I don't think that up to*

that time he had thought of it quite that way. In any case, he died before the council opened.

Some consider it a blessing that the aged churchman was spared the trauma which older traditionalists, and many younger Catholics as well, experienced during the prolonged and often heated sessions of the 1962-65 Council — a debate which was to continue on a universal scale long afterwards. Still, J. M. Fraser might have been more receptive to some aspects of Vatican II than many of his colleagues would have expected.

No one will ever know. It seems likely, though, that shortly before he died, Monsignor Fraser was having some second thoughts about the principal motivating conviction of his missionary life. Again Rogers Pelow is the source for this revealing insight into Fraser's last days. From interview notes:

Monsignor Fraser always talked about missions when we had lunch. Once he asked me what may have been a rhetorical question. This day, all of a sudden, he stared at me and asked: "Do you think all those unbaptized millions out there are going to Hell?"

"I never thought that way," I said.

"I don't think they are, either," was his reply.

We didn't discuss it any further. He must have been mulling it over. A lot of things were coming to the surface when Vatican II was about to start.

* * *

John Mary Fraser died in his sleep early on the morning of September 3, 1962 — 85 years after his birth, 61 years after his ordination and nearly six decades since his initial arrival in the Far East. Father Pelow found the body. As he wrote to Gerald Kelly:

The Monsignor was lying on his back, as if asleep. No trace of pain on his features . . . . He had been in good shape all summer and was not figuring on cashing in. I don't think he suffered at all and he must have been well prepared. He spent hours every day in the church.

The funeral Mass at the pro-Cathedral of St. Theresa of the Child Jesus in Shukugawa was conducted by Francis Diemert, SFM Superior General, assisted by Fathers Tom Morrissey and Pelow.

Rogers Pelow, SFM, was with Scarboro's founder in his last years.

Three native prelates were among the many Japanese Christians present for the requiem. The body was laid to rest in one of the clergy plots of the Catholic section within the huge Shukugawa cemetery.

A few weeks later a pontifical high Mass was celebrated in St. Michael's Cathedral, Toronto. Archbishop Philip Pocock joined many Scarboro, diocesan and religious priests in the memorial ceremony.

* * *

Even though numerous difficulties — civil war, invasions, bombings and virtual internment, plus his own shortcomings and those of his colleagues — hindered his tireless efforts, J. M. Fraser left a lasting legacy. The Canadian missionary Society he had founded — initially, almost single handed — was and still is flourishing. There exist two missionary societies in the U.S. and Ireland for which he helped to plant the first seeds in episcopal minds. And although China was "off limits" to foreign missionaries when he died, Scarboro priests by then were sharing the Good News in several lands as well as in Canada — in Japan and the Philippines, in the Dominican Republic, Guyana (or British Guiana as it was known previously), the Bahamas, the West Indies and Brazil.

By every human measure, the zealous young Scottish-Canadian "really started something" when he first arrived in China in December of 1902. But *who* was he in himself?

15 WHAT MANNER OF MAN?

"It has always been repugnant to me to speak of myself," J. M. Fraser, then in his late seventies, wrote in the foreword to his life story, **Pillar of the Kingdom**, which he completed in February 1955. "Obedience . . . . is my only excuse for writing these memoirs," he insisted, explaining that he could "no longer refuse" to record his experiences and impressions "in consideration of the many requests, some from the Superiors of the Society".

His task completed, he concluded with these words: "All I ask from the readers of these memoirs, if they have had any pleasure in reading them, is an occasional prayer for the conversion of China and Japan."

The autobiography was published by instalments in **Scarboro Missions** from January 1959 through January 1961, together with excerpts from some of Fraser's earliest letters from China. The memoirs provide revealing glimpses of the inner man — implicitly more often than explicitly.

Monsignor Fraser was almost wholly taken up, some would say obsessed, with the ambitious missionary goals he had set for himself as a young man. He had little or no inclination, it appears, ever to ponder the state of his physical or mental health — that self-regarding concern which so preoccupies many people nowadays. Whatever feelings he had about himself and about major happenings in his life, he kept mostly to himself. His Scottish inheritance of canny rectitude was reinforced by the disciplines acquired during studies for the priesthood in Genoa, and further strengthened, no doubt, by Scriptural admonitions neither to worry about oneself nor judge others.

In **Pillar of the Kingdom**, as in most of his reports and correspondence on record, it is clear that John Mary Fraser rarely commented publicly, favorably or unfavorably, on the actions or personalities of the men and women with whom he worked. This forebearance on the part of the Society's founder was not and is not always matched now by many "Fraser watchers" — including would-be storytellers.

* * *

Fathers John Mary Fraser and Vincent Morrison with some Chinese associat

Given the information and opinions at hand, what is a fair assessment of this man and the works that continue after him?

His many champions agree that Monsignor Fraser believed and lived quite literally, even rigorously, the Biblical injunction to

"Set your hearts on His Kingdom first, and on its righteousness" (Mt.6:33). In public print and speech, contemporaries tended to praise him as an exemplary leader virtually without human fault. Such a portrayal is, of course, too good to be true — whether of Fraser or any other person subject to the human condition, no matter how saintly. And we know from SFM records and recollections that some of his strongest traits had a negative side which contributed to internal tensions.

Later generations, especially among those whose perceptions of mission goals and methods differ, have been inclined to look critically at the man, his religious assumptions, and his evangelizing approach. Some see Fraser as a zealot pursuing an impossible dream which unwittingly served "Western imperialism" in a China already exploited by industrial nations.

A just appraisal of the Scottish-Canadian from Toronto and his endeavors lies somewhere between these laudatory and critical extremes. Any black or white assessment would fail to do justice to the complexity of his person and his ambitious undertakings. He was, after all, a leader who was both an inspiration and a trial to dozens; a man who was narrowly focused and yet far-seeing in his outlook; single-minded and yet adaptable, cautious and also courageous, childlike in his trusting faith and yet shrewdly practical when it came to money matters of any kind.

Would it be just to say that John Mary Fraser was something of a Francis Xavier and something of a Don Quixote as well? Certainly the Jesuit saint was his missionary mentor. On the other hand, this venturesome Canadian may not have known the story of Quixote — that fictional knight errant who pursued his fantasies with exaggerated zeal. Still, is there not some measure of Quixote, if not of Xavier, in every person who sets out in quest of goals judged impossible by almost all his or her contemporaries?

* * *

In search of a fair measure of Fraser and his missionary legacy, we can sample some opinions and observations on record, beginning with several passages from his memoirs that tell us something of the man's view of himself.

In the autobiography we find some expression of the lasting affection he felt towards family and a few other influential figures during his formative years. He recalled with admiration the loving and frugal care with which his parents raised 11 children on a workingman's meagre wages at the turn of the century. "Charlie and I were chums," he said in reference to the brother closest to him in age and affection. He expressed pride in his nephew, Francis Carroll, son of his sister Isabelle. Father Fraser was instrumental in making arrangements for his nephew's studies, which led to the priesthood and Carroll's subsequent consecration as Bishop of Calgary.

Monsignor Fraser remembered his first departure for China in 1902: "It was a sad parting for the family and the few friends who were there." One such friend and his mentor was Father John Mary Cruise, the curate at St. Mary's parish church in Toronto who later became archdiocesan chancellor. Fraser credited Cruise as the person most responsible for his vocation: "Only for him I might never have been a priest."

In the memoirs are brief yet unmistakably clear glimpses of Fraser as the single-minded churchman, for whom missioning — with all the ceremonial trappings — always came first. Two examples give the picture, beginning with this memory of his first year as a priest in Toronto:

> *I had intended to wear my soutane (floor-length black robes) even in Toronto but the Archbishop would not hear of it. I had, however, the pleasure of dressing in soutane in public all the time I was in China.*

He relished the attention his liturgical presence commanded soon after his arrival in the Orient:

> *All (the inhabitants of a Chekiang town) had heard of the Europeans but very few had seen them, and fewer still had seen a priest in ecclesiastical dress. There was a rush from all sides to see me. The word passed like wildfire throughout the whole town, and everyone made it a point to come and have a look.*

Careful spending was important for the missionary from Canada but extra expense was always justified when it came to "saving souls". The Monsignor's practical approach was also a major factor in his penchant for building, as he emphasized in an early letter from China:

> *If we wish to convert we must first build churches as fine as their temples. The Chinese, you know, are highly civilized, and for that reason a miserable structure of a church is a great drawback to the propagation of the Faith.*

Fraser enjoyed recalling occasions when his childlike trust, coupled with shrewdness, "paid off". An example already reported was the founder's success in selling the Society's first Scarborough property at a profit so as to fund a new seminary-residence on Kingston Road.

As he saw it, church properties never should be put to any other use, even in wartime emergencies. In describing experiences when the American forces defeated the Japanese around Manila, Fraser gave this revealing account of his priorities in a crisis:

> *The house had been thoroughly looted. Some poor people by the roadside had a sanctuary lamp. I demanded it. They let me have it but begged for the oil it contained. I met a boy carrying the sacristy tabernacle and a censer. I took them from him and gave him the artificial flowers. He went away crying. Poor boy, perhaps he was hungry . . . .*

Another telling example of his sometimes disconcerting blend of piety and practicality is seen in a letter he wrote from Rome to John E. McRae, rector of Scarboro seminary, in July 1925. Fraser enclosed a photograph of the Gesu shrine said to contain the relic of Francis Xavier's right hand. "Poor St. Francis Xavier dying on the coast of China, sighing for its conversion," Fraser wrote of Scarboro's patron saint. The Canadian founder was moved to prayerful exhortation, followed immediately by some brisk business advice to McRae:

> *May our dear Patron bless and protect us all — priests, students and benefactors, and may he soon lead us to the promised land — that part of China destined by Divine Providence to be evangelized by our seminary! Don't forget the slogan: "**A Big Fund for our first band of missionaries.**" This does not sound very apostolic; but no matter how big the funds, our missionaries will find so many pressing needs on their arrival that there will be nothing to spare. To this end we will cut down expenses in Canada to a minimum and bank every cent we can spare.*

* * *

Now to scan some of the many comments offered by others, beginning with a few official tributes.

"Monsignor Fraser is a great glory of the Archdiocese of Toronto," wrote James Cardinal McGuigan on the 50th anniversary of the missionary's ordination. His pioneering, the Cardinal said, "is in our own generation an unparalleled example of apostolic initiative and faithful perseverance".

Writing in the same jubilee issue of **Scarboro Missions**, Bishop James Boyle of Charlottetown praised Fraser and warned against the false faith of Communism: "His world vision of the Church presents a challenge to this generation of Christians who witness the greatest missionary program in history now taking place — with the unholy design of banishing Christ."

Bishop P. F. Pocock, then of Saskatoon, adopted a historical perspective that looked back and also ahead. "Missionaries of the gigantic stature of Monsignor Fraser never die," he wrote. "Like his intrepid predecessors — Paul, Xavier, Augustine, Boniface and Patrick — his apostolic influence will carry on."

In a tribute at the time of Fraser's death in 1962, Monsignor J. A. McDonagh of the Church Extension Society said that his colleague's passing "concludes the first chapter of Canada's most noted contribution to the conversion of the world". McDonagh observed that Fraser, like some other exceptional pioneers, had been very much an individualist:

> *His diplomacy was frontal assault. It may not have been a pleasure to be told that you are doing nothing for God's holy missions but the way he said it was convincing . . . It is easily seen why his heavenly impatience made him more fit for the lone saint than the sergeant major of a communal army.*

At the first SFM Chapter after Fraser's death — the fourth, held in 1968 — a carefully nuanced appreciation was expressed in the same committee report that recognized Monsignor McRae as foster founder of the Society:

> *There was . . . (in Monsignor Fraser's) character the needed courage to persevere in his plans at a time when his vision was not shared by all. But if it be said that the charism of the Founder did not extend to the solving of perplexities of organization, then perhaps we have come close to explaining the advent of Dr. McRae.*

* * *

And what of the more personal assessments among those who were J. M. Fraser's disciples and colleagues over a period of more than four decades from 1918 to 1962? In some of his associates he inspired lasting devotion; in others, considerable scepticism or even hostility. These and other reactions to the Society's founder are expressed in the following comments by more than a dozen members, almost all of whom knew Fraser personally and most of whom served with him in China or Japan. Other Scarboro priests no doubt would have somewhat different opinions to express. Still, the viewpoints reported probably are broadly representative of the spectrum of opinion within the Scarboro Foreign Mission Society. And to leaven this masculine testimony, there are the insights of two Grey Sisters.

Daniel Carey, one of the first missioners sent to China from Almonte in the early Twenties, voiced his lasting admiration for his mentor during SFM's 50th jubilee year in 1968. Monsignor Carey described his own efforts in China as "a labor of love" that afforded him "an opportunity to express deep and sincere appreciation of the apostolic zeal of the Society's dedicated founder".

Hugh Sharkey, another of the pioneers, shared some penetrating insights during an interview:

> *. . . he had the simplicity of a child, and the innocence of a child . . . . Yet he was a man with a one-track mind. Nothing was going to stand in the way of his missionary zeal. On the other hand, he found it difficult to work with other men. I don't know whether you would call it determination, or whether there was a bit of sternness about it. It was there and it carried him through. But his relations with other men weren't always successful.*
>
> *In my mind, Almighty God had designs on the man. God doesn't do violence to our characteristics, so his peculiarities remained. Because of these he was not a man who would have made a good superior general or a good bishop over a diocese.*

Lorne McFarland provided this vignette:

> *I remember one cold morning in Kinhwa, China. Since I was to get out on a mission trip that day, I had to get an early start . . . . As I plodded through the snow to the church door in the early hours I felt just a bit heroic. I was startled as I opened the church door to see the flickering light of an oil lamp in a background of darkness. And then I saw him. A thin motionless figure kneeling on a priedieu. It was*

Alex MacIntosh, SFM.

> *Monsignor Fraser. I was humbled to realize that what for me was heroic was for him a matter of daily routine.*

"He was a dour Scot, dourer than most," Alex MacIntosh reflected during a breakfast interview. "Under that hard Scottish veneer, though, there must have been a lonely man." Other insights from Father MacIntosh, paraphrased from notes:

> *Monsignor Fraser was the only one of his kind; they threw away the mold after that. He was single-minded. He had to be tough minded or we would never have had the Society. He must have written 10 letters a day on Feast days, like Christmas. This indicates to me that he was a lonely man. He did enjoy a little joke — on his own terms.*

Edward Moriarty served under Fraser in the Kinhwa district:

> *I was there for practically a year and I saw Monsignor Fraser was a man of great devotion to his work. He was also*

Allan McRae, SFM.

a man of great simplicity. I remember distinctly evening after evening seeing him in the church teaching catechism in the Kinhwa dialect to groups of little children. His whole life and his whole concern was with the Church and with the missionary work which he had done so much to establish . . . .

They say that the saints are hard people to live with, and if this is true, I think Monsignor Fraser could be classed with them.

He was a man who used church funds very meticulously. He could account for every cent he had received for the working of the mission, and his own personal needs were very, very few. This was also reflected in the clothes he wore and the food he ate. He was perhaps more ascetic than many monks who practise an ascetical life.

Allan McRae also worked under Fraser at Kinhwa through the tense and dangerous years of Japanese invasion:

Maybe because I was of Scotch ancestry, as he was, I got along well with him. He was a dour personality. He expected you to endure the same hardships that he had, under war conditions . . . . We (John Kelly, Tom Morrissey and McRae) were only 26 to 27 at the time and we found it difficult to emulate him.

Sister St. Angela shared her assessment of the pastor she had worked with in China:

For years I worked every day with Father Fraser. I really appreciated him. There were many ways of getting around him; there always are . . .

It's sad the way the poor man has been maligned sometimes. People forget that he spent many years alone in the missions. Anybody would have some eccentric ways after that. Also, there was quite an age gap between him and the younger missionaries.

Father Fraser gave himself for the Chinese people.

"Monsignor Fraser's history is one apart, but for those of us who knew him, his eccentricities could well be excused," wrote another member of the nursing community who served in China. Sister Susan Daly (formerly called Sister St. Joan) remarked, "His words of praise were consistently sparse for all men or womankind."

Harvey Steele thought the SFM founder "one of the great missionaries of the first half of this century".

Thomas McQuaid was Superior General when the Society's founder reached his 50th jubilee as a priest. In an article entitled "An Indomitable Spirit," Father McQuaid praised Monsignor Fraser as "Canada's greatest missionary". Nearly 20 years later McQuaid's enthusiasm was undiminished. Paraphrased from notes of an interview:

Monsignor Fraser is No. 1. He was away ahead of his time in seeing the importance of foreign missions. He was spearheading . . .

There were difficulties about his character but I got to love him. I had tremendous admiration for him. He always had the same determination on behalf of the missions; he never lost that. He never gave up hope. That's why he went to Japan, ready to return to China if the chance ever came.

Edward Moriarty, SFM.

> *Anyone who is doing something important in life is going to be criticized.*

Francis Diemert, Superior General after Father McQuaid, offered this appraisal:

> *I think he was a man who was motivated by one idea, a one-track mind, and there was nothing that could stop him from getting what he wanted. There may have been much more of a human quality that could have been developed, but perhaps he would never have accomplished what he did had he not had that strong determination to go ahead . . . Another type of character would have got discouraged and given up.*

Michael O'Kane, member of a younger generation and a recent Superior General, spoke of the founder during a conversation. In paraphrase:

Although he was a traditionalist in missiology, he saw that the Church is not completely Church unless it is missionary.

Some of the different experiments we're trying in mission today came about through men whose ideals were aroused by Fraser. There still are mavericks in Scarboro — men who are creative and open to other ways of doing things.

Rogers Pelow, who was with Monsignor Fraser when the founder died in Japan, wrote at the time: "His sole interest was, as ever, only the Church and the propagation of the Faith." During a later interview Father Pelow reiterated this point: "He was an ideal founder in terms of his singleness of purpose. Nothing could stand in the way of the missions."

Paul Flaherty, who also served in Japan, observed that Fraser "is not easily understood; he was a complex man." Father Flaherty shared some of his insights into this complexity. Again, paraphrasing from notes:

Monsignor Fraser was not a sociable man. He was mission-minded, period. He expected the Canadians working with him to be supermen — like himself.

He was not disturbed by the clamor of children when saying Mass, preaching or teaching. Their noise never seemed to bother him.

He died without any worldly possessions to speak of. You wouldn't have got $10 for what he left behind of his own.

Gerald Kelly was one of those closest to John Mary Fraser — if anyone could claim to have been close to this private person. Father Kelly, like Pelow and Flaherty, worked with Fraser in his latter years. Kelly's appreciation, written soon after his mentor's death, has been cited since then as one of the most discerning assessments. Excerpts:

God uses the weak and foolish things of the world to confound the wise . . . in any contest of so-called warmhearted, convivial human personalities, he, with his abrupt, independent Scot's heritage would have taken low marks. Respect and admiration he had aplenty, but of easy-going, warm intimate friendship with others, none. Let us hasten to add that age, and a natural temperament conditioned by over half a century of lonely and solitary work in foreign lands, are hardly conducive to the characteristics we arbitrarily deny him . . .

Except insofar as they promoted the work of the missions and the glory of God he had no time or thought for himself or for others, for places or for things . . . In this mode of action most will see the not entirely flawless yet blameless zeal and simplicity of the saints. Simplicity — this is the key word, the secret of the priestly and missionary success of Monsignor Fraser . . .

The serpent and the dove were well blended in this builder of churches. Simple enough in faith to secretly bury sacred medals in desired properties, he was still canny enough to raise the large sums necessary in the end to effect their purchase . . .

These kind of men are rare — those who are continually pioneering, building, founding, tracking the seven seas, crossing the continents, pursuing doggedly the goal set before them: the salvation of nations. He was one of these men. He was a good man. A good priest. A good missionary.

* * *

We can say with assurance that the Scarboro Foreign Mission Society — whose members were sharing the Good News in a dozen countries on three continents as the 1980s began — would not exist, at least in its present form, were it not for the single-minded vision, stubborn determination and courageous risks of John Mary Fraser. Given this continuing history, whether or not Fraser had a likeable personality now seems a secondary question. The primary point is that he made a difference. His life story is a Canadian testament to what can happen when a believer takes Jesus Christ literally at his word: "Go, therefore, make disciples of all the nations . . . ."

Perhaps Harold Oxley said it best in an editorial tribute on the occasion of Monsignor Fraser's 60th jubilee in 1961:

He has been a priest for 60 years and they have been 60 years of hard work. What are the results? It's hard to say. Most of his priestly life was spent working in China, and now the Communists are there. If he were looking for results there, he might be very disappointed. But he is not looking for results. That's God's part of the job. Monsignor Fraser is only concerned with the effort God expects of him.

Similarly, remembering the Scriptural warning not to judge one another, we know that the final assessment of John Mary Fraser is "God's part of the job," not ours.

At the same time the Chinese missioning experiences of the Society that Fraser founded demand some analysis. The next chapter reports on what was an ongoing, necessarily controversial process within the ranks of Scarboro and beyond.

16 REVIEWING THE CHINA RECORD

"I would say the Scarboro missioners were the best on the earth. Giants really," Sister St. Angela declared without hesitation in recalling her many years in China. "I saw the way they gave themselves, and they also gave us Sisters the leadership. They went over full of ardor and really spent it for the people."

* * *

The Grey Sister's praise of the Canadian priests in the Lishui-Kinhwa regions of Chekiang province would not be seconded by all members of the Scarboro Foreign Mission Society. Quite a number, including some China Hands themselves, became increasingly critical of the missionary methods followed during the Society's nearly 30 years in China.

The first member sent overseas, however, was not one of those who later questioned the evangelical approach which then prevailed in Roman Catholic missions. When Scarboro celebrated its 50th jubilee year in 1968 Daniel Carey offered some good-natured advice. "Perhaps," he said, with a sardonic touch, "an old veteran of the Rearguard may, by God's grace, be helpful to the new men of the Avant-garde, these enthusiastic young men with all the new words — aggiornamento, commitment, involvement, etc., etc."

He and other pioneers who replaced him in the Orient "did the planting," Monsignor Carey said in citing St. Paul, while the young Apollos who came after "did the watering". He continued:

> *As to missionary methods, I was then young enough and brash enough to be convinced that the renowned Jesuit missionary, Father Matteo Ricci (1552-1610), like St. Patrick in the 5th cenury, had the right approach to an ancient, cultured people like the Chinese; a people with profound respect for learning, lawful authority and family solidarity. This approach meant working from the top down, not neglecting those at the grass-roots but preparing these latter to consider seriously the doctrine approved and accepted by those whom they revered and trusted. I held then, and still hold, that this approach should, by God's Grace, guarantee in*

> *due time a native clergy with its own native hierarchy, ensuring permanence and continued development.*

But Daniel Carey acknowledged that Scarboro priests were "using new missionary techniques suitable to the social and religious demands of an age of renewal" in eight other "emerging and developing countries." He spoke for himself and for some others of his generation in pledging the solidarity that should exist between aging pioneers and their successors: "We of the Old Guard are with them, heart and soul."

In that anniversary year Terry O'Sullivan had become the 200th man to follow Carey as an ordained member of the SFM Society. O'Sullivan was asked by **Scarboro Missions** whether he thought he and Carey "might have anything in common". He replied that both tried to be men of faith, although each gave "a different expression of that faith". Father O'Sullivan explained:

> *Communications, education and specifically theology have changed our outlook. Before, we went out, preached the word, baptized and moved on, or so it seems anyway. Today, we tend to laugh slightly at this St. Francis Xavier method. We don't laugh at his faith, only the method. It was the numbers game. How many converts did you get this year? That isn't very important any more.*

The magazine interviewer had a last question for the newly-ordained member of the Society:

> *Q: Is there any danger that with all this emphasis on the social aspect of religion — self-help programs, etc., that we might lose sight of our real goals — implanting the faith; building the Christian community; and showing God to the people?*

> *A: It is quite possible but I don't think it's too likely. After all, Christianity is a very humanitarian thing. First and foremost is that we are dealing with man. Christ became man. He died a human death. He looked after the poor. Christ above all was humanitarian.*

* * *

Ten years later Scarboro members assembled at headquarters for a fraternal exchange preceding the Sixth General Chapter. That summer of 1978 they were asking questions such as these:

Are we to keep as a primary purpose the mission to the non-evangelized? In other words, are places like China and Japan and Indonesia more central to our Society's purpose than Brazil and the Dominican Republic where at least one finds a Christian culture and most of the populace have received baptism?

Approximately 20 of the more than 50 men who had been missionaries in China still were living and some of them were present when the assembly swapped memories and opinions about the Chekiang years. By then almost a quarter century had passed since SFM's expulsion from China. In the turbulent years that followed the withdrawal, most Scarboro members had weathered the shock waves — welcomed by some, tolerated by others, and resisted by some — of Catholic renewal, as initiated by the Second Vatican Council in the 1960s and then reflected in major decisions reached by the Fourth and Fifth General Chapters of the Society in 1968 and 1974.

These developments, together with societal changes in Canadian life and world affairs generally, induced most SFM members to reassess the China years from substantially revised perspectives. Sometimes the privilege of hindsight as viewed from later vantage points was unfairly indulged. Overall, however, the ongoing review of the Chekiang experience — ranging from remembered first impressions to critical analysis years later — was a valuable learning exercise within the ranks of the Society. Valuable, that is, for those prepared to relearn and revise their outlooks. When judiciously reappraised, yesterday's mission in China revealed useful lessons for missioning tomorrow — in Canada itself, in Latin America, the West Indies, the Philippines, Japan, Hong Kong — and perhaps some day once again in mainland China.

* * *

In retrospect, one of the most obvious lessons the Chinese experience taught was the decisive importance of cultural conditioning in every society. Religious beliefs aside (and such beliefs themselves are always colored by the surrounding social context), the predominant technoculture of North America in which Scarboro men were raised had implanted in them certain basic "givens": accustomed ways of perceiving and valuing, which were then "built in," unconsciously for the most part, to their missionary efforts in China.

Coming, for example, from a comparatively rich country to a poor one, the Canadians arrived in China as privileged messengers claiming to bring "good news" to these innumerable "least" among God's human family. While most SFM members themselves began life in modest enough circumstances, they could hardly have anticipated the extent and degree of systemic deprivation which for centuries had entrapped hundreds of millions of Chinese, nor how they must have been perceived by their impoverished hosts.

* * *

"It is strange how wary they are of the foreigner," Desmond Stringer wrote with evident puzzlement in March 1933. He was describing a visit to outlying chapels of Lungchuan, where he was parish priest. "Most of our Christians have merely a speaking acquaintance with the priests; for the most part, they lack that freedom which marks our relations with our pastors in Canada."

Travelling in a fleet of rickshaws.

Lawrence Beal also kept a mission diary that same spring as he visited missions in the Sungyang district. "We had spent nearly three weeks searching and seeking our flock in these subcentres," he wrote in summing up his labors:

> *Our spiritual fruits were altogether: Confessions (of duty), 19; Communions (of duty), 17; Confessions (of devotion), 6; Communions (of devotion), 39; Baptisms, 3; Marriages consolidated, 2.*
>
> *The total number of Christians in the two subcentres and environs is 136. Our three weeks' work succeeded in netting only 19 of them. So you can see what is the state of this mission. And, too, we consider this mission trip as* **fruitful.**

Within a few years Father Beal was among those asking questions about the narrowly focused approach to evangelization prescribed by superiors in Rome and Scarboro. While it remained his "holy ambition to get this church filled with faithful followers of the Gospel," Lawrence Beal was also persuaded by then that "unless people got some material help along with the doctrine, they were not interested in what the Church had to offer in the way of salvation".

Joseph Venini ventured further along the same line of thought. He predicted — accurately, as it turned out — that "the raising of the Chinese standard of living will call for the razing of practically every existing institution and custom." (In the 1950s this socially-sensitive priest joined a diocese in the Central American republic of Guatemala. Tragically and ironically, in 1972 Father Venini met a violent death through robbery, even though he was an old man who "lived poorly.")

Vincent Morrison, a member of the first mission band, later would say that he was mistaken in believing that "our way is best" in the Orient. So "we begin at once to impose our way and to interpret our ideas to have them (the Chinese) change . . . It is a fatal mistake which many have made before us, and by now we should have learned our lesson," he wrote in 1944.

Another pioneer, Craig Strang, was still more self critical when he reflected years later on his China experiences during an interview:

> *. . . I began to catch on that we weren't doing this thing in the right way. We did not adapt to the culture. We lived in our missions as closely as we could to the Canadian way. We had no close relationships with the people at all.*

In later years I began to see why they referred to us as a foreign religion. Everything about it was foreign except the prayers we taught them, which were in the classical Chinese — a language they couldn't understand, never having been educated in it . . .

It seems that everything we could have done wrong, we did it. It seems in looking back that we made as many obstacles to delivering the message of Christ as were humanly possible — without meaning to, of course.

"Recently a missionary of long experience in China said that it was his conviction that more converts are made through the practice of charity than through the preaching of the Gospel," Leo Curtin reported to readers of **China** in October 1938. Presumably speaking for himself, he added that "even to those with short experience here, that statement seems almost self evident."

* * *

By the time Harvey Steele arrived in the late Thirties several more Scarboro voices were questioning any perception of mission which was narrowly "spiritualized" and hence not incarnated in the daily life of the people.

Rarely in this story of Canadians in China do we hear from the local inhabitants themselves regarding their reactions to the foreign advocates in their midst. One we do hear from is a Mr. Lee — indirectly, that is, through Father Steele. Lee, a carpenter in Lishui, was not a Christian. He made a lasting impression on Steele. When he described his China years to Gary MacEoin, Harvey Steele spoke at length of this Buddhist who was "absolutely honest" and who lived next door to the mission compound.

One day the Canadian challenged Lee, who replied that "your religion has no relevance for us". Those who became Christians, he claimed, were less reputable citizens who wanted free medicine and schooling for their children — "rice Christians." Moreover, Lee said, "Sex is one enjoyment of the poor, who are 90 percent of our people. It makes their dreary lives tolerable . . . (yet) you tell them it is a sin."

Steele's neighborly critic then pointed out the noticeable living gap between the Chinese poor and the Canadian priests and sisters. The missioners were seen as rich by every local comparison. "You have a big compound, servants, good food, electric light."

Lee challenged Christian evangelizers along these lines, as Harvey Steele remembered:

> *Now, if you could create an alternative, if you could offer the poor some escape from their misery, then perhaps they would have the leisure and the understanding to reflect. Perhaps they would come to find something worthwhile in your message.*

Lee's counsel and the SFMer's later experiences in China brought Steele to the conclusion that would influence the rest of his active missionary life in Latin America. As reported in MacEoin's biography:

Grey Sisters with some younger patients.

. . . the important thing for the missionary to do was not only to offer the sacraments but to try to help the poor people themselves who were powerless; to save them from their exploiters, to show them how to band together and lift themselves out of their misery.

* * *

"Real mission is still to go into a pagan country. Go where no one else would go," Thomas McQuaid said in a 1979 interview long after his years in China and leadership as Superior General. "I hope China will be open again. People are the same all over and I couldn't say a bad thing about the Chinese."

Would he do anything differently if it ever became possible for Canadian missionaries to return to China? "I don't know what I'd do any differently," Father McQuaid replied. "You have to win their attention. Begin with charitable works. And by all means learn from them, from their culture, so as to lift up their culture."

* * *

Although wartime internment prevented Francis Diemert from ever reaching the Lishui area, his experiences at language school in Peking were instructive for the man who would become SFM Superior General in 1959. He presided in the Society during the challenging transitional period before, during and after Vatican II. His few years in China and his missioning time in Latin America deepened his appreciation of other cultures. Looking back over these eventful decades in his life, Father Diemert shared some reflections in 1981. As paraphrased:

The trend (since the China years) has certainly bettered itself when it comes to foreign missions. The old attitude of superiority is gone; the idea that we have everything to give and nothing to receive. Now we see that no matter where you go people have real values which we should learn to appreciate.

This change in mentality is a real advance for missions, and for everything else.

* * *

"Of course I'd go back if it was possible," Kenneth Turner said during a conversation early in 1980. However, he doubted whether foreigners "would ever be allowed to operate again as Christian missionaries" in the People's Republic.

"I admit now that I see it in a different way," Scarboro's first and last bishop of Lishui acknowledged. Up until their expulsion in the 1950s, the Canadian priests had "followed the rules of the European church" in China. "There was no getting around the Latin" in celebrating Mass in the years before Vatican II. "It was taboo to use any vernacular (local) language" in the sacramental services, Bishop Turner noted. (Ironically, the Catholic Patriotic Association in Marxist China still uses Latin in celebrating Mass, while proclaiming its independence of the Vatican.)

"My job is to preach the Good News," the SFM bishop emphasized. "That there's a loving God, not an avenging God." In that belief, he said, "we can leave the salvation of the pagans to the mercy of God".

* * *

Was Father Fraser's dream of mass conversions ever a realistic one? John Maurice, who served in China from 1936 to 1944, indirectly answered the question during a conversation years later. He described the limited conversion program followed by the small Canadian contingent with limited means, and he noted the social sacrifices required of those Chinese who did become Christian. Paraphrased:

> *We tried to adapt to the country and the people, who were quite thoroughly pagan. Radios were very scarce then but we did have a gramophone. We played records of Chinese music and dialogue. The people would come to hear the gramophone. Then we would shut it off and the native catechist would explain why we were there.*
>
> *Only about one in a 100 ever was interested in learning more about Christianity. Those who came to us were called catechumens. They were instructed by our catechists who said that although we were foreigners we had a message for all mankind.*
>
> *That there was one true God was a strange notion to them, since they had many gods in temples, which were abandoned by this time.*

"Whenever officials were Christians, most of the local population would follow their lead," Father Maurice continued. "Often the converts were called 'rice Christians,' but some of them were heroic Christians, I would say. They had to break with their families, go against the clan system, and give up all claim to any inheritance of property and crop sharing. So it involved a lot of sacrifice."

* * *

Added to these social impediments, "Murphy's Law" seemed to apply to the Scarboro missions much of the time. Just about everything that could go wrong, internally and externally, usually did sooner or later. Disruptive public events from the beginning hampered and later overwhelmed the Canadian presence in Chekiang province.

Conversions to Catholicism in the Lishui-Kinhwa regions assigned to the Society and the Grey Sisters, according to all available data, never numbered more than a small fraction of one per cent of local populations. Might this small but persistent evangelizing effort have converted appreciably more Chinese during a stable period of history? John McGoey was one inclined to think so. "Only God knows the work that might have been, the good accomplished, the suffering relieved, the developments attained," he wrote, "if China could have had peace."

Father Maurice said he never regarded the Canadian endeavor as a failure, even though "our role was a small one" compared to the Jesuits, Lazarists and the larger American and Irish missionary societies. Half a lifetime after leaving China, John Maurice believed that "the blood of their martyrs is the buried seed of the future Church in China."

* * *

Present-day critics of earlier missioning methods — whether that of Catholics emphasizing the Sacraments or Protestants stressing Scripture to the neglect of other central Christian beliefs and practices — tend to doubt that any limited evangelizing approach ever could have reached significantly more Chinese, no matter how abundant the manpower and other resources. According to this now popular viewpoint, the prevalent faith witness in pre-Maoist China was unconvincing because it usually was not accompanied by a vigorous commitment to social justice.

Nowadays, to cite the international Synod of Catholic Bishops in 1971: "Action on behalf of justice and participation in the transformation of the world fully appear to us as a constitutive dimension of the preaching of the Gospel or, in other words, of the Church's mission for the redemption of the human race and its liberation from every oppressive situation."

Mastering chopsticks: left to right — Fathers James McGillivray, William McNabb and Arthur Venadam.

In the China of the Twenties and Thirties, foreign Christian missions, often owning considerable property and employing Chinese servants as well as native helpers in teaching and nursing, must have appeared "rather elite institutions intervening in a society characterized by mass poverty, disease and oppression, and increasingly evidencing signs of massive social unrest".

Protestant mission teams, like their Catholic contemporaries, did much to lessen the people's immediate miseries through generous acts of mercy, but usually without drawing attention to the underlying causes of such persisting social wrongs. "It was assumed that this work of bringing the Good News of the Gospel to the Chinese was an urgent and immediate one," John Foster wrote in his appraisal of Methodist, Presbyterian and Church of England missions in China, "but that reform and reconstruction of the society would be a long and very gradual process."

Granted, it is much easier in retrospect to prescribe what should have been done than to anticipate all such requirements in advance. It is hardly fair now to insist that new arrivals in China during earlier decades should have recognized what is frequently evident in our time. Given the prevalent Western assumptions then and the kind of preparation prospective missionaries received in Canada, how many reasonably could have been expected to discern how privileged they appeared to the Chinese? Like their Protestant countrymen, probably most Catholic missionaries docked in China as unwitting "symbols of power" from the same Western world that had been exploiting Asia for gain.

Dr. Katharine Hockin, daughter of Protestant missionaries and herself a missionary in China until the early 1960s, states that all missioners from abroad arrived, knowingly or not, burdened by the excess baggage of "imperialist history". Because their hands were so full, they were not free to reach out to the poor but proud Chinese on terms of human equality.

This Canadian missiologist sees this basic and symbolic inequality as a major reason why the great majority of Chinese never responded to the Christian message. Visible privilege is a negating counter witness to the Christian Way proclaimed by Jesus.

Dr. Hockin said that she spoke as a believer who had "reached a new faithfulness" in a long process that began with her parents. One day her mother had acknowledged that her generation had been unconscious imperialists in their missionary labors. "Mother freed me to be as critical as I am now, and yet remain faithful."

* * *

In his analysis of the Canadian Catholic years in Chekiang province, Michael O'Hearn, editor of **Scarboro Missions,** identified four related motivations as the initial inner fuel that propelled the Scarboro-Grey Sisters' effort: save pagan souls from damnation through baptism, bring Western "progress" (later called "development") to supposedly backward peoples, resist the spread of atheistic Communism, and compete with Protestant missionaries in Christianizing pagans.

As a sequel to the O'Hearn articles, Timothy Ryan, Scarboro theologian with field experiences in Brazil, in 1981 wrote a generally sympathetic analysis of his predecessors' labors in Chekiang. Of all the rationales which had given inner drive to their endeavor, he said, "the motive of mission as a demonstration of the vitality of the Church is the one which survives most unchanged." Father Ryan continued:

> *. . . in spite of its flaws, the modern mission movement did more than demonstrate the vitality of the Church. It will undoubtedly prove to have been the condition of its survival. If Christianity is today where the newness of history is springing up amongst "the poor" of the world, it is because it is in its majority a Southern, a third-world Church. Not in its power structure or "official" positions and theology, but in its numbers, its vitality, its future.*
>
> *For this we must thank the missionaries of recent centuries, including that courageous and committed group of Canadians who have left to us in the yellowing pages of* **China** *and* **Scarboro Missions** *the witness of their motives and their faith.*

* * *

John L. McKenzie, a well-known American theologian, earlier took a more critical Catholic view of traditional evangelizing practices in other cultures. "The problems of foreign missions is that they must proclaim Roman — that is, Western — Catholicism," he wrote in **The Roman Catholic Church**, published in 1969:

> *An Indian or Chinese or African Catholicism has not yet come into being . . . These cultures are by no definition more in opposition to Catholicism than Hellenistic-Roman culture was, and the Catholic Church achieved a permanent identity with Hellenistic-Roman culture . . .*
>
> *These cultures must develop their own Catholicism with the*

same freedom which Europe developed its Catholicism. They can learn much from Europe, in particular how not to do a great many things.

* * *

And an instructive reminder from Anglican prelate and mission historian Stephen Neill. His studies suggest that Scarboro's China experience was only a recent and small-scale example in a long history of disappointing missionary ventures in the Far East. After surveying such efforts in the seventeenth and eighteenth centuries, Neill reached this chastening conclusion:

> *Almost every possible form of missionary work has been tried — accommodation and the fierce refusal of accommodation; individual conversion in China and group conversions in South India; the ordination of priests in Goa and the refusal of ordination in other areas; the appeal of the Jesuits to the rulers and the appeal of the Franciscans to the poor and outcast. Every method has had its at least partial successes; none escaped from the general disaster and collapse. At the end of two centuries there was remarkably little to show for so much heroism, labor and self-sacrifice.*

* * *

By the founding of the People's Republic 150 years later, there were fewer than four million professed Christians (if Peking's Bureau of Religious Affairs can be believed) in a China then counting well over a half billion souls, and growing fast. Given an Asian pattern that has been repeating itself for four centuries, can Christian evangelizers realistically expect that the future will be any different? Particularly in an officially atheistic China?

Whatever presence may be allowed foreign Christians in the People's Republic, the spirit if not the letter of advice given by Bishop Paul Yu Piu of Nanking in 1943 could prove timely. His counsel came too late in terms of his homeland's immediate future but it could prove prophetic in the long run. Said the Nanking bishop some 40 years ago:

> *Open to every influence from the West, . . . (the Chinese) people will receive what you offer them, whether it be industry or the Gospel of Jesus. Their culture has prepared them for this hour of grace. Their culture, already ancient when Greece was born, is still vigorous. Its power of*

adaptability is proven by the fact that after 50 centuries it still lives . . . .

A new China is being born . . . and we must furnish a new missionary. He must know the language, not merely to speak it but to read and write it. He must become a Chinese to the Chinese . . .

He must become imbued with our traditions . . . Send us a missionary who is looking for the good in us, who will extend to us a truly Catholic charity, and we in turn will follow him to the feet of Christ . . .

China will expect the missionary to instil the spirit of patriotism in its Catholics. This is the doctrine of the Church, but we have to prove it.

17 NEW DIRECTIONS AFTER VATICAN II

CATHOLICS' LIVES ON LINE
IN LATIN AMERICA

The Church is taking a new direction, tackling repressive regimes head-on and leaving its missionaries open to brutal retaliation.

In August of 1981 these headlines introduced a feature report in the **Toronto Star.** Val Sears had interviewed Scarboro members and lay-formation candidates who believed in a much more socially active (some critics would say "socialistic" or even "Communist") approach to mission than John Mary Fraser and his early disciples in China had ever practised.

Sears was persuaded to seek out these SFM opinions after the violent death of a lay mission worker belonging to the Quebec-based Société des Missions-Etrangères. Raoul Léger of New Brunswick had been shot to death in Guatemala by government troops. The Canadian activist had been working alongside poor rural families. Posthumously, government spokesmen claimed he had been an armed guerilla leader in the Central American republic.

"If the missionary is working for justice, he is often interpreted as working for the revolutionaries," Father Roland Laneuville subsequently explained at the Montreal headquarters of the companion society to Scarboro.

The tragic event brought home to advocate and critic alike the hazards involved in this combined "salvation and liberation" approach to evangelization. By the 1980s this was already a well established, if still controversial mode of missioning, particularly in Latin American republics. As early as 1965, in fact, Scarboro had seen one of its own priests, Arthur MacKinnon, shot to death at 33 in the town of Monte Plata, Dominican Republic. A colleague said that Father MacKinnon had been "one of the agents of change, real institutional change", and in the Dominican Republic "Padre Arturo" still is widely revered as "a modern-day prophet and martyr for social justice".

On the tenth anniversary of his death, **Scarboro Missions** published a special commemorative issue to honor the witness of Art MacKinnon and other pastoral workers — including another Canadian, Maurice Lefebvre of the Oblates — who had suffered violent death in Latin America. An introductory editorial attempted to explain why a "salvation and liberation" or "faith and justice" approach to evangelization could lead to assassination:

> *Without doubt they were men who believed in the peace and love of Christ and one wonders what led them to such a violent end.*
>
> *The answer seems to be both complex and simple. The complexity enters when we look at the way their thinking evolved in the environment of poverty and misery which they experienced. Some of them tell us a little about this evolution in their thought and attitude towards their vocation in Latin America. The simplicity enters when we reflect on the fact that they not only believed in the love and peace of Jesus but in His justice as well. They knew that to teach Christ's love and peace was to teach only part of his message, surrounded as they were with a people who daily bore the weight of gross injustice. These men saw the root cause of injustice to be in the political, economic and social system and it was this conviction that led them to work for change, some in a peaceful way, some in a violent way . . .*
>
> *Today the "Church of the Prisons" in Latin and South America knows persecution for the same reasons as the "Church of Silence" in the East. The perversion of torture is not less sinful because it is done in the name of the West and the defense of religion than when it takes place in the name of the East and the defense of atheism.*

* * *

Clearly the Society begun by a single-minded John M. Fraser had revised its approach to missioning to an extent the founder never foresaw — and which some SFMers opposed as strongly as a majority favored it when the 1970s were giving way to the 1980s.

A few days before the opening of the 1978 SFM General Chapter there was an assembly of Society members, some China Hands among them. As later described in **Scarboro Missions**, the leaders of the retiring and incoming General Councils wanted "to hear the honest concerns of many who had not been able to express themselves to the Scarboro family for quite some time".

Whether in fact there was a free and full exchange of views at the assembly was later a question in some dispute. In any event, editor Gerald Curry wrote that some senior members "reminded us of our roots, of our China days and of the spread of the Society to South America as well as Japan and the Philippines". Participants, for instance, were invited to reflect on the mission intentions of their founder, John Mary Fraser:

> *Did we believe as he did? Were we as concerned for the salvation of nonbelievers as he? Indeed it was time for us younger members to do some soul searching. We made it clear that we too believed, were concerned about the spread of His Kingdom. One way we express this concern today is in the area of Social Justice.*

This stocktaking was in keeping with the sometimes agonizing reappraisals that had been going on within the Society, as elsewhere in the Church across Canada and abroad, ever since the Second Vatican Council.

* * *

New directions charted by Scarboro leaders at General Chapters which followed Vatican II reflected more than this historic turning point in Church history. The renewal of missioning officially undertaken from 1968 onwards also was influenced by SFM members' pastoral experiences on three continents, and by the invaluable insights provided by the frustrating China years in earlier decades. Still, Vatican II was the catalytic event that threw new light on these Scarboro experiences.

In response to civil and religious changes in much of the world, Pope John XXIII surprised everyone in January 1959 when he announced his decision to convene an international council of over 2,000 Catholic bishops — the first such gathering since 1870. He proposed that this 21st Council in Catholicism's long history should update the expression and practice of essential Catholic teachings, take new steps towards the elusive goal of Christian unity, and join with the rest of humanity in the ongoing struggle for world peace with justice.

Vatican II, meeting for four fall-winter sessions between September 1962 and December 1965, approved 16 constitutions, decrees and declarations. Two of the major ones were the **Constitution on the**

Church and the **Pastoral Constitution on the Church in the Modern World.** Some of the key insights from these seminal constitutions were applied in the Council's **Decree on the Missionary Activity of the Church.** The stance of the decree was comparatively open:

> *The future missionary . . . must bring an open heart and mind to men, and gladly shoulder the duties entrusted to him. He needs a noble spirit for adapting himself to strange customs and changing circumstances.*
>
> *. . . (The Church) should search out ways and means for bringing about and directing fraternal co-operation as well as harmonious living with the missionary undertakings of other Christian communities. Thus, as far as possible, the scandal of division can be removed.*

Calvert Alexander SJ, writing in the first popular English collection of conciliar documents, said this decree showed that "the focus of missionary activity today is less on territorial expansion . . . than on making the Church an *active* presence within and native to the diverse and developing non-Christian cultures in which it exists".

The Council touched off an often painful reassessment of evangelization in a continuing debate that showed few signs of abating by the early 1980s. Some of the most significant analyses took place among theologians, activists and pastoral leaders in Latin America — the continent where, numerically at least, more than half of the world's baptized Catholics lived. And the region where Scarboro missioners worked in growing numbers.

In January of 1979, 20 years to the month after Pope John had announced his surprise decision to convene a global Council, the Third General Council of Latin American Bishops (CELAM III) met in Puebla de Los Angeles, Mexico. There the bishops adopted their historic **Puebla Document** as a pastoral guide for the coming decade. One of the many striking features of the continental episcopal statement was its attempt to describe the essential relationship between religious mission and public affairs. Or, as the bishops put it, between "liberating evangelization" on the one hand and "human development, liberation and the social teachings of the Church" on the other.

This linkage between faith and social justice was further interpreted in a **Synthesis of the Puebla Document** presented in April 1979 to an Assembly of the Brazilian Bishops by Aloisic Cardinal Lorscheider, who had been one of the three presiding officers at the CELAM III meeting. A sampling of the Cardinal's perception of missioning:

Francis Diemert, SFM — Scarboro's Superior General from 1959 to 1968.

To evangelize is to convert people and to transform society within the creative and saving divine will . . . . It is to form a new humanity with new men, guiding all to a new way of living, being, judging, giving and fraternizing.

* * *

Comparable developments in the way mission is seen and practised have taken place within the major Protestant denominations on other continents. In the 50th anniversary year of the United Church of Canada, for example, Reverend Len Keighley, a missionary with the Ecumenical Forum in Toronto, published a research paper, **New Occasions Teach New Duties**, which traced the evolution of missionary perspectives within Canada's largest Protestant denomination. The decade-by-decade development he described paralleled similar perceptual shifts within the Catholic Church, not least of all in Scarboro circles.

Before 1920, Dr. Keighley wrote, "An almost completely spiritualized version of the Great Commission in Matthew 28:18-20 provided the major impetus for mission." There was "little serious questioning of the generally accepted assumption that mission meant proclaiming the Gospel to the heathen — to those who had no chance to hear it". There seemed very little awareness then that evangelizing in pagan lands was "related to the promotion of Western culture . . . in the context of Western economic and political imperialism".

During the Twenties (when the first Scarboro mission bands were settling in the Chuchow region of Chekiang province) "the basic impetus did not stray too far from the Great Commission although there is more talk of God's love for the world (John 3:16) and perhaps a bit less of the 'heathen' ". As well, "new elements related to human need rather than simply to the salvation of souls emerge." Keighley cited as evidence this observation by a missionary of the time: "By learning hygiene and sanitation much superstition should be overcome . . . By learning about agriculture and nutrition they could overcome many of the illnesses."

In the Thirties (when the Grey Sisters' nursing and teaching care in China began to supplement the mission efforts of the Scarboro priests) the emphasis in United Church missionary circles was shifting "even more to the meeting of human need" at a time of world depression and approaching global war. "The need for personal salvation and the emphasis on church building remained central, however."

"In the Forties the decade opens in warfare and strife and ends in a period of reconstruction and relief (experiences in which the Scarboro-Grey Sister teams fully shared)."

By the 1950s (when the Scarboro presence ended in China through expulsion) the missionary thrust in Protestant circles, Len Keighley reported, was "leaving still further behind the idea of actively converting the heathen and of church-building in favor of . . . 'presence' and 'witness in doing' ".

This emphasis on witnessing continued in the Sixties, when ecumenical co-operation also became prominent, thanks largely to Vatican II and Protestant receptivity.

The Seventies were to see further development of the social dimension of mission, popularly summarized in such buzz words as "liberation", "solidarity" and "human rights". This continuing perceptual shift in United Church and other Protestant circles was paralleled to a large extent in Catholic groups, including the Scarboro Foreign Mission Society in the 1960s and 1970s.

* * *

Francis Diemert was SFM superior general during this difficult transition period. He took office soon after John XXIII's announced intention to call a Council. During and after Vatican II, Father Diemert guided Scarboro's divided household (something almost all religious societies experienced at the time) quietly yet firmly towards a more open stance: open to the whole Church, the laity included; to other Christians, and to the world.

"Things were just starting to change", he recalled during a conversation in 1981. "The old traditional ways were coming to an end and new ways were coming into view. It was quite confusing for a while." What was his position at the time? "I thought I was open", Father Diemert replied. Yes, there had been considerable opposition to a renewal of missionary methods — an opposition that lingered in some quarters.

Under Diemert's leadership, unprecedented preparations were made for the Fourth General Chapter in 1968, which coincided with the Society's 50th anniversary. Early in June the superior general convened this "Chapter of renewal". It would adjourn late in August after electing Paul D. Ouellette to succeed Father Diemert. Joining the new superior on the General Council were George Marskell and Kenneth MacAulay.

More than 200 pages were required to record the Acts of the 1968 Chapter, together with advisory reports prepared by six study committees on the nature and purpose of the Society, internal government, community life, modern missionary approaches, priestly formation and public relations. The careful preparations, long sessions and detailed documentation were in keeping with the Chapter's ambitious purpose, as later described in a message from the new General Council:

> *The problems of today, demanding as they do new answers and new solutions, made it imperative that the Society re-evaluate its position relative to the needs of the modern world. The Second Vatican Council gave the Church a new image. If Scarboro was to be faithful to the demands of the Council, it had to renew itself in order to reflect this new image . . . .*

"We do presume that these concepts will call for a new spirituality", the General Council continued. "They will help to add a whole new dimension to our lives as Christians and as missionary priests." At the same time the Council emphasized that during the 1968 Chapter, "The past was neither condemned nor rejected; rather, full credit was given to those who preceded us."

In fact, not everything was changing in the Society. Working with the poor, including pastoral service in less than affluent Canadian missions, had long been a Scarboro preference. Still, extensive renewal of mission was desired by a majority of SFM members, one committee reported to the General Chapter. Responses to a questionnaire the committee had circulated showed: "58 priests in our Society considered that an early change in our approach is necessary; 10 thought not. 26 priests called for a radical change and 32 want a moderate change."

The General Chapter's new perspective is particularly evident in its stress on adaptation. An excerpt:

> *The aim of the missionary is to see a community of the People of God, the Church, take root in a different socio-cultural setting. To take root means that it cannot be an artificial transplant; not an alien plant which is sheltered from the local environment by "hot-house" methods. Rather, it means that faith in Christ becomes the experience of the people in the context of their own culture . . . Relevant communication of the Gospel takes cultural relativism seriously, but not as final authority.*

The decisions of the 1968 Chapter permanently record one of the most significant turning points in the still young history of the Scarboro Foreign Mission Society. The transition it initiated, often stormy and never tranquil, continued into the Seventies, as reflected during the two Chapters in that decade.

* * *

The decisions of the Fifth General Chapter in 1974 were "the results of nine weeks of prayerful and reflective consideration by the delegates" who, before adjourning, elected Michael O'Kane as Superior General, with Clair Yaeck and Robert Smith as assistants. While reaffirming the general direction of the "Chapter of renewal" six years before, the 1974 Chapter did decide that some 1968 positions required revision in the light of subsequent experience.

Twenty years after the last Scarboro missionary had been forced to leave the People's Republic, "China and New Mission" remained a primary focus of attention in 1974. Said the Chapter:

> *We wish to reaffirm our concern for and love of the Chinese people. The work of evangelization impels us to seek to identify the movement of the Spirit in historical events and we are called today to locate the action of God in China . . .*
>
> *. . . we believe that we must make serious efforts to familiarize ourselves with the complexities of the China reality today, and therefore we recommend that the Society commit itself at this time: to encourage and support Society members to*

". . . the Spirit of God may be discerned at work in every society and social group."

> *undertake Chinese studies; to maintain and strengthen ecumenical contacts in relation to China concerns; and to co-operate in grassroots educational and informational programs concerning China among the Canadian people.*

Social Justice was seen as a key pastoral priority for Scarboro. The Chapter committed the Society "to a more simple lifestyle", and to management of property, resources and invested capital so as to "promote the ideals of full universal justice"; including payment of a "just, living wage" and fair retirement benefits to employees of SFM.

A dissenting minority in 1974 challenged what they saw as an exaggerated emphasis on the social dimensions of mission. Among their comments, which were submitted to the Chapter in one of several preparatory reports:

> *It may be easier to work for the betterment of man than to make men better . . . (but) we cannot afford to give up the preaching of the Gospel for "the serving of tables" . . .*
>
> *Christ did not come in the first place to place man in an ideal civilization. He came to lead man back to God . . .*
>
> *. . . the poor are canonized by virtue of their physical poverty which is an accident of race, birth or geography. The poor are certainly not less greedy than the rich, merely less successful in their greed.*

Concerning the formation and education of SFM members, the Fifth Chapter decided for the first time that single male candidates would be accepted, if qualified, for temporary mission service, "without imposing on them the prerequisite demand that they have the intention of proceeding on for ordination" to the celibate priesthood.

* * *

Those who took part in the Sixth General Chapter during seven weeks of 1978 reported their findings with a provisional tone similar to that of the 1974 legislators. The continuity between the two Chapters was noted in a subsequent message from the General Council newly elected to serve into 1982: Kenneth I. MacAulay as Superior General, with Gerald Curry and Fred Wakeham as assistants. The Acts of this Chapter, the new Council noted, "are basically those of our 1974 Chapter".

Sixty years after the Society's founding by John Mary Fraser in 1918, three dozen guidelines were formulated as "reaffirmation, clarification and development" of the Society's purpose and functions. Among them:

> *China: Today we are called to locate the action of God in China, for the primacy of our dedication to the non-evangelized has its historical roots in our mission to the Chinese people and we wish to reaffirm our love and concern for them . . .*
>
> *The Society will maintain and encourage a Scarboro presence in Hong Kong or China as an expression of our commitment . . .*
>
> *Our Society will continue to support the Canada-China Programme of the Canadian Council of Churches with personnel and money through 1982 . . .*
>
> *Asia and Africa: In view of the importance placed by this Chapter on creating an adequate Church presence where it does not yet exist, the General Council will give particular attention to mission possibilities in Asia and Africa . . .*
>
> *Indigenization: The Society reaffirms its commitment to indigenization. To be credible witnesses to the Gospel we must develop a genuine understanding of and affection for the people whom we serve and for their cultural values . . .*
>
> *Ecumenism: . . . We commit ourselves to continue working with our brothers and sisters of other Christian Churches towards that unity which has been willed by Christ, and to co-operate with them in the work of announcing the Good News . . .*
>
> *Social responsibility: The Society's role in the home Church would demand particularly that the General Council continue to work with the Canadian Church in bringing to the attention of our nation as a whole international issues of injustice and the ways in which we as Canadians participate in them, whether knowingly or unknowingly . . .*
>
> *Reverse Mission: The Society carries on mission work in Canada when it brings back to our own people, in programs of reverse mission, the Good News of God's saving presence in the world, which we are privileged to experience in our work in other cultures.*

Personal renewal and social liberation. Indigenization. Ecumenism. Social responsibility. Reverse mission. Probably these 1978 guidelines would have puzzled or irked Scarboro's founder. J. M. Fraser labored at another time, in a very different social and ecclesial climate. For him and his first collaborators in China, the missionary mandate was clear and simple: "spread the Faith among the heathen", to cite his own words in 1922.

Sixty years later, his followers were emphasizing "reverse mission" and a formation program that involved laity, including women, as well as candidates for ordination. Reverse mission and the revised formation program were based on recognition that the Spirit of God may be discerned at work in every society and social group. Further, every culture, non-Christian as well as Christian, has worthy values to share with peoples of other milieux. The partnership in mission pioneered by Scarboro priests and Grey Sisters in earlier decades had expanded to mission teams consisting of priests, with married and single lay members, who were to serve abroad and in Canada.

* * *

SFM's "work overseas has brought home to us in a special way the close ties we have with peoples all over the world", the Mission Information Department noted in a brochure promoting multi-media materials for small study-action groups. "What we learn from our own first hand, on-the-spot experience brings home to us more and more the urgency of making our fellow Canadians aware of their interrelatedness to the world community."

This was part of the rationale behind the reverse mission concept which Scarboro leaders made their own in the late 1970s. The year he became an assistant on the General Council, Gerald Curry described three examples of reverse mission for readers of **Scarboro Missions.** First, he said,

> *. . . having lived and experienced life in another country, the missionary is more able to sympathize, to understand what it is like for the many who have migrated to Canada . . .*
>
> *Today, Scarboro carries out reverse mission by having several of its members working with various parts of the immigrant community.*

Secondly,

> *Our missionaries from Third World countries return to the Canadian Church with a strong message of the injustice of the*

Western economic system and the burdens it places on the vast majority of Third World peoples. This message of suffering and the need for social justice plays a large part in the "reverse mission" of our Society. Many Canadian Christians are unable to hear this message and are especially unwilling to face the part Canada plays in the oppression of others, let alone attempt to do something about it.

And third,

Another lesson from the Third World Churches is the importance and emergence of a new kind of Church community called "Basic Christian Communities" . . . With the decline in vocations the Canadian Church could well heed the message of missionaries who speak of the development of new ministries and a new kind of leadership within the Christian community that is found in other countries . . .

Reverse mission, Father Curry declared, exemplified ways the whole Church could "become one with the poor and powerless and stand alongside of them and speak out for them."

* * *

Such aspirations also found expression in Scarboro's program of formation in the late Seventies. It was designed to graduate committed members of small, evangelizing groups not unlike the base communities of Latin America. Formation of candidates for the priesthood was tied to the training of lay missionaries. Ordained men as before would be making a lifelong pledge. Lay men and women would make a minimum two-year commitment to overseas service after 12 months of preparation. Men and women, priests and laity would work together in teams.

"People come searching for something and ready to give of themselves", Paul Ouellette, director of this renewed formation program, observed during an interview in 1980. "They're not prepared to go it alone but they are ready to try working together as a team."

There was considerable initial opposition to a formation program that included lay men and women alongside ordination candidates, the former superior general admitted. "For some members this was a traumatic break" in what had been an exclusively clerical, all-male Society. Some priests still opposed having the laity become associates of the Society. "But little by little candidates will sell the idea by their personal witness", Father Ouellette predicted. "They'll make mistakes, of course. It will take time."

The formation director noted that the preparation of lay candidates as well as that of prospective priests included Far East studies. Ideally, SFM mission teams should be in a state of readiness to "adapt to whatever becomes possible in China".

On May 3, 1980 an historic missioning service took place at Scarboro headquarters when 12 men and women were sent out. Included were students for the priesthood, single lay men and women and a married couple.

Lay missioning still was a comparatively new departure in the Catholic Church, Superior General Ken MacAulay observed at the commissioning ceremony. "It's not new for the Protestant churches; they've been in the field for a long time", Father MacAulay continued.

> *It's true that in the past there were a lot of lay Catholics overseas, but they were priest-helpers or sister-helpers. We don't want that today. We want lay persons who will have an impact especially on the people in countries where the institutional Church is looked on as a "foreign" imposition.*

"We stress very strongly the faith commitment", he continued. "We could not accept people merely as volunteers or do-gooders." Team members were expected to bring back information and insights for sharing in Canada by way of reverse mission.

"This is where I see the future of the Church: it is the role of the lay person", the SFM leader emphasized. He added, "As missionaries we can't go out just to listen. We have to share."

* * *

When these expectations are compared with those of Scarboro leaders 60, 50 or even 20 years before, it is immediately obvious how much mission perceptions and priorities in the Canadian Society have shifted in the span of an average lifetime.

The direction the Scarboro Foreign Mission Society was travelling by the 1980s certainly was new. But what did all this mean in terms of the "New China"?

18 BUT WHICH DIRECTION IN "NEW CHINA"?

Early in 1981 yet another ambiguous sign of the times emerged from the New China. **Time** magazine reported that a young woman named Pan Xiao published a letter which drew 60,000 replies from other readers of an official publication called **China Youth.** The 23-year-old worker had asked, "Life, is this the mystery you try to reveal? Is the ultimate end nothing more than a dead body?"

China watchers in North American mission circles took this poignant incident as one more indication of spiritual hunger in the officially atheist state. At the same time Christian observers had to admit that "foreign religions" still were widely suspect in the People's Republic.

Beginning in the latter half of the Seventies, an increasing flow of such signs and portents was detected as the People's Republic opened itself gradually to communications with the industrialized West. But these indicators did not point consistently in any one direction. Instead they tended to point first one way, then another. On one hand there was this piece of news from Peking; on the other hand there was a countering report from Shanghai, and so on.

Typical media headlines in these years summarized what was still an inscrutable story in the process of unfolding:

RICE BOWLS THAT ARE FULL AND FINGERS THAT ARE BROKEN — CANADIAN JESUIT RETURNS FROM CHINA

CHINESE RELIGIOUS LEADER ON OFFICIAL VISIT TO UNITED STATES AND CANADA

IMPROVED VATICAN-CHINA LINKS FORESEEN

CHRISTMAS MASSES DRAW CROWDS IN PEKING

SHUN LURE OF RELIGION, CHINA WARNS ITS ELITE

OVERCROWDED CHURCHES FOR EASTER SERVICES

LOYALTIES DIVIDE CHINESE CATHOLICS

* * *

When Sister St. Angela re-entered China in 1980 as a visitor she met, as expected, two groups of Catholics — those who remained loyal to the universal Church as personified by the Pope in Rome, and those who as "patriotic Catholics" adhered to self-governing norms for a Chinese Church that collaborated with the government in Peking. Among the Grey Sister's recollections, paraphrased:

> *In every city I visited there was an underground Church loyal to Rome and an above-ground patriotic Church. I met a number of both kinds of Catholics, and also Protestants. The nice thing about it is that we were all Christians meeting together. But the Catholics loyal to the Holy Father don't take part in any ecumenical services with the Protestants who have merged into one denomination.*
>
> *In Shanghai I was with about 80 people in a little chapel. Mass was celebrated in Latin, in the old-fashioned way that it was before Vatican II. Then we prayed the rosary together. The priests told me that as many as 3,000 to 4,000 people attend on major feast days . . .*
>
> *Bibles in Chinese are becoming available. Some of the Christians are breaking up their Bibles into the various books so they can share them more widely. Some even are copying out passages for circulation . . .*
>
> *In some places I was advised not to go into the churches. I didn't press the point so as not to bring any harm to the people who were my guides, or to local Christians.*

* * *

While Sister St. Angela was seeing the New China at first hand, veteran missioners and a new generation of leaders at the headquarters of the Scarboro Foreign Mission Society were foremost among those Canadian Christians who were trying to discern what was happening in the People's Republic, and what these developments might portend for their apostolate.

How could the Society founded in 1918 — now beginning to augment its aging and declining priest manpower with lay missioners

— best ready itself, like the ever watchful steward, for whatever future opportunities might come on the Chinese mainland?

This "bottom-line" question was the subject of intense debate within the Society, just as versions of the same question were argued about in other mission circles, both Catholic and Protestant, across Canada and beyond.

In the U.S., for example, John L. McKenzie, veteran Catholic theologian, had taken this controversial position on foreign missions generally:

> *The Roman Church must return to the missionary ideal of the New Testament: proclaim the gospel, form a group of believers, and leave them with their church. There probably is no future for "the foreign missions" as we have known them. There can be a future only for the Catholic Church, Roman or something larger.*

"Certainly nothing approaching the old missionary thing — that's a dead duck," predicted Reverend Francis Carey of the United Church in referring to prospects in China. He was speaking as a member of a U.S.-Canadian Christian group authorized to aid higher education but **not** religious proselytizing in China.

The Canadian Bible Society, meanwhile, campaigned for funds to finance the mass circulation of Scriptures on the mainland. Why? Because "China today is like a group of hungry guests sitting down to a banquet. The Bible societies of the world are the catering service."

This approach troubled Donald Wilmott, chairman of the Canada-China Programme. "The new receptivity on the part of Chinese authorities to religious activity within China," he warned, "will wither on the vine if we violate their budding trust."

* * *

Earlier, Raymond Whitehead, who for some years had directed the Canada-China Programme for the Canadian Council of Churches, had with his wife Rhea identified four possible approaches to the New China:

1 — The "Visible Church" approach emphasizes "the need for verbal evangelization of the people of China" — by the Chinese Christians themselves, or by Chinese believers with the outside assistance of mission teams of overseas Chinese, Third World

Some things, like the Great Wall, do not change.

Christians and possibly Western missionaries. A traditional Catholic version of this "up-front" approach was, of course, the route followed by Scarboro teams until 1954, and is the method generally favored by evangelical groups in the Eighties.

2 — The "Lord of History" perspective stresses "God's action beyond the Church". Advocates see "the possibility of significant saving works of God being manifested in non-Christian, even anti-religious contexts". The Whiteheads quoted Dr. E. H. Johnson, controversial Presbyterian missionary and frequent Canadian visitor

to China: "I can't imagine . . . anything more counterproductive and showing less faith in the Holy Spirit than blasting in the Gospel from the Philippines (by radio signals) or Bible smuggling." Instead, Johnson, argued, Western Christians should recognize that God is working in new ways among this "fourth of the human family". Don't we believe that "God created all, and is concerned to save all?"

3 — The "Values" approach affirms that the Chinese people's "way of living and interacting" under Communism "is in some way 'Christian,' aside from any considerations about religious adherence or belief". This paradoxical perception, as interpreted by Joseph Needham, a British Christian: "in China they are implementing the second great Commandment far better than has been done by Christendom at any period, while at the same time rejecting altogether the first one."

4 — The "Mirror" approach seeks to redefine mission theology in the light of China's unique experiences. China is seen as a "counterfoil, a positive but alien experience, through which we can see ourselves more clearly". This approach asks, "Where is the fullness of salvation?" and answers, "If we look at our community life, or that of China, we can see that fullness of salvation cannot be claimed by any society. We are involved in continuing search and struggle . . . (So) might it not be useful to have a dialogue about what each of us is observing in our search?"

Another prominent observer of the China scene also took a broad view of the situation. Katharine Hockin, daughter of a missioning family in China, recalled in **Servants of God in People's China**, that most missionaries in 1949 had to decide "whether to remain in the new regime or leave before the Communists arrived". The Protestant missiologist was one of those who stayed for a time in the belief that "God would use his servants there too".

While critical of the Maoist revolution she had witnessed in its early stages, Dr. Hockin reminded North American Christians in 1962:

> *It may well be that God has lessons for his Church which will only be learned in Marxist lands. And which will still be true whether we happen to like it or not. The Church is there in China because of God's grace and power. The Body of Christ, there as here, is in his hands. What is God's word to us . . .? Where is our obedience?*

* * *

"Any movement on the part of Christians towards China should be done ecumenically," Gerald Curry of SFM's General Council maintained in a report to the Canadian Conference of Catholic Bishops in June 1979. This interchurch collaboration "should be based on lessons we have learned from our own historical involvement with the Chinese people."

With this in mind Father Curry invited the Canadian prelates to give financial support to the Council of Churches' Canada-China Programme. Curry's point of view was shared by his colleagues on the SFM General Council but not by all Scarboro members by any means. Some veterans of the China years were not persuaded in the least by the Council's stance nor by Canada-China Programme researches and arguments. And they were not impressed by the religious official from China, K. T. Ting (sometimes called Bishop Ding Guangxum), whose Canadian tour in the fall of 1979 was co-ordinated by the Canada China group.

Ting became a ranking Christian spokesman in New China as director of the Nanking University Centre for Religious Studies and vice-chairman of the Three Self Movement among Chinese Protestants. Consecrated as an Anglican Bishop, he later became the best known leader of the Protestant denominations fused under the threefold banner of "self-government, self-support and self-nurture". He came to the U.S. and Canada in this capacity.

Dr. Ting's nuanced statements on the position of Christianity in the New China and the very minimum role expected of foreign believers were positively received in some Christian quarters in Canada. Protestant hosts usually sounded convinced by their Chinese guests, while some leading Catholics expressed reservations, in part because of the unresolved religious and diplomatic differences between the Vatican and the Catholic Patriotic Association in China, whose relations with the Peking government parallel those of the Three Self Movement among Protestants.

Some Scarboro veterans were among the critics. John McGoey did not accept the Ting thesis. While he attended an exchange session when the Chinese leader visited SFM headquarters, some others did not.

Like it or not, what Professor Ting came to say to Canadian Christians was unquestionably significant. His message, as the first Christian spokesman to visit this continent in any official or quasi-official capacity since 1949, was the clearest indicator up to that time of the likely direction of Peking policy towards religious practice in general and any foreign participation in particular.

What exactly did Ting say to his Canadian and American hosts? In addition to many interviews and public talks, he also committed his basic position to paper. One example is a short document, prepared for limited circulation, which he entitled, "Facing the Future or Restoring the Past?" In the paper Dr. Ting brusquely dismissed any would-be missionary who would look on the Chinese as "just objects of his dreaming and fantasy, objects of his theologizing."

"New China means liberation for the overwhelming majority of our people," he wrote. "The price of grain has remained steady all through the last 30 years. There are problems and mistakes and excesses in a revolutionary situation, but we need to allow our people to learn to do better." These preliminaries stated, K. T. Ting reached the key issue:

> *Authentic Christian witness to China requires us to struggle for a Chinese Christian identity, a selfhood that is both Christian and Chinese and definitely not crypto-Western. The movement for self-government, self-support and self-nurture . . . is the embodiment of that struggle to overcome the de-nationalizing and alienating effects of the missionary movement and has made considerable achievements.*

There was no encouragement in this for those North American evangelizers who might still think in terms of "restoring the past" on the Chinese mainland. And lest anyone doubt what he was saying, Dr. Ting spelled out the strict limits of foreign collaboration in answer to a questioner at Carleton University, Ottawa, in October 1979:

> *We can have exchanges; we would like to have more. My colleagues feel that my presence here is only a beginning. But we have to be selective and discriminating . . .*
>
> *And we are not going to have missionaries go back to China. No matter how well intentioned, that will mean undoing our Three Self Movement.*

* * *

Shortly before the Ting visit to this continent, Scarboro leaders had been studying an assessment of future prospects in China prepared by their own Brian Swords. After some years in Hong Kong, where he had worked with "freedom swimmers" escaping from the People's Republic, Father Swords accepted an 18-month English-teaching assignment inside the People's Republic, in the northeastern port city of Darien. These experiences had brought him to this conclusion:

Once a busy centre of Catholic worship.

> *The Church in China is now in the hands of Chinese and will be for all practical purposes . . . It will take a lot of dialogue and work to form a good bond of understanding and support between the Chinese Catholics and Catholics of other cultures.*

Not many months later the relevance of Brian Swords' patient approach became painfully evident. Just when the public image of the late "Great Helmsman" Mao was being officially refashioned by the new Politburo leaders in Peking, the Holy See was sharply rebuked for alleged interference in the internal autonomy of the Catholic Patriotic Association. The public chastisement came in the early summer of 1981 after Pope John Paul II had named Bishop Dominic Tang as Archbishop of Canton. It was the first such episcopal appointment by the Vatican since 1955, while the Patriotic Catholic Association inside China reportedly had consecrated over 40 bishops without Rome's concurrence in that interval.

With evident government backing, a leader of the dissident Patriotic Catholics accused the Vatican of acting like a colonial power and then repudiated Tang's appointment — even though he had previously been invited to assume the same post by both Patriotic and loyalist Catholics of Canton.

"Apparently Rome thought that he (Tang) would be a bridgehead but it has backfired," Brian Swords told the **Catholic New Times** when asked for comment. He offered an explanation for the fierce opposition on the part of the Patriotic Catholic wing:

> *It's very hard for Westerners to understand the profound pride of culture in China. To let the Pope make an appointment like that is to be under a foreign power.*

Father Swords said he was not surprised by the Chinese reaction. Again in his words, as reported by the Catholic weekly of Toronto:

> *I was kind of hoping that Rome would stand off and let the Church in China take its own pace . . . After all, the Catholic family in the world is a big family. There's nothing wrong with having a member of that family who's trying to find himself. We should give the Church in China space and time to find itself. The seeds of Catholicism are in China. If we wait patiently, they will flower, and in time, the Chinese Catholics might be coming over here to help us to a deeper form of the faith. If we try to manipulate the situation, then I think we're not honoring the leadership of the Spirit among that people.*

* * *

Exploring alternative approaches was advocated by an American evangelical scholar — Ralph R. Covell, acting academic dean at Conservative Baptist Seminary in Denver. Writing in the January 25, 1980 issue of **Christianity Today**, Covell concluded:

> *The People's Republic of China has some very obvious felt needs. Most of them relate to their goal of modernization, and embrace economics, agriculture, industry, science, and education. Religion has no priority at all . . . Can we give more creative thought to how we — individually and institutionally — might help to meet some of China's pressing needs? . . . Then Jesus Christ will not be seen as a stranger — an intruder whom they do not presently want or need — but as one who sees their plight and waits patiently to show how only he can deal with it at the deepest level.*

* * *

The American Baptist's observation that in the New China "Religion has no priority at all" also was noted by a Canadian Jesuit leader on his return from the Orient. Consequently, W. F. Ryan SJ cautioned other China-watchers, "I hope we don't try to answer too quickly the question of what God is doing in China today."

The superior of English-speaking Jesuits in Canada visited the Communist-run nation in the late summer of 1979. He went as a member of a scientific-religious delegation organized by the Kennedy Institute of Bioethics. Some of the following impressions and insights were later shared in a paper prepared for the Washington-based Institute by this leading spokesman for a "social faith that does justice":

> *"My friends, religion is no big thing in China today!"*
>
> *This self-assured caution, stated categorically by our Chinese guide as we emerged from our visit to the old Catholic Cathedral in Peking, remains uppermost in my mind as I jot down for you my impressions on the present state and possible future of Catholicism in China. Our Chinese hosts were frank. If there is some thaw in their hardline treatment of believers, it does not stem from a newfound interest in religion, but rather from the keen desire of its new leaders to win cooperation of all Chinese — and even of friendly foreigners — to work together strenuously to achieve their primary goal of "modernization"...*
>
> *Active Christians presently represent less than one half of one per cent of the population. Even allowing for 10 million Muslims and millions more "lingering" Buddhists, modern China is, in fact, the most secular of states, for whom belief in God is not a threat but only a superstition for the old, a curiosity for the young. If indeed Christianity's mission is truly universal, then we must still be very early in our human history, since more than a quarter of humankind remains almost totally untouched by revealed Christianity.*
>
> *If evangelization is to have any success in future, then its carriers must give compelling and credible witness to the Gospel's clear bias in favor of the poor, and that human advancement and social justice are integral to its message. In the immediate future the Chinese will open their doors and their hearts only to people who are as preoccupied as they are with overcoming the poverty of their masses.*

* * *

John McGoey took a different view. In his critique of the first draft of this chapter, the Scarboro missionary who was in China during the Forties commented:

> *"If religion is really no big thing in China today," how come it has not been wiped out? How come the government is so worried about it? How come it led to so many imprisonments and deaths? . . . The truth remains, that Christianity had the most profound influence on modern China until it was suppressed with the gun. And even then it has greater influence.*

* * *

Katharine Hockin returned from a visit to China in 1981 with quite another perspective. As a United Church representative with a delegation organized by the Canadian Council of Churches, this

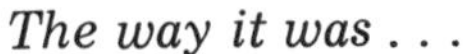

The way it was . . .

veteran missiologist later wrote that she had been reminded repeatedly of "deep missionary complicity" in "the evils of the last century of colonial and imperialist exploitation" in China:

> *As a former missionary I feel that I have been trying to recognize this history, to learn from it, and to be part of the missionary community seeking new goals of mutuality. But there remains a deep regret that this history has scarred relationships so deeply, and that perhaps a justified bitterness continues to be effective in shaping policies and attitiudes. Granting this however, we can perhaps understand that the Chinese church feels it must keep up all its defenses against all that might fracture the unity and rooted indigeneity that has been achieved. There is to be no foreign intrusion on their integrity and selfhood. The Chinese church is deeply committed to God's mission. In this we can hope to deserve to be partners! But in fact we are both fractured and deprived by a history which we tend to forget and which they cannot!*

* * *

"This is no time to build walls . . . This is time for bridges," Archbishop Gilles Ouellet of Rimouski, Quebec told the **Catholic New Times** after his return as a Catholic representative with the same CCC delegation. The former superior of the Société des Missions-Etrangères and past president of Canada's Catholic bishops added: "We are groping to understand the New China. It calls for a new presence of the Church. It's not in the dictionary. We will have to discover it by living."

* * *

As 1981 was ending, reports from China told of new arrests of Catholic priests and lay Christians in the Shanghai area — a development that revived fears of more religious harassment and perhaps selective persecution in the interests of government goals.

* * *

Several months before the Seventh General Council of the Scarboro Foreign Mission Society was scheduled to convene in May of 1982, mixed evidence coming out of the People's Republic still was more ambiguous than enlightening. It remained very uncertain when, if ever, the Canadian mission Society might help in some modest way to compose a new and different chapter in the land of Confucius, Sun Yat-sen and Mao Tse-tung.

19 FROM THE AMAZON TO TOKYO

Scarboro is not waiting for some clear answer to emerge from the New China; the Society has never waited. Even before the People's Republic was proclaimed, the Canadian missionary organization began reaching out to other parts of the world, beginning in the Dominican Republic in 1943.

By late 1981 more than 70 SFM members and lay associates were ministering in 11 localities from Brazil's Amazon to Tokyo in Japan, while another 50 were living in Canada: serving in parishes from Newfoundland to British Columbia, in the social justice apostolate, as hospital or military chaplains, in administration at Kingston Road headquarters or among Scarboro's sick and retired members.

Abroad and at home, the mission thrust in most localities by now was a still experimental mixture — one that saw clergy and laity working together to promote both faith and social justice, quite often in co-operation with neighboring Christians.

Sixteen priests were in Japan, among them the pioneering Gerald Kelly, a veteran of 32 years of missionary labor overseas when he died in December 1981. In the Philippines were six members and two lay collaborators. Other counts: Dominican Republic — 12, Brazil — six members and one lay missionary, Peru — two members and three associates, St. Vincent and neighboring Caribbean islands — five priests, Mexico — three laity and a priest, the Bahamas — four priests, Guyana — three Scarboro members, and Panama — one priest and one associate member.

* * *

"As a lay person actively involved in the Peruvian mission," Tom Walsh recalled in **Scarboro Missions** during the Society's 60th anniversary year, "I faced the problem of integrating myself into parish work structured by clerics." Opportunities soon surfaced as he faced up to "the actual pastoral needs" of the people. By 1978 he said, "I think what I am learning in Peru is the truth of the Gospel, that Christ is very present to the poor."

Tom Walsh's experiences, which led to his appointment as a lay representative at the Sixth General Chapter that same year, personify the renewed approach to the mission apostolate that Scarboro is testing in different parts of the world.

Several priest members also reflected on these new directions in articles carried by the SFM magazine in 1978. A sampling gives a bird's eye view of Scarboro's wide-ranging activities as the Canadian Society began its seventh decade.

The mission team in Leyte, the southern Philippines, reported to the Sixth Chapter:

> *We are committed to the development of lay leaders and the development of small Christian communities and to helping the people become more aware of what the Gospel means in the present-day Philippines context.*
>
> *The actual implementation of our mission theory varies from parish to parish, depending on the local factors, previous groundwork and, to no small extent, on the personality of the particular priest involved.*
>
> *The priests and the sisters have been supportive of the people in their struggle, believing that the official representatives of the Church must identify more and more with the struggles of the poor in their reaching out for some measure of justice.*

Fred Wakeham, then regional co-ordinator for the Philippines, provided some pastoral details in another article:

> *Because most of the inhabitants of the area are Catholic, the sacramental ministry is a prominent part of the priest's work. Today of primary importance are the numerous programs and seminars aimed at deepening the understanding of the Christian faith. Based on the Bible these seminars involve a lot of dialogue on questions of faith, morality and social involvement. Lay men and women are emerging to lead paraliturgical services in their own communities and take part in programs for community development. Preparing for these seminars and attending these sessions, which are held mostly at night, is now seen by priests as their primary work.*

During a 1978 interview with Sister Doris McMullin, c.s.m., of Scarboro's Mission Information Department, Gerald Kelly in Japan talked about the building of Christian community. People and priest, he said, "begin with nothing except a shared belief in the Good News". Gradually this becomes "a sharing of all things, save evil. Supply any good you wish — love, forgiveness, truth, food . . . anything. It is sharing. It is always understood in this context that God the Father in Christ and the Holy Spirit are the centre of the Christian community."

Clergy and laity working together, 1982.

Asked what he saw as "the work of our men" in Brazil's Amazonas, Douglas MacKinnon replied:

> *Well, we should have a trade or some skill. Some might have a theological background in lay leadership. What we have to do*

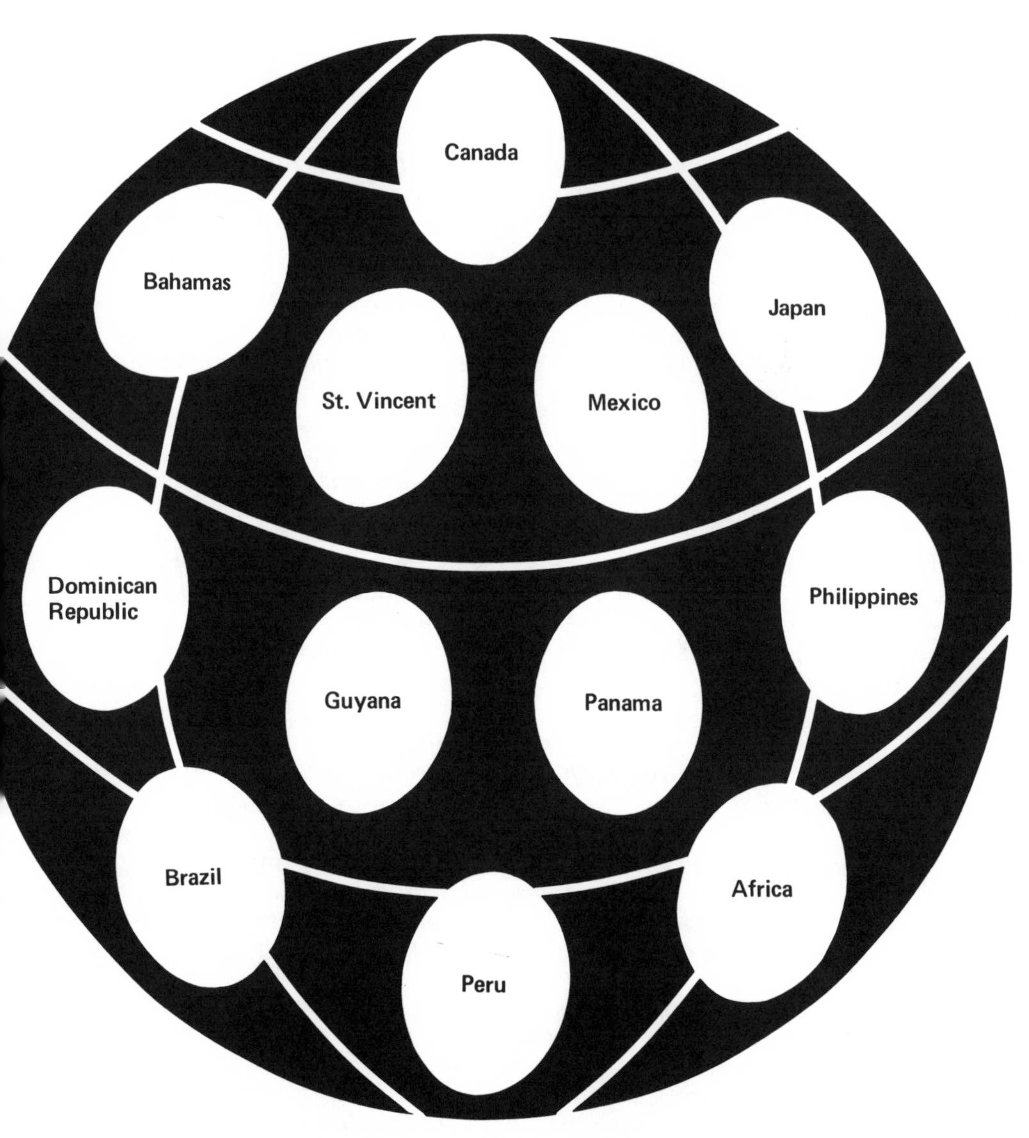

Scarboro's missions, 1982.

is fulfil the needs of the present moment, which is the formation and preparation of some kind of ministry. Thus I see Scarboro's involvement becoming less in the sense we no longer need to send men down to run the parishes. Rather, we have to form lay leaders, who are going to be able to take over parish functions within the parish structure.

Joe Young offered a similar assessment in describing his experiences in Guyana:

First of all, the indigenization of the Guyanese Church, that is the building up of the local Church, has high priority for the members of the Scarboro team. Positive steps have been taken in that direction . . . with emphasis being placed on a leadership training program . . .

There is some evidence in the various parishes that priests want the lay people to have a more meaningful role in the Church. This means that they want them to become more than deacons or 'mini-priests.' It means that they want them to be more than just readers, distributors of Communion or even being catechists . . . They want them to become more involved in the life of the parish and it is not quite clear at present just how this can come about.

In Panama, the Interamerican Co-operative Institute (ICI) founded in 1963 by SFM's Harvey Steele had conducted more than thirty 100-day courses by mid-1982, for many hundreds of local leaders from numerous Latin American countries. **Scarboro Missions** reported:

ICI is a private, non-profit, educational organization that does not distinguish between creed, race or sex and which operates under the laws of the Republic of Panama . . .

The primary objective of ICI, that of the promotion of social justice among the oppressed sectors of Latin America, is accomplished through the action of co-operatives of every kind and of community development projects . . .

The following kinds of people are selected for the programmes: farm leaders, people connected with co-operatives, farmers' movements, popular associations and trade unions, people with experience in working with the grassroots, people who wish to broaden their vision of the global and local situation.

During the anniversary year Rollie Roberts recalled how he had initiated a day-care nursery on St. Vincent Island in 1963. Mothers who had to work in the farm fields or road maintenance crews were his most enthusiastic collaborators. Each paid 50 cents weekly towards the cost of caring for their children, from seven o'clock in the morning until four each afternoon.

After three years in the Dominican Republic, Gary McDonald reported some of his convictions as a Scarboro missionary:

> *I feel for myself that the only possible way of working is with small groups of people and there is no emphasis on my teaching them but rather we learn together. Since it's their country and their problem, I am only sort of an adopted son. I think I have a role to play because I look at their reality with a whole different background. I'm sort of a catalyst — people come together because I am there.*

Father McDonald spoke of "using the New Testament as a kickoff point, trying to figure out what Jesus is saying, or what was being said at that time, 2,000 years ago, and really trying to get into it, to see it, and then trying to apply it today. And of course economics comes into it, politics comes into it, everything comes into it."

Members like Gary McDonald, and now lay men and women associates as well, follow in the steps of both their founder, John Mary Fraser, and a more recent mentor — Art MacKinnon, the SFM priest who was assassinated in the Dominican Republic in 1965. As the Sixth General Chapter observed in a 1978 letter to his parents, Father MacKinnon "symbolized by his life and death" the Society's "commitment to justice and human rights" in the perspective of Christian faith.

* * *

During the anniversary year, Bishop George Marskell of Itacoatiara, Amazonas in Brazil interpreted the continuing Scarboro story in the same perspective. In taking this longer, larger view, he challenged fellow SFM members to renew their mission commitment "not just to announce the Gospel but to live it". Help the Good News become a reality, not merely a postponed promise, for those who are least and last, he said. From Bishop Marskell's homily in 1978:

> *For 60 years now we are a Society precisely because we have not kept the Good News of God's Kingdom to ourselves. And for 60 years we have not even contented ourselves with just announcing the Good News. We have attempted in many*

parts of the world to help create conditions whereby the Kingdom could become a reality and whereby it could grow . . .

God continues to reveal Himself throughout history. Historic events question our conscience. Faith makes us search for God's will at the present moment. Concrete situations in the world must be interpreted in the light of Christ and His message.

I think most of us would agree that our mission experience tells us that two questions face us today, more perhaps than ever before in our history. How can we call God Father, and our neighbor brother/sister, in a world where so many people are exploited and living in misery? What changes are necessary so that the Good News of faith in God as Father and in all men as brothers and sisters becomes Good News in reality?

* * *

This commitment to a "social faith that does justice," and does it with compassion, is the heart of the matter. This is the aspiration that most motivates Scarboro priests and lay members in a dozen scattered mission fields today.

Their many-sided and continuing story on three continents and in the Caribbean area deserves further telling by other chroniclers. After all, as the authors of the Gospel discerned, telling the story is an essential part of the action.

Appendices

Roster of Scarboro Men in China 1902–54

Name	Birth Place	Born	Arrival in China	Death	SFM Status
John Mary FRASER	Ontario	1877	1902/ 1926	1962	Founder
John Joseph SAMMON	Ontario		1920	1951	Associate
Daniel CAREY	Ireland		1921		Member. Excar-dinated.*
(*Excardinated: Left Society but remained a priest)					
Joseph LACHAPELLE	Quebec	1891	1923	1961	Member
Paul KAM	China	1897	1926	?	Member
Vincent MORRISON	P.E.I.	1893	1926	1950	Member
Ramon SERRA	Spain		1926	1972	Associate
William FRASER	Ontario	1867	1926	1952	Associate
Joseph VENINI	Ontario	1898	1926	1972	Member Excard.
William AMYOT	Ontario	1898	1928	1968	Member
Lawrence BEAL	Ontario	1900	1928	1978	Member
John E. McRAE	Ontaro	1875	1928*	1955	Foster Founder
	(*First of two visitations to China)				
Bernard BOUDREAU	U.S.A.	1905	1929		Member Excard.
Michael DUNNE	Ireland		1929		Laicized*
	(*Laicized: Returned to lay state)				
Aaron GIGNAC	Ontario	1902	1929	1940	Member
Hugh F. X. SHARKEY	New Brunswick	1904	1929		Member
Desmond STRINGER	Ontario	1900	1929	1959	Member
Joseph KING	Ontario	1905	1931	1979	Member
John J. MacDONALD	Nova Scotia	1903	1931	1978	Member

Name	Birth Place	Born	Arrival in China	Death	SFM Status
Arthur VENADAM	Nova Scotia	1899	1931	1958	Member
James MacGILLIVRAY	Nova Scotia	1897	1932	1935	Member
William C. McGRATH	New-foundland	1896	1932	1970	Member
William McNABB	Ontario	1907	1932		Member
Gerald DOYLE	Ontario	1903	1934	1978	Member
Hugh McGETTIGAN	New-foundland	1909	1934		Member
Craig STRANG	New-foundland	1909	1934		Member
Leo CURTIN	Ontario	1898	1935	1966	Member
Leonard HUDSWELL	Ontario	1911	1936		Member
James LEONARD	Ireland	1909	1936		Member
Lawrence McAULIFFE	Ontario	1912	1936	1962	Member
Lorne McFARLAND	Ontario	1911	1936	1976	Member
William MATTE	Quebec	1911	1936	1973	Member
John MAURICE	Romania	1908	1936		Member
Patrick MOORE	Ontario	1911	1936		Member
Harold MURPHY	Ontario	1912	1936	1965	Member
Ronald REEVES	England	1909	1936		Member. Excard.
Michael CAREY	New-foundland	1911	1938	1968	Member. Excard.
Edward LYONS	Alberta	1915	1938	1975	Member. Excard.
Alex MacINTOSH	Nova Scotia	1912	1938		Member
Gerard McKERNAN	Scotland	1897	1938	1978	Member
Daniel MacNEIL	Nova Scotia	1911	1938		Member
Allan McRAE	Ontario	1911	1938		Member
Edward MORIARTY	New-foundland	1914	1938		Member
Thomas MORRISSEY	New-foundland	1914	1938		Member
Charles MURPHY	Nova Scotia	1912	1938		Member

Name	Birth Place	Born	Arrival in China	Death	SFM Status
Harvey STEELE	Nova Scotia	1911	1938		Member
Armand CLEMENT	Quebec	1913	1940		Member
Francis DIEMERT	Ontario	1915	1940		Member
John KELLY	Ontario	1913	1940	1972	Member
John McGOEY	Ontario	1915	1940		Member
Thomas McQUAID	Ontario	1908	1940		Member
Michael MacSWEEN	Nova Scotia	1911	1940	1967	Member
Joseph MURPHY	Alberta		1940		Member. Excard.
Andrew PINFOLD	Ontario		1940		Laicized
Gordon STRINGER	Ontario	1912	1940		Laicized
Kenneth TURNER	Quebec	1905	1940		Member
Russell WHITE	New-foundland	1910	1940		Laicized

Roster of Grey Sisters in China 1929–52

Name	Birthplace	Arrival in China	Death
Sr. Mary Anthony (Catherine McHugh)	England	1929	1968
Sr. Mary Catherine (Catherine Doyle)	Baptized in New York St.	1929	1981
Sr. St. Oswald (Christine McDonald)	Ontario	1929	1963
Sr. Mary Daniel (Annie C. O'Connor)	Ontario	1932	1943
Sr. Mary Genevieve (Jean Jedrzejeszyk)	Ontario	1932	
Sr. St. Angela (Mary Helen Lynch)	Ireland	1932	
Sr. St. Julitta (Mary Jane Fleming)	Ontario	1932	1970
Sr. Mary Angela (Mary McCarthy)	Ireland	1934	
Sr. St. Martin (M. Catherine Gervais)	Ontario	1934	1958
Sr. Mary Vianney (Iona Bertrand)	Quebec	1938	
Sr. St. Kenneth (Kathleen Radey)	Ontario	1938	
Sr. Mary Esther (Margaret Devenish)	Ontario	1947	
Sr. St. Joan (Susan Daly)	Saskatchewan	1947	
Sr. St. Matthew (Florence Pinfold)	Ontario	1947	
Sr. St. Nicholas (Genevieve Grace)	Newfoundland	1947	

Main Sources

Acts, General Chapters of the Scarboro Foreign Mission Society, 1941, 1949, 1959, 1968, 1974, 1978.

SFMS Archives.

Interviews and conversations with numerous members of the Society, and with a few Grey Sisters of the Immaculate Conception, Pembroke.

Research findings and archival selections made by C. J. Eustace and Pat Jamieson.

Issues of **China**, 1919-1950, and **Scarboro Missions**, 1950-1981.

Walter J. Abbot, S.J., General Editor, **Documents of Vatican II**, The America Press, New York, 1966.

Pat Barr, **To China with Love, The Lives and Times of Protestant Missionaries in China 1860-1900**, Secker and Warburg, London, 1972.

Stephen Endicott, **James G. Endicott: Rebel Out of China**, University of Toronto Press, Toronto, 1980.

Episcopal Conference of Brazil, **Synthesis of the Puebla Document**, Canadian Conference of Catholic Bishops, Ottawa, 1979.

Allan S. Evans, Riley E. Moynes, Larry Martinello, **What Man Believes**, McGraw-Hill Ryerson Limited, Toronto, 1973.

J. M. Fraser, SFM, "Pillar of the Kingdom", published in **Scarboro Missions**, January 1959 - January 1961 inclusive.

John Fraser, **The Chinese — Portrait of a People**, Summit Books, New York, 1980.

John Foster, "The Canadian Enterprise," an analysis of Protestant missions in China 1885-1933, United Church of Canada.

John A. Hardon, S.J., **Religions of the World**, Volumes I and II, Doubleday Image Books, Garden City, New York, 1968.

Katharine Hockin, **Servants of God in People's China**, Friendship Press, New York, 1962.

Philip Hughes, **A Popular History of the Catholic Church**, Burns Oates, London, 1949.

Len Keighley, "New Occasions Teach New Duties," Ecumenical Forum, Toronto, 1965.

K. S. Latournette, **The Great Century in North Africa and Asia AD 1800-1914**, Volume VI in **A History of the Expansion of Christianity**, Harper & Row, New York, 1944; republished by Zondervan Publishing House, Grand Rapids, Michigan, 1970. And **A History of Christian Missions in China**, London, 1929.

Sister Mary Lawrence, "Challenge to Serve: A Missionary to China," Grey Sisters of Pembroke.

Jacques Leclercq, **Thunder in the Distance, The Life of Pere Lebbé**, Sheed and Ward, New York, 1958.

John McGoey, SFM, **Nor Scrip Nor Shoes**, McClelland and Stewart, Canadian Best-Seller Library, Toronto, 1968.

William C. McGrath, SFM, **The Dragon at Close Range**, St. Francis Xavier Seminary, Scarborough, 1938.

John L. McKenzie, **The Roman Catholic Church**, Holt, Rinehart and Winston, New York, 1969.

Stephen Neill, **A History of Christian Missions**, Volume VI in the Pelican History of the Church, Penguin Books, London, 1964.

W. F. Ryan, S.J., Toronto, untitled paper prepared for the Kennedy Institute of Bioethics, 1979.

Hugh F. X. Sharkey, SFM, **Stairway to the Stars**, 1975.

Ninian Smart, **The Religious Experience of Mankind**, Collins Fontana Library, London, 1971; and **The Long Search**, Little, Brown and Company, Toronto, 1977.

Harvey Steele, SFM, **Agent for Change**, as told to Gary MacEoin, Orbis Books, Maryknoll, New York, 1973.

K. T. Ting, "Facing the Future or Restoring the Past?", 1979.

John Walsh, SFM, editor, **Scarboro Missions — Chapter V**, 1974.

Theodore H. White, **In Search of History, A Personal Adventure**, Warner Books Edition, New York, 1978.

Raymond L. and Rhea M. Whitehead, **China — Search for Community**, Friendship Press, New York, 1978.

Some issues of the **Catholic New Times, Catholic Register**, both of Toronto; **The Prairie Messenger**, Muenster, Saskatchewan; **Globe & Mail, Toronto Star, Time** and other periodicals.

Acknowledgements

Grateful acknowledgement is made for permissions to cite the following texts:

From THE CHINESE — PORTRAIT OF A PEOPLE, by John Fraser, Summit Books, New York, 1980. Used by permission.

From SERVANTS OF GOD IN PEOPLE'S CHINA, by Katharine Hockin, Friendship Press, New York, 1962. Used by permission.

From A SHORT HISTORY OF THE CATHOLIC CHURCH, by Philip Hughes, 1949 edition. Reprinted by permission of Search Press Ltd., London, U.K.

From NOR SCRIP NOR SHOES, by John H. McGoey, reprinted by permission of Little Brown and Company (Canada) Ltd.

From THE ROMAN CATHOLIC CHURCH, by John L. McKenzie. Copyright (C) 1969 by John L. McKenzie. Reprinted by permission of Holt, Rinehart and Winston, Publishers.

From A HISTORY OF CHRISTIAN MISSIONS, by Stephen Neill (Pelican Books 1964), pages 207, 409, 411-12. Reprinted by permission of Penguin Books Ltd.

From AGENT FOR CHANGE, by Harvey Steele, as told to Gary MacEoin. Reprinted by permission of Orbis Books, Maryknoll, New York.

From CHINA — SEARCH FOR COMMUNITY, by Raymond and Rhea Whitehead, Friendship Press, New York, 1962. Used by permission.

PEKING
JAPAN
MONGOLIA
RUSSIA
NANKING
YEL
SEA
SHANGHAI
CHUNGKING
HANGCHOW
SHAOHING
NINGPO
CHINA
CHEKIANG
YUANLING
LANCHI
KINHWA
SUNGYANG
LISHUI
PIWA
WENCHOW
LUNGCHUAN
EAST
CHIN
SEA
FOOCHOW
1942 EXODUS
TAIWAN
BURMA
INDOCHINA
INDIA
N
W
S
CANTON
HONG KONG